In Search of Angels

IN
SEARCH
OF ANGELS

Travels to the Edge of the World

◆

ALISTAIR MOFFAT

BIRLINN

First published in 2020 by
Birlinn Limited
West Newington House
10 Newington Road
Edinburgh
EH9 1QS

www.birlinn.co.uk

ISBN 978 178027 672 4

British Library Cataloguing in Publication Data
A catalogue record for this book is available from the British Library

Designed and typeset by Hewer Text UK Ltd, Edinburgh
Printed and bound by Clays Ltd, Elcograf S.p.A.

FSC
www.fsc.org
MIX
Paper from
responsible sources
FSC® C018072

'Son mo charaidean Gaidhealach uile

For all my Highland friends

Contents

Acknowledgements

When Hugh Andrew approached me with the idea of this book, I was immediately attracted. There is much more to the story of the Christian conversion of the west and north of Scotland than Columba. But sources for the lives and works of the other holy men who sailed amongst the islands and sea lochs from the sixth to the eight centuries are vanishingly scant. Sometime only names and the whispers of half-forgotten stories survive. And so it seemed to me that I should do what they did, go on a journey and try to discover something of their passing, and why they founded their communities on the islands and remote places of the Atlantic shore. Blessed with sun, calm seas and enough solitude, I spent a summer in the company of the saints who came to the Hebrides all that long time ago and who did so much to shape modern Scotland.

I'm grateful to Calum Macdonald for permission to reproduce the text of *An Ubhal as Airde* (copyright © C. & R. Macdonald and published by Chrysalis/BMG). The lines from Sorley MacLean's 'Hallaig' are copyright © the estate of Sorley MacLean. The poem appears in *A White Leaping Flame/Caoir Gheal Leumraich: Sorley MacLean, Collected Poems*, edited by Christopher Whyte and Emma Dymock, published by Polygon in association with Carcanet Press.

Patricia Marshall is a mistress of her craft and edited this book with immense skill and sensitivity, while Andrew Simmons produced it with tact, patience and persistence. I would like to thank them both, kind and considerate professionals that they are. Jan Rutherford completes the quartet who brought this book to life. As ever, I am immensely grateful to her. My agent, David Godwin, also encouraged me greatly. And finally, for wonderful Highland hospitality, I would like to thank Mrs Flora MacRae.

Alastair Moffat
Summer 2020

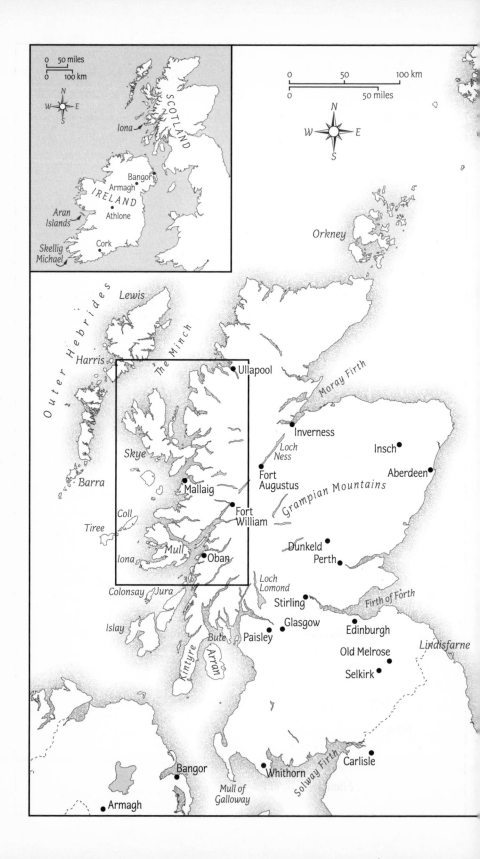

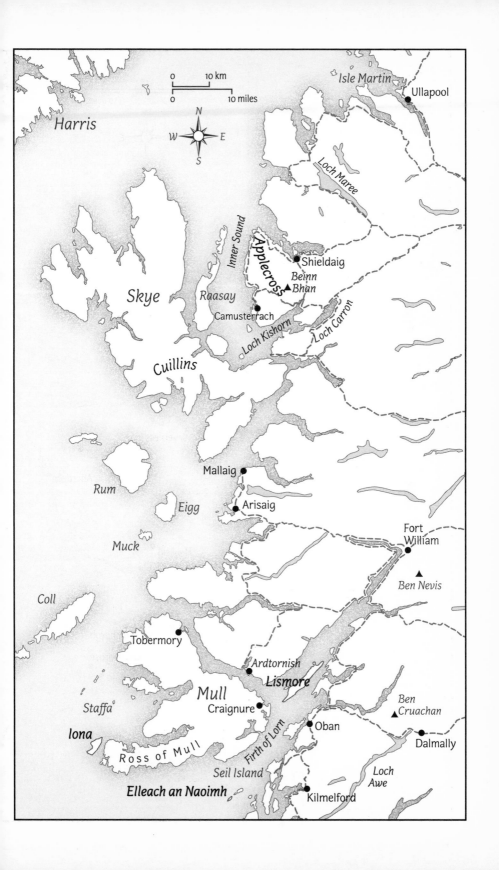

Preface

Thirty years ago, in another life, I stopped for a moment to look up from the morning mist on Loch Awe and across to Ben Cruachan. Snow-crowned, majestic, its mass dominates the Pass of Brander, the dawning sun dazzling, glinting in the distance off the white summit. As the tide of yellow light slowly unfolded over the land, I put my briefcase on the back seat of my car, checked my inside pockets for wallet, passport and tickets, and drove away through the mountains to another world.

With friends from Edinburgh, we had hired the west wing of Ardbrecknish House on the eastern shore of Loch Awe. High on a ridge, it commands long vistas up and down the loch and across to the Argyll mountains. But early on Easter Sunday morning I had to leave all of these unfurling glories behind and drive to Edinburgh Airport to catch a plane bound for a very different landscape. In those days, I worked in television and, having recently been appointed Director of Programmes at Scottish Television, I had to attend the Marché International des Programmes de Télévision (MIPTV), the largest international market for buying and selling what was known as content – programmes. It is held each Easter at Le Palais des Festivals in Cannes on the French Riviera and I was to stay at the five-star Carlton Hotel on the long, curving seafront called La Croisette. I was not looking forward to it and, as I drove down through the twists and sudden turns of the Pass of Leny, where the Highlands suddenly becomes the Lowlands, I thought of my family and friends waking up in the peace of Ardbrecknish by the lochside.

In the windowless bowels of a concrete monstrosity at one end of the Croisette, misnamed a palace, hundreds of trade stands are set up by those with programmes to sell, and buyers cruise the aisles, often stopping to pick up brochures or look at excerpts. Producers and sales staff from all the major networks are there – ABC, CBS, NBC, BBC, ITV, Disney, Warner Brothers and many more. Co-production deals are discussed, expensive gourmet dinners eaten, promises made and sometimes kept. For ITV we made several game shows for adults and for children, and my main purpose in going to Cannes was to consolidate those deals with American format owners and sometimes renegotiate terms. The cost of all this, the conspicuous consumption, was vast, as were the potential rewards. It was the market economy working at full throttle. To remind me of the scale of expenditure, I recently looked online at the cost of a room in the Carlton Hotel for one night and it was £500, probably more at MIPTV. I knew that our network production business depended on shaking the right hands at the right time and saying the right things but I found it all very uncomfortable, claustrophobic and ultimately repetitive.

Such is the pressure on hotel accommodation in Cannes that some companies used to prefer to hire large luxury yachts that were moored at the jetty on the seaward side of Le Palais des Festivals, only a few hundred yards from the windowless basement and its suffocating atmosphere. In the yachts, television companies could both hold meetings and sleep in what was often a set of very well-appointed bedrooms. The year before I decided to leave my work in TV, I received an intriguing invitation. Would I like to join a group of American executives on their very fancy yacht for a series of meetings? These would take place not in the tranquil waters of the harbour but on a short cruise down the coast, the fabled Côte d'Azur. It sounded like a very welcome relief from the chatter and racket amongst the trade stands in Le Palais.

The size of a two-storey house, the yacht was white and the sundeck at the stern high above the water was very attractively shaded by bright striped awnings. We made our stately way out of

Cannes harbour and, over coffee, as I talked with my American hosts, the mood amongst us was also bright, having left behind the hurly-burly for a few hours. We were bound for the Lérins Islands, a small, low, wooded archipelago only a few miles out to sea off Cannes. Having found a brochure in the Carlton Hotel the night before, I knew that one of the islands was the Île Sainte-Marguerite. It was the location of a citadel where the Man in the Iron Mask had been imprisoned at the end of the seventeenth century. Made world famous in Alexandre Dumas's d'Artagnan sagas, there was, by coincidence, a film about this strange story made that year (1998) starring Leonardo DiCaprio, Jeremy Irons and Gerard Depardieu. When I asked if we were to visit the prison of the man rumoured to be the brother of Louis XIV, I was a little disappointed to hear that we would not. Instead, the giant white yacht glided around the Île Sainte-Marguerite and set a course for the smaller island of Saint-Honorat.

The island turned out to be a magical place – quiet, unhurried, peaceful. It is dominated by Lérins Abbey, which maintains its own vineyards. This imposing monastery was founded by St Honoratus around 410. Having tasted some pleasant white wine and been given a presentation pack of soap, liqueur and honey, we ate a simple lunch before dispersing to have a look around this beautiful little island. Finding myself alone and a little relieved not to have to make conversation with people I did not know well, I walked past the vineyards and through a green tunnel lined with tall trees to the coast of the Île Saint-Honorat. Behind me were the jagged littoral of the Riviera, the bustle of Cannes and the dense clusters of the bright and white buildings of other ports and towns. In front of me stretched the unbroken horizon of the Mediterranean.

I walked west along a brick-red path through pine trees and shaded by them was a bench. I sat for some time and felt my shoulders loosen, my back relax. It was as though I was exhaling a long breath. This corner of the little island seemed to me to be different, to have a palpable *genius loci*, to be a place of settled peace. As I gazed out over the rocky foreshore, my mind seemed to empty, surrendering itself only to what I could see or sense. I stopped thinking and, if the phrase had been current then, I found myself in the moment and only in the moment.

After a time, I seemed to wake from my reverie and began to wonder if my hosts might have been waiting for me, checking their watches, anxious to be back in Cannes for the next round of meetings. When we docked and tied up at the jetty below the Palais des Festivals in the late afternoon, we all shook hands and made our way back into the world of business. Less than a year later, I decided that I had had enough of corporate life and resigned from a highly paid, prestigious job to return home to the Scottish Borders to work alone as a writer and producer. But I never forgot that time amongst the pines on the Île Saint-Honorat and more than once I have wondered if its magic worked on me then.

Many years later, my publisher, Hugh Andrew, asked me if I would consider writing a book about the Irish monks who sailed to the Hebrides in the sixth, seventh and eighth centuries to found communities on the islands and the Atlantic coast. The most famous is, of course, Columba but my preliminary reading told me that he was by no means the only missionary to sail from Ireland. Hugh was right – this was a rich and too-little-told story, and work began.

Like these pious mariners, I decided that, as far as was feasible, I would embark on a journey, a series of voyages of discovery that would take me to the remote islands, to the places of solitude they so eagerly sought. Instead of a seagoing curragh, I would plan my summer explorations with the help of the timetables of Caledonian MacBrayne ferries or hire local sailors to take me where I needed to go. In the spring, I began to read more widely and deeply. Very soon, I found myself again bringing to mind those few hours spent on the Île Saint-Honorat and discovering how important the life of Honoratus and the monastery he founded on that unexpected and atmospheric little island was.

Introduction

Eilean Mhartainn shimmers on the edge of eternity. A lost cathedral of the elements, the little island is also a recurring metaphor. When the sun rises over mighty Beinn Dearg, 'the Red Mountain', then splashes on to the sea, reaches the gently sloping eastern shore and breasts the rounded heights of the island's hill, a tiny lochan sparkles like a natural font. Beyond it lies Nuill Dhuirch and the vast sweep of the ocean. It can mean 'the Edge of Beyond' and, below it, dark cliffs drop sheer into the ocean. Westernmost is Clach an Nuill Dhuirch, 'the Great Rock of Beyond', and it is where the unceasing waves of the Atlantic break at last and make landfall.

Isle Martin, in English, is a place where the everlasting can be compassed. Mariners know where waves come from – what they call the length of fetch. A westerly wind can blow up off the cold coasts of Labrador and make waves three thousand miles away – over the open water they roll endlessly towards the little island before breaking on the rock of beyond. North of Eilean Mhartainn, rising from the shores of Loch Broom, there is more metaphor – the mass of Beinn Mor Coigach looms. It translates as 'the Great Mountain of the Hand' and, above it, clouds billow across huge Hebridean skies spread like a vast canopy over sea and land.

No one lives on Isle Martin. Only the gulls and divers fish its shores and, hidden in the abandoned fields, the croak of corncrakes can be heard in June. Now the island is a place of ghosts and echoes. Carried on the westerlies off the wastes of the Atlantic come whispers of prayers and psalms and hints of an ancient sanctity. In the eighth century and probably long before, a community of solitaries lived here – monks who built cells on the sheltered eastern shore – and their sole relic is a strange stone cross that stands in the grave-yard of a much later chapel. It has been described as a triple Latin cross and is unique in Scotland.

These hermits sailed to this lonely little island because they believed that there, cut off from the tumult of the world, they might move closer to God. Living lives of extreme privation, shivering at their prayers in small, draughty, beehive cells, they fasted and induced trance-like visions. These tiny, cramped spaces were ante-rooms to eternity. Often too small to stand up in, they were places for kneeling in prayer. With only the music of the winds, the monks sang the early psalmody and recited the creed. On many days, they climbed the hill behind their cells, looked out to the west, past a scatter of small islands, and watched the sun set on Creation. Some gratefully suffered many hours of shivering discomfort as they morti-fied their flesh by immersing themselves in the chill waters of the lochan on the hill's summit and in the seas around the island. These men suffered all this so that they might know the mind of God and so that, when death came racing across the oceans of eternity to take them, they would be born aloft over God's Great Mountain of the Hand. They prayed they would be gathered up in the arms of angels at the gates of Heaven to begin the glories of life ever after.

Isle Martin is named after their inspiration and exemplar, St Martin of Tours, one of the first in the West to embrace and adapt the beliefs and practices of a group of Middle Eastern ascetics known as 'the Desert Fathers'. To escape the periodic persecutions of the Roman Empire and to lead hermetic lives, these men fled into the deserts and remote regions to worship, meditate, pray and fast. Most famous was St Anthony of Egypt and a brief biography of him by St Athanasius of Alexandria began to circulate widely in the fourth century.

St Martin also understood that the complete and perfect faith sought by the hermits was impossible without departure. The temporal world and all its temptations and distractions had to be left behind. Anthony entered the empty vastness of the desert so that he could do battle with his demons, give himself entirely to prayer and privation and find perfect communion with God. His suffering would be rewarded with the gift of eternal life. Martin substituted the woodlands of the Loire Valley for the deserts of the East and founded the first monastery of solitaries in Western Europe at Marmoutier near the town of Tours. It derives from the Latin *Maius Monasterium*, 'the Great Monastery'.

This initiative made Martin deeply unpopular with the bishops of the established Church. Gaul was still part of the Roman Empire and Christianity was almost exclusively urban. He appalled his urbane contemporaries by insisting on missions of conversion, preaching in the countryside to those who still held pagan beliefs. In Latin, the word *paganus* meant 'a country person, a peasant' and, as now, it had pejorative overtones – 'a bumpkin', 'a yokel'. When he came upon a pagan shrine, the saint showed great physical courage by breaking it down and setting up a cross in its place. His behaviour scandalised the wealthy bishops of Gaul and they branded him as unfit for his holy office as well as sniffing grandly at his 'insignificant appearance, his sordid garments and disgraceful hair'.

Just as with Anthony and most saints who became famous and the focus of a cult, a biography of Martin was written soon after his death in 397 and, again, it was widely circulated. St Ninian had certainly seen a copy for, when he founded his monastery at Whithorn in the early fifth century, he called it Taigh Mhàrtainn, 'the House of Martin'. In fact, it may have been a more direct tribute to a mentor, for scholars now believe that Ninian studied and worked at Marmoutier before he ventured west on his mission to Galloway. Not far from Whithorn, Kirkmadrine, 'the Church of Martin', was founded, near Stranraer. In his biography, Sulpicius Severus described the community at Marmoutier near Tours:

He [Martin] made himself a hermitage about two miles from the city. The place was so secluded and remote that it had all the solitude of the desert. On one side it was walled in by the rock-face of a high mountain, and the level ground that remained was enclosed by a gentle bend of the River Loire . . . His own cell was built of wood as were those of his brethren; but many of them hollowed out shelters for themselves in the rock of the overhanging mountain.

Almost three centuries later, when St Aidan came east from Iona to become Bishop of Lindisfarne, he founded another monastery on a site in the Scottish Borders that is closely similar to Marmoutier. Bounded on three sides by the Tweed, Old Melrose is further enclosed by a high and sheer river cliff carved out by an ancient glacier. When Aidan first set eyes on this place, it must have seemed like God's will that a monastery should be built there.

In a small yard by the River Lee, opposite the Beamish brewery in the city of Cork, I watched Padraig O'Duinnin build a boat in a morning. In the midst of the clutter of half-finished repairs to rowing boats, bundles of tree branches and sheets of canvas, he had lain on the ground two curved lengths of timber and arranged them into an oval shape, like a flat rugby ball. In what would become the gunwales of his boat, Padraig had bored a dozen small holes on each side. A fluent Irish speaker, he flecked his talk with Gaelic words. 'Craobh nan sithean – magic wood,' he said, when he picked up a bunch of green hazel rods of differing lengths. Whittling one end to fit, he jammed them in the holes in the gunwales before bending them and tying them together with twine. When all twenty-four rods were in place (with Padraig constantly measuring and adjusting by eye alone – I never saw him with a tape or a rule), the skeleton shape of the boat became clear.

Laths were then tied lengthwise from bow to stern and then black canvas stretched over the frame. So that the boat stayed rigid and did not fold under the pressure of water, benches were fitted crosswise to act as thwarts. Only wood, twine and canvas were used, and no metal fittings of any sort were needed. In only a few hours, Padraig had built a seagoing curragh. The sole change from those that sailed the coasts of Ireland two thousand years ago was the substitution of canvas for cowhide. With a broad smile, its builder picked up his curragh and, through a gap in the wall, shot it out on to the River Lee before clambering aboard.

These ancient boats were the vessels of the Lord. The monks who prayed on Isle Martin came there in curraghs. They and many other holy men came from Ireland in these simple craft, their voyages themselves acts of faith. 'When the sea is big,' Padraig told me, 'you must have faith, must not panic or move around. At times like that I imagine a seagull sitting quiet on the waves, letting the swell carry it up and down. The curragh is so light that it sits like a bird on top of the water. When we go out on choppy seas, I tell my crew that we should think of it as a treat that we are sailing like those brave old monks.'

PART ONE

THE WORD
MUST BE SPREAD

I

The Lauras

In the beginning the Word was in the East. Across Judaea, where Christ had lived and died, there were seven flourishing Christian communities by AD 100 and, through the energetic missions of St Paul, many more in Asia Minor and Greece. In the western Roman Empire, the new faith was barely represented. There were active communities only in Rome itself and nearby Puteoli (present-day Pozzuoli) and Pompeii. By the end of the fourth century, thousands of churches had been established across Egypt, Judaea, Syria, Asia Minor and Greece, while in the provinces, in what are now France, Belgium and England, there were only thirty. The rise and subsequent triumph of Islam in the East has induced a variety of historical amnesia and we forget that, for the first six centuries since Anno Domini, the cradle of Christianity was in the cities of the eastern Mediterranean. The fundamentals of the Nicene Creed were formulated at the Council of Nicaea in 325 in Asia Minor and there were major churches in the cities around the shores of the Aegean at Miletus, Ephesus, Smyrna, Pergamum, Athens and Corinth. After the conquests of the Rashidun Caliphate between 632 and 661, when Arab armies overran the old provinces of Egypt, Judaea and Syria, and much later Turkey and then Greece, many of these communities faded from prominence and their stories were forgotten. Only Jerusalem was remembered.

The early expansion of the Christian Church was spasmodic, inhibited by periodic bouts of persecution that drove worship and membership underground. Perhaps most famously the Emperor Nero made Christians scapegoats for the Great Fire of Rome in

AD 64 and probably martyred St Paul and St Peter at around that time. The public torments meted out to hundreds of martyrs in the amphitheatres were hideous. After torture, Christians were crucified or hung on poles to be set on fire while they still lived or torn apart by starved and goaded wild animals such as bears and lions. But most emperors ignored what they saw as the followers of only one of several oriental cults. By the middle of the third century, conversion had gathered pace and the kinder, more forgiving precepts of the Gospels had persuaded many in the ruling classes to become believers. Not all emperors were tolerant. Decius saw Christianity and its principles as a threat to the state, and in 250 he issued an edict requiring all citizens to sacrifice to the traditional gods of Rome.

Many of those Christians who could not comply suffered martyrdom, sometimes after torturers had attempted to force them to recant their beliefs. Here is a moving passage from *Ecclesiastical History*, an early account of the beginnings of Christianity, written by the historian, theologian and bishop of Caesarea, Eusebius:

> Ammonarium . . . a virgin of irreproachable life, endured unheard-of torments without opening her mouth, only to declare that no arts or power should ever prevail with her to let drop the least word to the prejudice of her holy profession. She kept her promise inviolably, and was at length led to execution, being, as it seems, beheaded. The second of these holy women was named Mercuria, a person venerable for her age and virtue; the third was Dionysia, who, though a tender mother of many children, cheerfully commended them to God, and preferred his holy love to all human considerations; the fourth was another Ammonarium. The judge blushing to see himself shamefully baffled and vanquished by the first of these female champions, and observing the like fortitude and resolution in the countenances of the rest, commanded the other three to be beheaded without more ado.

Ever more appalling cruelties were inflicted before many died as martyrs for their faith. Their resolve to endure unspeakable pain and a grateful death was kept in place by a certainty that their sacrifice would earn them a place in the Kingdom of Heaven and the glories of everlasting life. It was a straightforward understanding and it fostered a faith that was often unbreakable. In 303, Emperor Galerius abandoned the policy of toleration that had been followed by his immediate predecessors and enforced more edicts against Christians. Churches were destroyed and, once again, the grisly spectacles of more public martyrdoms could be seen all over the empire. But it turned out to be the last such spasm.

On 28 October 312, the army of Emperor Constantine met that of Emperor Maxentius, his rival for power in the western empire, at the Milvian Bridge over the Tiber, not far from Rome. Eusebius recounted a much-repeated tale. The day before battle was joined, Constantine saw a vision sent by God. He looked up at the sun and, above it, saw a cross of light with the Greek words '*En touto nika*', taken to mean 'In this [sign] you will conquer'. Banners and shields were painted with the chi-rho symbol. Of course, those carrying them triumphed and the godless Maxentius drowned in the Tiber. Eusebius claimed to have heard this story from Constantine himself even though the chi-rho symbol (which comprises the first two upper case letters of the Greek form of Christ – *chi* and *rho* ☧) was used by persecuted Christians as a secret sign to identify each other during dangerous times of the persecutions.

The political and cultural consequences of this for Christianity were epoch-making. After victory at the Milvian Bridge, Constantine converted and, in the Edict of Milan, he and his co-emperor in the East, Licinius, agreed that Christianity should become the state religion. It was a decision that would transform the simple, unadorned beliefs of Christ, his disciples and St Paul. An indelible link was forged between Church and State and, very importantly for some, it removed the possibility of blood or red martyrdom, as persecution seemed to have been consigned to history.

Genuinely interested in the story of Christ's life and in Church doctrine – he presided over two Church councils – Constantine appointed his mother, Helena, as Augusta Imperatrix and furnished her with lavish funds to find relics relating to the stories of the New Testament. Eusebius listed the beautiful churches she had raised in Bethlehem and Jerusalem and in Sinai at the place where the Bush had burned. But, most spectacularly, Helena claimed to have found the True Cross on which Christ was crucified. A pagan temple had been built over the site of his tomb in Jerusalem, and when it was destroyed, workmen, who seemed more like archaeologists, found three crosses. A terminally ill woman was brought to the site: when she touched two of the crosses, her condition remained unchanged, but when she laid hands on the third cross, she made a miraculous recovery. Over the place where the True Cross had been found, Constantine decreed that the splendid and ornate Church of the Holy Sepulchre should be built.

A few miles east of Jerusalem, God was being sought in a very different place. During the Emperor Aurelian's persecution of Christians in 275, a man named Chariton had been cruelly tortured and then flung in prison to rot. Aurelian was murdered and Chariton was unexpectedly released. His principal emotion had not been one of blessed relief but disappointment. Chariton had wished fervently to die as a red martyr for Christ. To console himself, he embarked on a pilgrimage to Jerusalem but was captured by bandits and taken to their cave in the Pharan Valley, a dramatic, sheer-sided cleft now called Wadi Qelt. The stream that runs through the valley joins the River Jordan near Jericho. Miraculously, all of the bandits died after they had drunk wine poisoned by a snake.

Chariton realised that divine providence had placed him alone in this cave so that he could become a hermit and embark on a life of extreme austerity mixed with prayer, psalm singing and fasting. He had discovered another form of martyrdom, what later became known as white martyrdom, second only to red martyrdom as the highest form of sacrifice. Chariton had abandoned all comforts, renounced all the pleasures of the senses and left the temporal world behind to lead a solitary life in the presence of God. It could scarcely have been a more different approach than the contemporary co-option of Christianity by the imperial family and its vast empire, as money was lavished on opulent churches and gilded reliquaries.

Chariton was not alone for long. Because his hermetic life in the extremes of the desert echoed the wanderings of the Old Testament prophets, of St John the Baptist's voice crying in the wilderness and of Christ's forty days and forty nights of fasting as he endured Satan's temptations, others began to join him at the '*laura*' or '*lavra*' in the Pharan Valley. *Laura* is a Greek word that means 'a narrow lane' and it may have been adopted as a metaphor for the straight and narrow path to an understanding of the mind of God. The well-worn phrase comes from the Gospel of Matthew, 7:14, 'Because strait is the gate, and narrow is the way which leadeth unto life, and few there are who find it.' Nevertheless, many sought it and groups began to cluster in communities that became known as 'lauras' or 'lavras'. For a time, Chariton coped with intrusions but so many were attracted to the starkness of the hermetic life that he eventually abandoned his cave. Near Jericho, he found more silence and solitude, but when that was broken he moved once more.

Most famous of these early ascetics was St Anthony of Egypt. Profoundly affected by a sermon around 270, he believed that spiritual perfection might be achieved if the material world was entirely renounced. Anthony was modestly wealthy, and he sold his farm and possessions, giving almost all of the proceeds to the poor. In summary fashion, he kept aside a little money and used it to bundle his sister into a nunnery. Once all had been disposed of, the young man walked out of the lushness of the fertile Nile Valley and into the dust and heat of the desert. Like Chariton, he lived a life of extreme privation, spending many solitary years in the ruins of a Roman fort, but, unlike him, Anthony became the subject of a biography, more precisely a hagiography. Athanasius of Alexandria wrote that so many followed the hermit in pursuit of white martyrdom that 'the desert had become a city'.

The early Church was often riven with controversy as doctrine took time to settle. Arius of Alexandria believed that the Father, Son and Holy Ghost were materially distinct beings and it therefore followed that there was more than one God. The Arians were opposed, vehemently, by the Trinitarians, who held the more orthodox view that all three were a single entity. During the debates between the followers of each party, the urbane bishops of the cities of Egypt were shocked when large bands of hermits suddenly appeared in the streets of Alexandria, having walked out of the desert to make their views known. Many were unnerved at the sight of so many ragged, wild-haired, wide-eyed scarecrows prowling the streets.

However, most of them agreed – bishops *and* hermits – that early Christianity was transactional, a relatively uncomplicated system of sacrifice and reward. If a mortal life was given to God alone, however uncomfortable that might be, then the reward of everlasting life could be expected. The more the flesh was mortified, the purer the soul became and, as a result of prayer and contemplation, the closer to God one could approach. Some of the sayings of these hermits have been preserved and they believed that the repetition of prayer was effective. And the simplest and best prayer was known as the Jesus Prayer: 'Lord Jesus Christ, Son of God, have mercy on me, a sinner.'

By the early decades of the fourth century, the informal communities that had clustered around charismatic ascetics, such as Anthony, Chariton and others, began to become more organised. Pachomius had been conscripted into the Roman army around 310, as recruiters scoured the city of Thebes on the upper reaches of the Nile. It may have been his military service that instilled a need for order. Having converted to Christianity, the veteran soldier founded a monastery at Tabennisi, not far from Thebes, and he laid down rules and a structure that eventually formed the foundations of western monasticism.

Adopting the Hebrew word *abba* for father and *amma* for mother – nuns were admitted to the new monastery – Pachomius insisted on discipline, obedience, manual labour for all, silence, fasting and long periods of prayer. Men and women lived in separate quarters and, unlike the caves and cells of Anthony and Chariton's followers, several monks might live together. Each was taught how to weave baskets from willow withies or cloth from local yarn and these were sold or traded in exchange for essential supplies. All property was held communally. In a central building all of the monks came together to eat in silence and, at least twice a week, they fasted for a day, taking only water. Simple clothing was worn and the monk's habit with a hood was adopted. At prescribed times each day, the community came together to pray and to hear readings, but each member was also required to spend time alone meditating on what they had heard and on the scriptures. These communities were described as coenobitic, from the Greek for 'common life'. They may have been better organised than the informal clusters of hermits in the Pharan Valley or those who flocked to Anthony, but life was not designed to be comfortable. Sleeping on hard, earthen floors covered only with a prayer mat, monks will have shivered through the cold nights of the desert or baked in the noonday sun.

As *abba*, Pachomius was responsible for the spiritual welfare of the monks and nuns, and the choice of this title made clear that when they left their birth families they were admitted into another – the family of the devout. Even though they spent much of their time alone, they had the consolation of being part of a close group, united by a deep faith. But admission was conditional. New monks and nuns had to complete a three-year probation before becoming full members of the community. For those who were illiterate and innumerate, Pachomius organised classes and also invented a method of counting that entered Christian tradition.

Made from twisted strands of wool, the prayer rope originally had thirty-three knots, one for each year of Christ's life. Later versions could have as many as one hundred or one hundred and fifty. The rope and its knots were used to keep count of the number of repetitions of the Jesus Prayer and other devotional formulae. Not only did innumerate monks find this useful, it helped others meet their quotas, as they passed each knot through their fingers when they closed their eyes and offered up the sonorous, almost hypnotic repetitions of piety. The prayer rope is still used in the Orthodox churches; for Catholics, it became the rosary with beads rather than knots.

By the time Abba Pachomius died in 348, there were many lauras in the desert places of Egypt and Judaea where thousands of monks and nuns had left behind lives in the towns and cities of the late Roman Empire. These communities of hermits doubted that religion mixed with imperial politics could ever bring about a truly Christian society. Instead, they began to embrace a mystical tradition known in Greek as hesychasm. It means 'stillness, rest, quiet, silence' and it was seen as a necessary precondition for prayer. These ideas were at first transmitted orally in Coptic, the late Egyptian language spoken by most of the hermits. By the end of the fourth century, a Greek translation called *The Apophthegmata Patrum*, 'The Sayings of the Desert Fathers', had begun to circulate. These brief pieces of advice were very influential: 'Take care to be silent. Empty your mind. Attend to your meditation in the fear of God, whether you are resting or at work. If you do this, you will not fear the attacks of demons. Sit in thy cell and thy cell will teach thee all.'

Around 400, the Greek text was translated into Latin, the language of the western empire, by Pelagius. A pivotal figure in the early Church, he was almost certainly a Celt from the west of the province of Britannia, perhaps what we might think of as a Welshman. Pelagius is a Greco-Roman calque of his original name, probably Morgan, and it means 'Son of the Sea'. Also known by his friends as 'Brito', he was a theologian much involved in doctrinal disputes, especially those that revolved around the notion of free will as opposed to divine grace. These debates were complex, ferocious and fascinating, but the importance of Pelagius in the early history of British and Irish monasticism lies in his origins. It seems very likely that the ideas of the Desert Fathers first made their way westwards through his translation of *The Apophthegmata Patrum*, but because Pelagius eventually fell on the wrong side of doctrine and was seen as a heretic, his influence has been submerged.

Another earlier and very likely conduit for the transmission of the ideas of the laura may have been St Athanasius, the biographer of St Anthony. Sometime before 336, he was expelled from his bishopric at Alexandria, having been on the losing side of the debate between the Trinitarians and the Arians. Banished to the farthest ends of the Roman Empire, Athanasius arrived at Augusta Treverorum, modern Trier, on the banks of the River Moselle. What the Egyptian bishop made of the Rhineland winters is not recorded but he did find himself close to power.

Trier became one of the capital places of the later empire, a much-used residence for the western emperors and the imperial court. From 318 onwards, the city was the seat of the Gallic prefecture, the central government of all of the western provinces, from Britain in the north to Morocco in the south. Constantius II, the son of Constantine I, ruled the west from there from 328 to 340, and Trier grew into the largest city north of the Alps. As such it was the centre of an extensive and extremely busy communications network, one that certainly could have carried the ideas and the influence of a prominent and exotic churchman such as Athanasius all over the western empire.

The fame and sanctity of the lauras certainly seem to have reached the Loire Valley in France. Like Pachomius, St Martin of Tours was a soldier before he converted to Christianity and his most famous act of charity supplied another of the staple terms of the spreading faith. A cavalryman, Martin took pity on a ragged beggar he came across while travelling through the depths of winter and, with his sword, he cut his cloak in half. The Latin term for a small cloak is *capella* and it came to mean 'a chapel'. The more precise original meaning was a shrine, the place where this relic of St Martin was placed as his cult grew and people flocked to the places made sacred by his tread.

Like Anthony, Martin had a near-contemporary biographer who recorded incidents such as the halving of the military cloak, and Sulpicius Severus's writings contributed greatly to the saint's renown. When he left the cavalry, Martin became a follower of St Hilary of

Poitiers, but their relationship was cut short by the imposition of exile to Asia Minor. A Trinitarian, Hilary opposed the Arian beliefs of the imperial court and was banished to Phrygia – what is now central Turkey. While he appeared to continue to rule his bishopric at Poitiers from an immense distance, Hilary almost certainly became aware of the monasticism of the lauras. The austerity and purity of a life apart from the world and the turns and twists of imperial politics may have appealed to him at that time.

It certainly attracted Martin. The exile of his patron persuaded the young convert to leave the Loire Valley and make his way to Italy. After a series of miraculous incidents faithfully reported by Sulpicius Severus, Martin sought the peace and silence of the hermetic life on Isola d'Albenga in the Ligurian Sea, off the coast of north-west Italy. A humped, rocky outcrop, the home of a huge colony of herring gulls, it was uninhabited and some low, ruined walls on the southern side of the island may once have been all that sheltered Martin as he followed the precepts of hesychasm and the advice of the Desert Fathers.

Two unlikely snapshots of how outsiders saw the hermetic life can be found in the long poem '*De Reditu Suo*', 'On His Return', by Rutilius Claudius Namatianus. In 416 he sailed from Rome to his home in Gaul and, on the voyage, passed by two more islands off the Italian coast where communities of ascetics had established themselves. Rutilius's view of them may be more highly charged because he himself had converted to Christianity but did not admire the hermits' total withdrawal from secular society.

As we advance at sea, Capraia [part of the Tuscan Archipelago, not far from Elba] now rears itself – an ill-kept isle full of men who shun the light. Their own name for themselves is a Greek one, 'monachoi' [monks], because they wish to dwell alone with none to see. They fear Fortune's boons, as they dread her outrages: would anyone, to escape misery, live of his own choice in misery? What silly fanaticism of a distorted brain is it to be unable to endure even blessings because of your terror of ills? Whether they are like prisoners who demand the appropriate penalties for their deeds, or whether their melancholy hearts are swollen with black bile . . .

And a little further on in the text, more of Rutilius's own bile:

There rises in the midst of the sea the wave-girt Gorgon [Isola Gorgona, further north than Capraia and now a prison] with Pisa and Corsica on either side. I shun the cliffs, which are memorials of recent disaster; here a fellow-countryman met his doom in a living death. For lately one of our youths of high descent, with wealth to match, and marriage-alliance equal to his birth, was impelled by madness to forsake mankind and the world, and made his way, a superstitious exile, to a dishonourable hiding-place. Fancying, poor wretch, that the divine can be nurtured in unwashen filth, he was himself to his own body a crueller tyrant than the offended deities. Surely, I ask, this sect is not less power-ful than the drugs of Circe? In her days men's bodies were trans-formed, now 'tis their minds.

On Bishop Hilary's return from exile in Phrygia, both he and Martin came back to the Loire and founded Ligugé Abbey, now the oldest monastery in Europe. In keeping with the urban Roman tradi-tions of institutional Christianity, Martin was consecrated Bishop of Tours (rather than *abba* or *abbatus*) in 371 and he began a vigorous campaign against paganism. Eventually, the lure of the hermetic life proved too strong and he set up the community at Marmoutier a few years later. But even then, Martin continued to involve himself in the doctrinal battles of the Church and he travelled to the imperial court at Trier to plead for mercy for Priscillian. He was the leader of an ascetic sect that owed much to the legacy of Anthony, Chariton and the other hermits of Judaea and Egypt. Sulpicius Severus was at pains to make clear that Martin did not agree with the Priscillianists but he did not think they should die for their beliefs.

At the same time as Martin was searching for his God in the skies above Isola d'Albenga and listening to the cries of the herring gulls, another hermit prayed on a small island about seventy miles to the west. Caprasius had built a shelter on the smaller of the two large islands of Lerina, later the Lérins Islands, before he was joined by the young man who would eventually give his name to it. Honoratus rowed across the bay with his brother, Venantius, to join the hermit and imitate his exemplary life. Perhaps in pursuit of even more understanding and inspiration, the three men decided to board a ship at Marseilles that was bound for the ports of Judaea. They had embarked on a pilgrimage, fervently wishing to visit the famous laura of the desert. In the event, they travelled only as far as Greece before turning back. Venantius died there and his brother and Caprasius decided to go no further. With the permission of Bishop Leontius, the two men built a hermitage in the hills near Fréjus in modern Provence. Eventually they abandoned it and returned to the wild islands of Lérins so that, surrounded by the wastes of the sea rather than the sands of the desert, they could live in closer imitation of the laura and, as a community developed, they adopted the rules of Pachomius.

Amongst those who joined Honoratus and the ageing Caprasius was Lupus, the son of a wealthy patrician and a recent convert. Like Anthony, he had sold his estate and given the money to the poor. An outstanding young man of great piety, Lupus was soon appointed Bishop of Troyes, probably in 427. Two years later, with Germanus, Bishop of Auxerre, he was sent to Britain by the Council of Arles to help the bishops there combat the spread of the heretical teachings of Pelagius. Such was the spite and hatred for what was seen as heresy, the mild-mannered St Augustine of Hippo raged against this British theologian as 'a fat hound weighed down by Scotch porridge'. For the times, the visit of Germanus and Lupus was well documented and, even though accounts of the events were undoubtedly salted with propaganda, it appears to have been successful. And it seems a historical irony that, through the journeying of both heretical and orthodox admirers of the hermits of the lauras, their ideas and sayings were probably transmitted to Britain and eventually to Ireland.

A year after Lupus and Germanus returned, Pope Celestine I ordained Palladius as a bishop and sent him 'to the Irish believing in Christ'. This mission of conversion may well have been pre-emptive since the Pope and his councils of bishops seemed constantly anxious about the spread of Pelagianism. It is possible that Germanus of Auxerre sent Palladius to Rome to receive a commission directly from Celestine. The later Irish annalists recorded that the new bishop made landfall at Arklow in County Wicklow, where he began the labour of conversion.

Palladius's role in the creation of Christian Ireland has been submerged by the fame and promotion of Patrick, thought of as the sole 'Apostle of the Irish'. It is likely that this earlier mission was much more successful than has been allowed. The 'Irish believing in Christ' may have been led by St Ciaran of Saighir. Pushed into the background by the hagiographers of Patrick, his work probably predates his mission and some scholars believe he was active in the late fourth century. Tradition holds that he went to Marmoutier to learn directly from St Martin. On his return, Ciaran retreated into the wooded hills of Ossory, an ancient kingdom in south-eastern Ireland. There, in the Slieve Bloom Mountains, he lived the solitary life of a hermit, wearing animal skins, perhaps in imitation of St John the Baptist. But soon, like Anthony and Martin, Ciaran was joined by others and a monastery of cells grew up around him. It was said that his mother, Liadan, led a group of devout women into the mountains.

Palladius probably brought three men with him. Auxilius, Secundinus and Iserninus are obscure figures but later sources associate them with origins in France and even Italy. It seems likely that they were well aware of the teachings of St Martin and others and that may be the reason Pope Celestine was anxious to send a bishop to Ireland. In 428, the pope wrote an irritated letter to the bishops of Vienne and Narbonne in Gaul, objecting to the election of a monk to the vacant see of Arles. He wished to see the local clergy promoted and not 'wanderers and strangers'. Here is part of the text of the letter that show how sniffy he was about sainted solitaries:

They who have not grown up in the church act contrary to the church's usages . . . coming from other customs they have brought their traditional ways with them . . . clad in a cloak and with a girdle round their loins . . . Such a practice may be followed . . . by those who dwell in remote places and pass their lives far from their fellow men. But why should they dress in this way in the churches of God, changing the usage of so many years, of such great prelates, for another habit?

The urban, Roman church had been organised along clear, hierarchical lines, following the example of imperial civil administration. Order, custom and practice, to say nothing of clean clothes and bathing, were being threatened by what seems to have been the growing reputation of these unkempt and unwashed holy men who emerged from the woods and the deserts.

The oral transmission of ideas and experiences is very difficult to trace with any certainty. Men like Pelagius, Hilary, Martin, Honoratus, Caprasius and Lupus certainly admired the Desert Fathers and imitated their beliefs and customs in the West, but the most emphatic link was a fascinating figure known as John Cassian. Some scholars believe that his origins were on the western shores of the Black Sea, others that he came from a wealthy, patrician family in Gaul, modern France. Fluent in Latin and Greek, Cassian was certainly well educated.

As a young man, he travelled to Judaea and entered a hermitage near Bethlehem. After three years in that community, he moved on to the Desert of Scetis – now known as Wadi El Natrun – west of the Nile delta. Doctrinal disputes divided the different laura and, in search of resolution, presumably in some sort of leadership role, Cassian went first to Constantinople to plead for the interpretations he had come to believe in and, from there, he travelled to the papal court in Rome. What took place there is unclear but it is certain that his experience and interpretation of the laura impressed those who listened to him.

In 415, John was invited to found a monastery at Marseilles that would follow the teachings of the Desert Fathers and be a laura in the west. The Abbey of St Victor still stands, much changed from the simple cells and communal buildings of the first monastery. It was to become a fount of ecclesiastical wisdom, not only enormously influential in the western provinces of the decaying empire but also in places where Rome had never ruled, principally Ireland. Cassian also began to write. Sometime after 420, he produced two major devotional works – *The Institutes of the Coenobia* and *The Conferences of the Desert Fathers*. The first focused on detailed advice on how to set up and manage a monastery and the second concerned 'the training of the inner man and the perfection of the heart'.

It seems that John Cassian was critical of Marmoutier and the work of St Martin as it had been recorded by Sulpicius Severus. He believed the movement was indeed inspired by the example of the Eastern hermits but that the new foundation was chaotic. *The Institutes* were an attempt at a prescription for much greater order, in particular insisting on the central importance of manual labour. But Cassian did admire the community at Lérins, presumably because it followed the precepts of Pachomius more closely and certainly because he was impressed by the pious example of Honoratus. Part of *The Conferences* was dedicated to the Abba of Lérins.

This work was based on recollection. Cassian recorded what he had learned from the elders of the Egyptian laura at Scetis and *The Conferences* were to prove immensely influential. In the late sixth century, Benedict of Nursia, an Italian monk who founded several communities before he died at Monte Cassino in 547, was inspired. He based much of his famous monastic rule on what Cassian remembered and wrote down. These principles of the spiritual and ascetic life were read aloud in later Benedictine monasteries after the evening meal and from the Latin subtitle of *Collationes* comes the term 'collation' for a meal.

According to the Desert Fathers, hermits and monks who wished to move closer to God should follow a process of three stages. In the long hours of solitude in their cells or while they practised mortification of the flesh, novices had first to clear the high hurdle of *purgatio*

in Latin. Through prayer and self-denial, they needed to triumph
over the temptations of the flesh by purging their gluttony, banish-
ing their lust and dismissing all desire for possessions. This was a
long and often arduous journey and it relied heavily on a moral
strength that might be bolstered by grace, with the help of the Holy
Spirit.

The second stage was *illuminatio*. Using the New Testament and
in particular Christ's Sermon on the Mount, monks attempted to
build a life based on holiness and on charity as they looked after the
poor and the sick, sharing all they possessed unstintingly. If they had
the will and power to move on, these men and women could expect
at last to come to the final stage of *unitio*, a union of their soul with
God. If this level of understanding was attained, it often came
towards the end of a life of prayer and mortification and many would
retreat into the desert or into uninhabited or remote places so that
they could meet their maker in perfect solitude.

In common with other contemporary theologians, John Cassian
believed that Christians were constantly at war. Satan and his
demonic armies were everywhere. Here is a characteristic extract
from *The Sayings of the Desert Fathers*: 'It happened that as Abba
Arsenius was sitting in his cell that he was harassed by demons. His
servants, on their return, stood outside his cell and heard him praying to God in these words, "O God, do not leave me. I have done
nothing good in your sight, but according to your goodness, let me
now make a beginning of good."'

In *The Institutes*, Cassian wrote of what became known as the *laus
perennis*, 'perpetual praise'. In each community, groups of monks
would take turns to pray out loud or recite or sing psalms or read
scripture at all times, even through the night. It was believed that
demons loved the darkness and were especially active at night, so the
unceasing recital of the Word of God would create the best barrier
against the assaults of the hellish hosts of Satan.

Cassian's work offers the clearest sense of how these early communities of ascetics were run, or aspired to be run, and what their daily
lives were like. The spiritual heft of *The Institutes* and *The Conferences*

was clear and compelling; both undoubtedly influenced two men who were central to the growth of the early Church in Britain and Ireland and, in particular, the holy men who sailed their curraghs in the sixth and seventh centuries to the western islands and the Atlantic shores of Scotland in search of angels.

2

The Deserts of the North

'My name is Patrick. I am a sinner, a simple country person, and the least of all believers. I am looked down upon by many.' So begins *The Confession of St Patrick*. Probably composed around 470, this very rare example of contemporary written record appears to be authentic, a clear and vivid voice, and its contents offer precious insights, unravelling some mysteries and deepening others. These self-effacing opening lines may be more than a formula. *The Confession* can be read as a defence against some undisclosed sin or offence, but it is also a declaration of faith that hints at the influence of John Cassian's *Conferences*.

Patrick continues: 'My father was Calpurnius. He was a deacon; his father was Potitus, a priest, who lived at Bannavem Taburniae.' These two sentences are central, critical to any clear understanding of Patrick, his origins and the nature of his faith. In the summer of 2002, I visited a remarkable man, a very great scholar and archaeologist, and, on an evening I shall never forget, their meaning was explained to me. Professor Charles Thomas had written an elegant account of Celtic Britain and I had been commissioned to make a television series called *The Sea Kingdoms*. A journey up the western coasts of Britain and Ireland that began in Cornwall, at Penwith, on the high and windy cliffs of the Lizard Peninsula, the programmes would pick up many of the themes in Thomas's book. He had agreed to do an interview and, after some wrong turnings, we found his very beautiful house near Truro. It was wonderful, warm and inviting, a place where I learned a great deal.

There seemed to be several sitting rooms, all furnished with deep, comfortable sofas, warmed by crackling fires, and every wall was lined with bookshelves. But in his study, Professor Thomas did not work sitting at his desk. Instead, his doggedly manual typewriter was perched on what looked like a cut-down classical column. It stood at the right height for him to be able to rattle its ancient keys while standing up. A chronically bad back was the reason. 'What do you want me to say? And how long do you want it?' Professor Thomas had clearly done many television interviews and in less than an hour, a very short time in TV production, the crew were packing up their gear.

Mrs Thomas had gone up to London 'to some concert or other' and so, with glasses full to their winking brims with at least three measures of gin and tonic, we sat down in front of a vast roaring fire that spat sparks on to an ancient carpet. It was spring and unseasonably cold on the Cornish Riviera that year. As Professor Thomas stamped out the bigger sparks, I talked about the long book I was writing about the history of the Scottish Borders. Since I wanted it to encompass Galloway, Dumfriesshire, Cumbria and Northumberland as well as the Tweed Valley, I told Thomas I had read his work on early Christianity, specifically what he had deduced about St Patrick's origins. 'I've been at this a while and, even when the evidence is thin to the point of invisibility, you get a powerful sense of the past in particular places.'

It was Thomas's firm belief that Patrick had been raised near Carlisle in the early fifth century – just at the time when the Roman province of Britannia was being cut adrift from the Western empire. Around 410, the embattled Emperor Honorius faced several barbarian invasions, Rome had been sacked by Alaric's Gothic army and a letter was sent to the cities of Britain telling them that they had to look to their own defences. But while the Vandals, Alans, Visigoths, Suebi and Goths trailed destruction in the Continental empire, Britannia was left relatively untouched, for perhaps thirty or forty years. The cities of London, Bath, York – and Carlisle – managed to extend their existence as the Continental empire gradually descended into chaos. The only threat came not from the east but from the west – from Ireland.

As Professor Thomas talked, I made notes, scribbling quickly as he disappeared into the kitchen to replenish our glasses. In essence, these two sentences in *The Confession* could be plausibly interpreted to mean that Patrick was Romano-British, he had been born and raised near Greenhead, between Haltwhistle and Brampton on a modern map of North Cumbria and on an ancient one near the large Hadrian's Wall fort at Birdoswald. It was known as 'Banna' and Professor Thomas had recognised it in the first element of Bannavem Taburniae. Also a skilled and very experienced archaeologist, he knew that after the end of the province of Britannia in 410, the fort had remained occupied and that there existed a *vicus* – a civilian settlement – beyond its walls.

Towards the end of the fifth century, a substantial wood-built hall had been raised on the stone foundations of one of the Birdoswald's granaries. Other buildings – stores and stables – had also been built inside the stone-walled perimeter and the heavily fortified eastern gateway appeared to have been refurbished. Birdoswald had been no post-imperial shadow or shell, a ruin used as shelter by local farmers. Long after the empire in the west had faded, it had become a power centre, a place where a British king or warlord held court.

That extended continuity was persuasive but the remainder of the place-name in *The Confession* added more substance to Professor Thomas's deductions. Dialects of Old Welsh were spoken all over Roman and post-Roman Britain and *burn* or *bern* meant 'a mountain pass'. At Greenhead, immediately to the south of the Vallum, the huge ditch dug behind the Wall, there is indeed a steep-sided pass. Geography seemed to fit Patrick's text. Parking that piece of parsing for a moment and allowing me to scribble even more, Thomas talked about a wider geography and the sentence that immediately followed in *The Confession*: 'His [Potitus's] home was near there, and that is where I was taken prisoner. I was about sixteen at the time. At that time, I did not know the true God. I was taken into captivity in Ireland, along with thousands of others.'

Patrick's abduction argued for his origins to be located somewhere near the north-west coast of Britannia in the early fifth century

– somewhere Irish pirates and slavers could reach in their seagoing curraghs. It is clear from *The Confession* that after he was captured, Patrick spent a long time in the north of Ireland and so it may well be that his family had an estate near Carlisle, Luguvalium on ancient maps, somewhere easily and quickly available to northern Irish raiders.

The city had grown in importance in the fourth century when the administration of the province of Britannia had been reorganised. In 369, Carlisle was probably designated as the capital place of Valentia, one of five smaller administrative units. It was still a functioning town in 685 when it was visited by St Cuthbert and the Queen of Northumbria. Here is a passage from the anonymous *Life* of the saint: 'Cuthbert, leaning on his staff, was listening to Wagga, the Reeve of Carlisle, explaining to the Queen the Roman wall of the city.' And, in his *Life of Cuthbert*, Bede added some detail: '[T]he citizens conducted him around the city walls to see a remarkable Roman fountain that was built into them.' This implied that a water supply, probably via an aqueduct, was still working almost three centuries after the Roman province of Britannia ceased to exist. And, much later, in the twelfth century, the English historian William of Malmesbury visited the city and marvelled at a large, arched stone building that carried an inscription to Mars and Venus.

The reason the survival of Roman Carlisle into the fifth century and beyond mattered, according to Professor Thomas, was the information Patrick supplied about his family. He tells us that his father was Calpurnius and that he held office both in the church and in a Roman city. The role of a deacon in the early Church was that of a lay helper who may have looked after secular matters. It certainly means that Calpurnius was a practising Christian and a member of an established Church, one that was at least twenty or thirty years old. Patrick also wrote of his grandfather, Potitus, saying that he had been ordained a priest. That speaks of a wider Church, with bishops who could perform these ceremonies. Written records note that there were bishops in Britain as early as 314. Alban was probably the earliest British martyr, a soldier killed at Verulamium, St Alban's.

Two later martyrs, Aaron and Julius, also suffered death for their faith, either at Carlisle or Chester – the evidence is unclear.

Elsewhere in *The Confession*, Patrick wrote that he lived on a *villula*, a small estate, and that his father was sufficiently wealthy to have male and female servants, some of whom were also abducted by the Irish raiders. When Patrick returned home after a long captivity and a journey that would change his life, his father tried to persuade him to stay and undertake *munera*, or duties of public office, in Carlisle. Calpurnius was also a *decurion* of the city, a member of a group known as the *ordo*. They were a hundred men of means and standing who essentially acted as the city council and his father was anxious that Patrick should follow him into public office. All of which, taken together, argues for the origins of Patrick and the sort of Christianity that he first knew to be located in the far north-west of the old Roman province of Britannia.

When Professor Thomas and I shook hands on the doorstep of his lovely house, it was growing dark and my patient and long-suffering driver wanted his supper. It had been a magical meeting, and when I came to write my history of the Borders I leaned heavily on my notes of Thomas's brilliant deductions and the voluminous reading he recommended. We corresponded and he kindly read my manuscript, saving me from a few blunders. In 2016 I was sad to read Professor Thomas's obituary but glad he had lived a long and productive life. I had taken his advice and acquired a copy of St Patrick's *Confession* and a careful re-reading of it helped me towards some understanding of the atmosphere of early Christian Ireland and the minds of the saints who sailed their curraghs to Scotland's Atlantic shores a century later.

Here is another fascinating passage from *The Confession*:

After I arrived in Ireland, I tended sheep every day, and I prayed frequently during the day. More and more the love of God increased, and my sense of awe before God. Faith grew, and my spirit was moved, so that in one day I would pray up to one hundred times, and at night perhaps the same. I even remained in the woods and on the mountain, and I would rise to pray before dawn in snow and ice and rain. I never felt the worse for it, and I never felt lazy – as I realise now, the spirit was burning in me at that time.

The resonances of this account of what amounted to a hermetic life in the hills of northern Ireland are unmistakable – the mortification of the flesh, the solitude of the young shepherd isolated by his growing faith, and the constant recital and counting of the number of prayers. The woods and the mountains were the deserts of the north. Throughout *The Confession* are whispers of John Cassian's two stages in the journey towards *unitio*, a union with God. The images of Patrick praying in the snow, shivering for the love of the Lord God, rising early and forcing himself to stay awake at night, repeating his devotions over and over are the very essence of *purgatio*. But, if Patrick was abducted at the age of sixteen, 'did not know the true God' and led a solitary life in the hills far from any place of learning, then he can have had no knowledge of *The Conferences*. This passage may be a case of understanding history backwards – because, by *c.*470, when he wrote *The Confession*, Patrick certainly knew Cassian's work. Flecked through the account of his life and faith are strong hints of the second stage of *illuminatio* and the third, *unitio*.

What follows is the tale of Patrick's escape from captivity:

It was there one night in my sleep that I heard a voice saying to me: 'You have fasted well. Very soon you will return to your native country.' Again after a short while, I heard someone saying to me: 'Look – your ship is ready.' It was not nearby, but a good two hundred miles away. I had never been to the place, nor did I know anyone there. So I ran away then, and left the man with whom I had been for six years. It was in the strength of God that I went – God who turned the direction of my life to good; I feared nothing when I was on the journey to that ship.

At first, the sailors refused to take Patrick on board, but then:

one of them shouted aloud to me: 'Come quickly – those men are calling you!' I turned back right away, and they began to say to me: 'Come – we'll trust you. Prove you are our friend in any way you wish.' That day, I refused to suck their nipples, because of my reverence for God. They were pagans, and I hoped they might come to faith in Jesus Christ. This is how I got to go with them, and we set sail right away.

The invitation to suck these men's nipples is startling – jumping out of the text, it is an incident that reminds us how little is understood of pre-Christian society and its beliefs. Several historians have interpreted it as a pagan practice that signified an acceptance of the need to be obedient, or perhaps loyal. In any event, the ship sailed for three days before making landfall. Patrick gives no details of where he and his shipmates were and where they went inland. The text seems to imply more than one journey and another short period in captivity. 'A few years later', Patrick returned home to Carlisle, perhaps in the decade after 420, before he made another voyage, this time to Ireland to begin his famous mission of conversion.

Before he boarded a ship that took him west down the Solway, towards the Ulster coast, Patrick must have taken holy orders of some kind. The Church in Carlisle could have ordained him, and because of his family's close connections that must seem likely. But a later passage in *The Confession* suggests other possibilities: 'I would like to go to Gaul to visit the brothers and to see the faces of the saints of my Lord.'

Added to this clear evidence that Patrick certainly knew of and had probably visited communities in what is now France after he had slipped the bonds of slavery are powerful traditions that he studied at Marmoutier and that he accepted the monastic tonsure at Honoratus's community on the Lérins Islands. In both places, he will definitely have come into close contact with the ideas and precepts of John Cassian and the Desert Fathers.

Made around 450, the Latinus Stone is the oldest Christian monument yet found in Scotland. For many years, it was thought to have been a tombstone, but Professor Charles Thomas argued that it was almost certainly something else – something even more intriguing. His re-translation of the Latin inscription reads: 'We praise thee, o Lord! Latinus, grandson of Barravados, aged thirty-five, and his daughter, aged 4, made a shrine here.' It is not a grave marker but instead the commemoration of the foundation of a shrine or a monastic retreat. Above the inscription are the faint traces of a chi-rho symbol. The man who paid for the stone, and was perhaps the patron of the shrine associated with it, was not only the first Christian in Scotland whose name has come down to us, he was also someone who had it rendered in a Roman style. Two generations after the fall of the province of Britannia and the consequent military irrelevance of Hadrian's Wall, the link between Christianity and the memory of the empire was still powerful, even in a region of Scotland that is still thought to be remote. But, in fact, Galloway was almost certainly part of the province of the Roman city of Carlisle and it is the modern obsession with road travel that suggests remoteness. By sea, the settlements, churches and shrines were much closer, much easier to visit.

The Latinus Stone was found at Whithorn in Galloway, also the site of Scotland's earliest known church. Indelibly associated with St Ninian, it was first known as Candida Casa, 'the White House', because it had been built in stone and probably limewashed. About twenty-five miles to the west at Kirkmadrine, there are three more inscribed stones, probably from the early sixth century. They commemorate two bishops, Viventius and Mavorius. The name of Kirkmadrine is a version of the Church of St Martin, a very early dedication to the much-admired St Martin of Tours that was shared with Candida Casa at Whithorn, Taigh Mhàrtainn, 'the House of Martin'.

Ninian is a shadowy figure, his name a Latin version of *Nynia*, but he was probably sent by a bishop at Carlisle to minister to existing Christian communities in Galloway around 400. He may have taken some of the relics of St Martin of Tours with him to establish a shrine at Whithorn. More tradition encourages the notion that Ninian also visited Marmoutier and the Lérins Islands. The earliest notice of his mission of conversion is to be found in *The Ecclesiastical History of the English People*, written around 731 by Bede of Jarrow, a truly great scholar.

> The southern Picts, who live on this side of the mountains, are said to have abandoned the errors of idolatry long before this date [AD 565] and accepted the true Faith through the preaching of Bishop Ninian, a most reverend and holy man of British race, who had been regularly instructed in the mysteries of the Christian faith in Rome. Ninian's own episcopal see, named after St Martin and famous for its stately church, is now held by the English, and it is here that his body and those of many saints lie at rest. The place belongs to the province of Bernicia and is commonly called Candida Casa, the White House, because he built the church of stone, which was unusual amongst the Britons.

As ever, Bede is anxious to underline the achievements and reach of the Kingdom of Northumbria. In the seventh century, they over-ran Galloway and made it part of the Anglian kingdom. But what matters more than the politics is the sense of influences. There are mostly only gossamer traces. Nevertheless, I have come to believe that churchmen of the Dark Ages – such as Patrick, Ninian and others whose names survive only in obscure dedications or have disappeared entirely – travelled a great deal more than we realise. Even though four thousand miles separate the Antrim Hills from the deserts of Judaea and Egypt, I am certain that the teachings of the Desert Fathers travelled right across Europe. And, in Ireland, they exerted a powerful spiritual magnetism: they persuaded holy men to sail north into the unknown, to seek the deserts of the sea and to search for God in Hebridean skies.

3

The Colours of Martyrdom

Old and faded maps of the Atlantic shore of Scotland are speckled with dedications to ghosts – Irish saints who left behind little more than their names and memories of a forgotten piety. Kildavie in Kintyre, another Kildavie on Mull and Cladh Da-Bhi near Flodigarry on Skye were the churches of Da-Bhi and his graveyard. No one is sure when this holy man lived or died – the sole certainty is that he gave his life so completely to God that communities were moved to commemorate his sacrifice by naming their churches in his honour. Da-Bhi may be linked to a more substantial figure. Mo-Bhi mac Beoain, also known as Berchan, was abbot of a monastery at Glasnevin, near Dublin. Later hagiographers listed him as one of the Twelve Apostles of Ireland, saints associated with the mission of St Patrick in the fifth century. Mo-Bhi is said to have died in 544.

During the sixth century, and perhaps before, Irish monks began to seek martyrdom and Da-Bhi was probably one of the first to sacrifice his life for his Lord in this way. But what he sought was not the horrific deaths suffered by Christians in the amphitheatres of Rome. Here is a text known as the *Cambrai Homily*.

> Precious in the eyes of God:
> The white martyrdom of exile
> The green martyrdom of the hermit
> The red martyrdom of sacrifice.

Written in Early Irish in the seventh century, it is a concise expression – a drawing together of different strands of Christian thought.

In the Gospel of St Matthew, Jesus called upon his disciples to 'take up his cross' – in effect to submit themselves to the blood sacrifice, to red martyrdom. Christ's crucifixion and the beheading of John the Baptist were understood as martyrdoms. From classical Greek *martus*, the word originally meant 'a witness, one who brings testimony'. In the case of Jesus, St John and the many who died during the periods of imperial persecution, they stood witness to their faith, to the Word of God, and were prepared to die for it. Their reward was eternal life in the Kingdom of Heaven.

With the adoption of Christianity as the state religion of the Roman Empire, the possibility of red martyrdom largely disappeared. St Jerome was amongst the first to use the term 'white martyrdom'. A scholar and a desert hermit, he translated the Old and New Testaments from the original Hebrew into Latin while living in a cave near Bethlehem – allegedly where Christ had been born. It must have been a well-appointed cave, furnished with books, pens, ink and parchment, and it seems that a group of pious ladies looked after the saint as he worked. By the time of his death in 420, Jerome's work was beginning to exert great influence. He believed that the revered Desert Fathers had sought white martyrdom through their departure from cities and towns into the lonely wastes.

They had also practised strict and unbending asceticism. The *Cambrai Homily* elaborated: 'We carry the cross of Christ in two ways, both when we mortify the body through fasting, and when out of compassion for him, we regard the needs of our neighbour as our own. A person who has compassion for the needs of his neighbour truly carries the cross in his heart.'

Not only does this passage owe something to the stages of *purgatio* and *illuminatio* set out by John Cassian, it also reflects another absolutely central role for those who were prepared to endure extreme privation. The homily goes on to invoke the example of Christ once more: 'Everyone's sickness was sickness to Him, offence to anyone was offence to Him, everyone's infirmity was infirmity to Him.'

Lay people and especially powerful magnates and kings understood that the monks and nuns who fasted and mortified their flesh
in other ways were fighting a spiritual battle on behalf of everyone,
all who lived in the communities and kingdoms where they knelt in
their devotions. Their prayers and their example kept the tide of sin
(much of it committed by those magnates and kings who supported
them) and the Hosts of Hell at bay. Monasteries and hermitages
were fortresses of virtue defended by the pious with the help of God
and His angels.

During the fifth and sixth centuries, the colours of martyrdom
became more vividly defined. An Old Irish treatise, *De Arreis*,
describes green martyrs as those who underwent 'the fearsome
penances' of hunger and hard labour as well as passing entire nights
immersed in the chill waters of rivers, lochs and the sea or lying
naked but for a loincloth in a bed of nettles or on sharp nutshells or
beside the putrefying flesh of a corpse. And, if this was not virtue
enough, white martyrdom came to mean a complete separation
from all that an ascetic loved, a departure from the comforts and
consolations of home, family and friends and a pilgrimage into the
unknown on behalf of Christ as a witness to the Word of God. These
were the impetuses that persuaded the pious to sail north from the
coasts of Ireland across the trackless wastes of the sea and trust in the
Lord that He would protect them from storms and sea monsters.

Other dynamics were also at work. When he left Carlisle to begin
his mission in Ireland, St Patrick had rejected his father's urging to
take up *munera*, the duties of public office in the old Roman city.
Instead of becoming a *decurion* serving in the *ordo*, he saw himself as
a white martyr, abandoning all that was familiar and comfortable to
set out on a pilgrimage at God's bidding. As a Christian himself,
Patrick's father may have found that choice difficult to argue with.
As he set sail for Ireland, the young man took something of the
Church at Carlisle with him. In keeping with the traditions of the
Roman Church, Patrick saw himself as a bishop and not an *abba* like
Pachomius. At Armagh in the north of Ireland, he created the centre
of an episcopal diocese and began the work of conversion.

As the surprising invitation to suck his shipmates' nipples suggests, the new bishop found himself in a largely pagan society. *The Confession* contains very few details, few mentions of places and people and no dates, but it does seem that Patrick's approach was to seek out the powerful and attempt to bring them to God. If local kings could be converted, then their people would probably follow their example. The saint seems to have been successful in introducing the Word of God to women, especially aristocrats who gave him gifts in return. An undisclosed charge alluded to in *The Confession* may have been Patrick's acceptance of gifts from converts, particularly well-born women. These were probably not solicited. Gift giving was part of the fabric of early Irish society. Patrick's account also describes the baptism of thousands, what must have been large groups of ordinary farmers and their families.

Later hagiographers greatly accentuated the achievements of Patrick over the work of other Christian missionaries to Ireland, especially Palladius, the papal envoy. The balance of influence is difficult to weigh but it is clear that the diocesan structure based on Armagh did not flourish. Unlike Roman Britain, fifth-century Ireland had no cities or even small towns. A wholly rural society of farmsteads, fortresses and scattered townships, its demographic structure was very dispersed. Instead of urban bishoprics on the British and Continental model, what developed was a Christian society based on monasteries. By the sixth century many had been founded all over the Irish countryside, often at junctions of road and river routes. Usually, monasteries were little more than a cluster of simple cells protected by a vallum, or ditch and bank, and sometimes without a church, but they became a focus for the faithful. Behind the palisade were low wattle-and-daub huts of wooden plank structures. If there was a church, it too would have been built of wood. In Irish, the word for this type of church is *dairthech,* and it means 'an oak house'.

Immediately beyond the monastic vallum were the huts of the lay servants of the community, some of them slaves like Patrick. At first, these religious settlements looked very like the farms that surrounded them. These were circular palisaded enclosures known as *raths*. Having been given gifts of land, produce and sometimes precious objects by secular magnates in return for prayers and privileges, monasteries became larger, more elaborate, more powerful and central to the dispersed communities around them. And, instead of dioceses, the large monasteries formed the core of *paruchiae* – parishes of smaller communities, often those that had been founded by the mother house.

On the banks of the River Shannon, near Athlone, Clonmacnoise was founded in the middle of the sixth century by another St Ciaran where the Slighe Mhor, the great east-to-west land route, crosses the river. He cultivated the kings of Connaught and soon his monastery began to flourish. Its central precinct was surrounded and protected by impressive stone crosses, several churches were eventually built in the innermost sanctuary, the holy of holies, and wooden buildings were replaced by stone. Around these grew up the huts, houses and streets of a large secular community whose role was to support the monastic establishment and those visitors and pilgrims who began to come more and more frequently. Clonmacnoise and other foundations developed into monastic towns with populations of between 1,500 and 2,000 by the eleventh century.

Monks rarely took vows of poverty or chastity. What mattered was obedience to the abbot. Many were married with children, while others even became warriors. As centres of great wealth and prestige, monasteries needed to be protected – sometimes from each other. Wars between communities of monks occasionally broke out. In 664, there was heavy fighting at the monastery of Birr in County Offaly, in the centre of Ireland, and in 760 its monks fought a battle with Clonmacnoise, presumably over a dispute about property and rights of income. Soon afterwards, more than two hundred monks from the community at Durrow, founded by St Columba in the decade before he left for Scotland, were killed in a pitched battle with the belligerent monks of Clonmacnoise.

At the same time as most of Ireland's early monasteries were founded, and as some began to behave like miniature city-states, there was a parallel, very different impetus. Just as the Desert Fathers had rejected the imperial adoption of Christianity and all that it implied in the fourth and fifth centuries, some holy men turned away from the growing monastic towns. Like many of the early saints, Enda appears to have had royal connections, perhaps he even ruled for a time as a king in the north. Later accounts also hold that, after conversion, probably around 480 (there is no mention of Patrick's involvement even though it falls into the middle period of his ministry in the north), Enda sailed to Whithorn, to Ninian's Candida Casa. There, he was ordained a priest and the influences of what he learned in Galloway seem to have been profound.

Realising that literal isolation from the temporal world was an essential condition for a truly ascetic life, Enda founded a monastery on Inishmore, the largest of the Aran Islands, which lie off the Atlantic coast of Ireland in Galway Bay. In Irish, Inishmore is known as Árainn Mhór. *Arainn* means 'a ridge' and the island is an extension of the spectacular landscape of limestone pavements known as the Burren. To Enda, this flat, bleak, wave- and windswept island must have seemed like a bare, rocky, desert place – a desert in the ocean lashed by waves, a place at the mercy of God's grace.

For those who followed him, the holy man insisted on a severe regime of regular fasting and extreme mortification of the flesh. Monks were expected to lower themselves, clad only in their loincloths, into the frigid waters of the wild Atlantic, all the while praying aloud or reciting the psalms. Instead of sandy beaches, some of the shorelines of Inishmore are shelves of smooth limestone that slide under the incoming tide. Some monks intent on mortification may have simply walked out to sea on a pavement, a shivering pathway to the purification of their souls. Onshore, the monks built stone beehive cells, rock being much more plentiful than wood. They slept on the beaten earth of these draughty little huts, ate frugally when they were not fasting, and gave themselves willingly to God. Enda's monks called themselves 'the men of the caves' and 'the men of the cross'. Their unbending, iron rule certainly harks back to Pachomius and John Cassian and the revered Desert Fathers.

Attracted by Enda's reputation for piety, many came to his island for instruction and inspiration. Amongst them was St Brendan, a remarkable man who would later embrace both white and green martyrdom by sailing north to the Hebridean shores. The curraghs used by him and others are still made and sailed out of the harbour on the island. Another visitor was St Columba, also an aristocrat and later to be the founder of the community on Iona. Revered in Ireland as well as Scotland, he came to Inishmore as a young man and called it 'the Sun of the West'. It was said that before he came to Enda's community St Finnian had first visited St Martin's monastery at Marmoutier before returning to Britain to sit at the feet of St Cadoc at Llancarfan in South Wales. Another follower of the teachings of the Desert Fathers and the founder of many communities, Cadoc was a very influential figure.

Many groups of solitaries sought to move apart from the secular world by building their cells on islands off the Irish coast – Rathlin Island, off the coast of County Antrim, Tory Island, off the Donegal coast, and dozens of other islands around the rocky shores of the Dingle Peninsula in County Kerry – but none can match the spectacular Skellig Michael, the twin peaks of an undersea mountain that rises sheer out of the Atlantic eight miles off Ireland's southwestern coast. The most westerly point of Europe, on the very edge of eternity, it is a belly-hollowing place and the site of a most dramatic act of devotion, of complete belief. Probably founded by St Finnian in the early sixth century, the monastery perches five hundred and fifty feet above the roiling ocean on the narrow shelves of the sheer cliffs of Skellig Michael.

The peaks of the undersea mountain are connected by a ridge known as Christ's Saddle. Not far below the South Peak there are six large beehive huts, an oratory, a graveyard, many stone crosses and a series of drystone walls protecting narrow terraces. All are reached from sea level by a staircase of six hundred steps carved out of the rock. In high winds, low cloud, rain or all three, the climb to the monastery can be dangerous (in 1999, a German visitor fell to his death). On the North Peak, more stairs lead to a hermitage and these are even more hazardous.

What visitors see now are the remains of a completed monastery, but when Finnian sailed to Skellig Michael with several companions – usually there were said to be twelve, in imitation of Christ and the Apostles – there was nothing but wave-washed rock and screeching seabirds. Nothing at all, except a fierce piety and a determination to build a place where God would be worshipped with a wind-blown purity of purpose. Surely their prayers would be heard from the summit of the sea mountain. Devotion carved the steps from the cliffs and built the beehive huts, the walls and the oratory from rocks gathered and shaped to fit. But not quickly or safely. How did the first monks survive? Skellig Michael can be cut off from the mainland for many days in bad weather. What did they do when food ran out? Where did they sleep after their great labours on the vast rock? Was the work only undertaken in the better weather of the summer months?

What is unquestionable is that many will have died in the perilous construction of this utterly remarkable monastery. When a monk plunged to his death in the ocean, breaking bones as he fell, ricocheting off the jagged rock at the base of the cliffs, that was a moment of red martyrdom, a blood sacrifice for the love of God. Prayers will have been offered up immediately. In the midst of the fury of the elements and on days when the ocean was calm and the sun warmed their backs, these men were building a vast shrine, a cathedral of rock that reached up from the deeps of the world to the vaults of Heaven, a city of the godly. Skellig Michael was named after the archangel Michael, a celestial warrior, the leader of God's armies against Satan.

But the monastery was not enough. Once it had been established – and the work must have taken many years – the monks decided upon even more dangerous isolation. On the North Peak a hermitage was built. Another dizzying staircase was hacked out of the rock, and on a shelf in the cliff an oratory was raised. In this place, monks could separate themselves from the small community on the South Peak and lift their eyes upwards on this most extraordinary expression of piety. The love of God and the certainty of eternal life, nothing else, made Skellig Michael possible.

As well as its monastery and hermitage, there is a small, low structure built in drystane fashion without mortar known as a *leacht* on
Skellig Michael. *Leachta* are to be found at or near early Christian
sites all over Ireland. The one on Skellig Michael and another on
Inishmurray off the Sligo coast are the most famous but there is a
dense concentration of them in County Monaghan on the border
with Northern Ireland.

The builders of *leachta* keyed together stones to form what looks
like a square platform little more than a metre high and about four
metres square. Often a decorated slab was raised up in the centre,
like a thick candle on a birthday cake. There has been some specula-
tion as to what the function of a *leacht* was – an outdoor preaching
station, a stone pulpit or simply a means of keeping a carved stone
upright. But, in his *Illustrated Gaelic to English Dictionary*, Edward
Dwelly is unequivocal – *leac* means 'a tombstone' or 'a flagstone'. It
can also mean 'a ledge of rock jutting out from the foot of a cliff on
the foreshore and covered by the sea at flood tides'. The latter is a
wonderful example of how lexically tight and precise Gaelic can be
about the natural world. To explain the meaning of a four-letter
word, Dwelly is forced to use twenty-three English words. If a *leac* is
a tombstone, the obvious question is 'Who was buried underneath
it?' Clearly it was someone to be revered, and in Ireland human
remains have been found under some *leachta*. The habit of building
these unusual structures sailed across the North Channel and several
are to be found in Scotland. A few years ago, archaeologists discovered a *leacht* at Baliscate, near Tobermory on Mull. Their excavations
have shown it had been a religious site for centuries. Remnants of a
chapel and burial ground have been dated to between 610 and 690
while remains of a later chapel suggest the site was in use between
the twelfth and fifteenth centuries. Perhaps there are more *leachta* to
be discovered in Scotland – the resting places of saints whose sole
relic is their name.

4

The Land of Promise of the Saints

St Brendan soon after selected from his whole community fourteen monks. Taking these apart, the venerable father Brendan retired with them into an oratory where he thus addressed them: Dearly beloved fellow soldiers of mine, I request your advice and assistance, for my heart and mind are firmly set upon one desire; if it be only God's holy will. I have in my heart resolved to go forth in quest of the Land of Promise of the Saints . . . What do you think? What is your advice? But they, well knowing the purpose of their holy father, replied, as with one voice: Father-Abbot, your will is our will also. Have we not forsaken our parents? Have we not slighted our family prospects? Have we not committed into your hands even our very bodies? We are therefore, ready to go with you, whether unto life or unto death, provided only we find such to be the will of God.

. . .

St Brendan and the chosen brethren then decided to make a fast of forty days, at three days' intervals, and afterwards to take their departure. Those forty days having elapsed, St Brendan, affectionately taking leave of his monks, and commending them to the special care of the Prior of his monastery, who was afterwards his successor there, sailed forth towards the west, with fourteen brethren, to the island wherein dwelt St Enda, and remained there three days and three nights.

. . .

Having received the blessing of this holy father and all his monks, he proceeded to the remotest part of his own country . . . and there he fitted up a tent, near a narrow creek, where a boat could enter. Then St Brendan and his companions, using iron implements, prepared a light vessel, with wicker sides and ribs, such as is usually made in that country, and covered it with cow-hide, tanned in oak bark, tarring the joints thereof, and put on board provisions for forty days, with butter enough to dress hides for covering the boat and utensils needed for the use of the crew.

He then ordered the monks to embark, in the name of the Father, and of the Son, and of the Holy Ghost.

These extracts form the core of chapters two and three of *Navigatio Sancti Brendani Abbatis*, the fabled *Voyage of St Brendan*. It was a tale composed to be recited around 700 and was first written down sometime between 900 and 1000. It became so famous that its hero was forever after known as St Brendan the Navigator. Having sat at the feet of St Enda on Inishmore and clearly still seeing him as a mentor of some sort, he himself founded several communities, including the monastery at Clonfert in County Galway in the Irish Midlands, not far from the River Shannon. It appears to be the setting for the opening of the *Navigatio*.

The first chapter, more like a preamble setting up the premise of what follows, recounts the visit to the monastery of Barinthus, a monk with royal connections to the great Ui Neill dynasty of the north of Ireland. He told Brendan about Mernoc, a member of his own community, and his flight into the wastes of the sea to find a hermitage where he could become a solitary. 'Nigh unto the Stone Mountain' – a possible reference to Skellig Michael – he found an island 'full of delights'. When Barinthus caught up with Mernoc, the monk and his abbot set sail and headed even further west, 'towards the island called the Land of Promise of the Saints, which God will grant to those who succeed in latter days'. The 'latter days' is a phrase usually understood to mean the time of the Second Coming of Christ, when the world would be created anew.

Dazzled by these revelations, Brendan decided to see for himself and set sail for this remarkable island that sounded like an Edenic resort and a reward for all those saints (amongst whom he clearly included himself) who had served their Lord faithfully. The following twenty-four chapters of the *Voyage of St Brendan* see him and his band of fourteen (sometimes seventeen) monks sail to many clearly mythical islands – one of them surprised the monks as they lit a cooking fire because it turned out to be the back of a whale known as Jasconius – and spending seven years at sea. It is an early example of the Irish storytelling form known as *immram* (plural *immrama*). These were tales of voyages of discovery and many included fantastical elements intended to awe and amuse. But in this narrative, the story of the pious Irish monks who sailed to the Hebrides in search of angels, there is also much that is informative.

St Brendan did indeed sail away from Ireland and was one of the very earliest of the holy men to found monasteries on Scotland's islands. The opening chapters of his mythical voyage have something to say about how he and others who followed him set about sailing to real places and their motivation for risking their lives on unpredictable and unknown seas.

Most striking is the set of precise instructions on how to build a seagoing curragh. These vary very little from what I watched Padraig O'Duinnin do in his boatyard by the River Lee in Cork. It is very likely that Brendan's boat was much bigger than the one I saw shot into the river. It sounds as though it was a seven bencher since Brendan chose fourteen monks to accompany him, seven pairs of oarsmen. This appears to have been the standard for a large, seagoing curragh. The *Senchus Fer n-Alban* is a unique document, fascinating in its detail. A muster roll for the naval forces at the disposal of the kings of Dalriada, the Irish-speaking dynasts who began to colonise Argyll and the southern Hebrides in the sixth century, it was probably compiled in the eighth century. The various kindreds are bound to supply warriors who sail in seven-bench seagoing curraghs and are counted as paired oarsmen.

The seven pairs of oarsmen were not expected to row constantly. Brendan's boat almost certainly had two sails, one stepped amidships and the other a smaller foresail. Anticipating the need for running repairs on a hull that was only as thick as the hide of a cow, the monks stowed several spare hides and what they called butter to seal the sewn joins between them or around patches. This was also known as wool grease or lanolin and sheep secrete it from skin glands. Human beings also have a little lanolin, especially on our faces and necks, and it is intended to protect our skin against wet weather. With provisions for forty days, probably a stock phrase that just meant a long time, it is clear that Brendan was planning a long voyage. And, if the curragh had room for all of that cargo – 'all utensils needed for the use of the crew' – as well as sundry other items, then it must have been a large boat.

Even though they were made at the outset of a literally incredible journey, these preparations would have been little different for a real one. The rest of the text of the *Voyage* is full of sailing lore, composed by men who understood the ways of the sea and how their hide boats behaved in different conditions. And their audience will also have understood these subtleties. From the *Navigatio* and many other sources, it is clear that early Irish monks, along with secular society, were well acquainted with seafaring.

More context can be found in a famous biography. *The Life of St Columba* was written towards the end of the seventh century by Adomnán, his successor as Abbot of Iona and also his descendant. He had much to say about boats and sailing and especially about *immrama*. Adomnán is one of the very earliest sources for these stories. One of the most striking concerned Cormac Ua Liathain, a sixth-century Irish saint who did not appear to have had much luck – 'A truly holy man who no fewer than three times laboured on the ocean in search of a place of retreat yet found none.' His third and last voyage is described in detail by Adomnán:

He found himself in such danger that he came close to death. His ship had been driven with full sails by a steady wind from the south for fourteen summer days and nights, so that a straight course brought them to an area under the most northerly skies. They reckoned they had passed beyond the range of human exploration, and had reached a place from which they might not be able to return. There it happened after the tenth hour of the fourteenth day, that a source of terror appeared, rising up on all sides, most fearsome, almost unendurable. To that day, assuredly, no one had ever seen such a thing: the whole sea was covered with deadly, loathsome little creatures. They struck with horrible force against the keel, against the sides of the boat, against the stern and the prow, and the pressure of them was so great that it was thought they would pierce the skin covering of the boat. These creatures (as those present afterwards described) were about the size of frogs, but exceedingly troublesome because they had spines, though they did not fly but merely swam [possibly jellyfish?]. They were also a great nuisance to the blades of the oars. Nor were these the only prodigies that Cormac and his fellow sailors saw, though there is not time here to describe them. They were greatly disturbed and frightened, and with tears they prayed to God, who is a loyal and ready helper in time of trouble.

By remote control from Iona, Columba managed to persuade the wind to change direction. Instead of a southerly, a north wind blew Cormac's curragh out of the sticky clutches of the sea monsters. This episode was recounted in such a matter-of-fact tone that it seemed to be well understood that not only did extraordinary things happen at sea, it was also very dangerous, a place where sailors took their lives in their hands. And that turned out to be part of the attraction, a welcome, random facet of white and green martyrdom.

By the time Adomnán was writing, the seagoing search for a hermitage, a watery desert or 'diseart', had become an end in itself, an attempt at martyrdom that accumulated virtue even when it was not successful. Sometimes monks took extraordinary risks by going to sea in curraghs that did not have a tiller attached to the stern or even oars to pull it along. The winds, the weather, currents and tides would take them wherever God's will wanted them to go. They were in His hands. No doubt some were swept far out into the vastness of the Atlantic Ocean, where they died a martyr's death of starvation and thirst. Others fetched up in surprising places.

In the year 891, the *Anglo-Saxon Chronicle* recorded that three Irish monks had come ashore on the English coast. Presumably with no idea where they were, these disoriented, disappointed martyrs were taken to the court of King Alfred. When the adventurer and sailor Tim Severin read the *Voyage of St Brendan*, it sparked his imagination and his curiosity. Reading through the itinerary of visits to fantastic islands, it occurred to him that some of them might not be so fantastical after all. As he read and researched more and spoke to academics, it began to dawn on him that the *Navigatio* might not be a fable but a gilded, much embroidered version of a real journey. Hidden beneath the stories of whales, Islands of Delight and the Land of Promise of the Saints, Severin saw what he came to believe was an account of the discovery of America. Four centuries before the Vikings and almost ten centuries before Columbus, had St Brendan sailed his boat clear across the Atlantic Ocean? In two stages, in 1976 and 1977, Tim Severin decided to find out if he had, not with more research but by doing it and in exactly the same sort of craft built by Irish monks – the fragile, thin-skinned curragh.

Following Brendan's instructions in the *Navigatio* to the letter, Severin began to source the materials needed. Cowhides had to be tanned in oak bark, a process that had become all but obsolete. The framework was built from Irish oak and ash at Crosshaven, near the city of Cork. Once it was complete and the hides were ready, the most critical and difficult phase began. The oak-bark tanned hides had to be sewn together into a watertight skin, fitted snugly on to the frame and caulked with wool grease. A highly skilled job, it was done slowly and painstakingly under the supervision of an expert harness marker and saddler.

Once the boat had been completely fitted out with two masts, leather sails and flax ropes and a crew of five assembled, sea trials began. From generations of experience, Irish monks were steeped in sea lore and knew how to sail ocean-going curraghs in all weathers and conditions. Before they could risk themselves and their fragile boat on the face of the mighty Atlantic, Tim Severin and his crew had to learn all of these ancient skills. Something incidental that surprised them seemed to me to make a link with Brendan and the solitaries who sailed in search of angels. As it made its way through the waves, the curragh was very quiet. There was of course no thrumming engine but also no keel for the waves to wash and slap against. As Padraig O'Duinnin observed, the boat sat like a seagull on the waves. Such was the peace of sailing that at times there was very little conversation amongst Tim Severin's crew.

When the curragh, named appropriately *Brendan*, was finally launched, Eamonn Casey, the Bishop of Kerry, dressed in his splendid cope, read a poem he had composed. It harked back to Brendan, his spiritual ancestor.

> Bless this boat, O True Christ,
> Convey her free and safe across the sea.
> You are like a blessing of Brendan's time,
> Bless this boat now.
> Guide our journey in it to sheltered land,
> To go to the Land of Promise is your right,
> You are like a guide of Brendan's time,
> Guide our boat now.

Soon after they had set out from the Dingle peninsula, the crew of the curragh began to sail through history. They tied up at the little harbour of Inishmore so that they could visit St Enda's island, just as the young Brendan had done. Hugging the coast, they passed Scattery Island and then the lonely hermitage of St MacDara's Island and several other deserts in the ocean. But then near-disaster struck. A storm blew up and drove *Brendan* far out into the Atlantic. In mountainous seas, Severin found it impossible to manoeuvre the curragh and he feared they could be swamped or might capsize at any moment. Tiny and almost invisible, they were nearly run down by a big fishing boat as night fell. It missed them by inches, its crew having no idea the curragh was there.

When the storm abated and the wind changed to a kinder south-westerly, they managed to run before it and steer a course back to the Irish coast. Tim Severin realised that *Brendan* was at the mercy of the winds and the weather conditions. And, with all of the repeated references to fair and foul winds in Adomnán's *Life of St Columba*, it is clear that the monks who sailed the oceans in curraghs understood that too.

The crew of *Brendan* put in at Ballyhoorisky on the north coast of Donegal, rested after their battle with the Atlantic storm and readied their boat for their voyage to the Hebrides and beyond. On the afternoon of 30 May 1976, they were towed out into the open sea and set a course to the north, north-east, bound for the island of Iona and Columba's monastery. And instead of being tossed about by gales, they were immediately becalmed. There was no alternative but to wait for the wind. When it finally picked the following morning, the curragh began to make good, steady progress. In these waters and up the west coast of Scotland, the prevailing wind tends to be a south-westerly and, despite the collapse of the cross yard, the horizontal arm that carries the mainsail, *Brendan* made landfall on Iona only twenty-four hours after leaving the Irish coast. They then sailed onwards to Tiree, where the curragh's very shallow draught saved them from running aground, or worse, on dangerous reefs. In Tim Severin's excellent account of their voyage up the Minch to Stornoway, he marvelled at the speed *Brendan* could achieve as it ran before the prevailing wind.

The curragh and its hardy crew did achieve their unlikely goal. Having avoided ice floes, repaired a hole in the cowhide in freezing water, survived more storms and endured much, almost monkish, privation, *Brendan* successfully crossed the vastness of the North Atlantic and was hauled ashore on Peckford Island, one of the Wadham Islands off Newfoundland. The voyage did not prove that St Brendan discovered America before the Vikings and Columbus, but it showed that he *could* have. And, more than that, it suggested that, from the fifth and sixth centuries onwards, there was a great deal of rapid and frequent communication between Ireland and

Hebridean Scotland. People and ideas flowed up and down the Atlantic shore as those who sought green and white martyrdom turned their gaze northwards.

The magnetic pull of the ocean and its islands certainly predated the time of the saints. Long traditions sang of Tír na nÓg, 'The Land of the Young', a version of the Celtic Otherworld that lay in the west, out of sight across the sea. It was the resort of the pagan pantheon, the Tuatha de Danann – 'the Goddess Danu's people'. Echoes of this ancient, beguiling, mythic geography can be clearly heard in the *Navigatio*. Beyond the waves lay Tir Tairngire, 'the Land of Promise', and the voyage to it could be sailed across a beautiful image. Mag Mell is 'the Plain of Honey' and it described the golden path made by the sun setting over the ocean. The monks who took their curraghs to the Hebrides knew that they sailed along the edge of the world and perhaps they also believed that they were moving along the edge of Heaven.

PART TWO

THE ROCK
OF THE SAINT

Eileach an Naoimh

5

Setting off for the Edge of the World

The day dawned dark and foreboding. Only three days after midsummer, the solstice and the bright sun at its zenith, storm clouds were massing. Out to the west, thunderheads loomed, smoky piles of gigantic cumulus clouds were blowing in rain as I packed my car. It was 5 a.m. and our farm was still fast asleep when I turned down the long track to the tarmacked B road and then north on the A7. Ahead of me was a long drive to Oban, the mighty Atlantic and the wave-worn shores of its islands.

I had decided to follow Brendan to Eileach an Naoimh, 'the Rock of the Saint', an island on the windward edge of a tiny archipelago known as the Garvellachs. The name means 'wild rocks' and to the west of them lie the vast wastes of the ocean with no shelter from any storm. Just like Skellig Michael, it was the sort of raw, elemental place that attracted these ascetic men. Eileach an Naoimh is uninhabited now and difficult to reach by boat. For a price that would have bought me a ticket to cross the entire Atlantic instead of only about six nautical miles, I had persuaded a local charter company to take me to the island, get me ashore and then return at the end of the day to pick me up. But the weather was shutting down and rain spattered my windscreen as I drove through the Border hills.

Drawn from Irish annals often compiled a long time after the events they list, the chronology of the conversion of the West is both approximate and provisional. It is important to bear in mind when reading the early accounts, including Adomnán's *Life of Columba*, that these were not intended as history. Their purpose was to relate stories of sanctity, of the exemplary lives of holy men, and they paid little attention to the need to sort out who did what, where, when and with whom. There are few certain dates, some identifiable places, some mysterious allusions and many omissions.

The first white martyr to steer his curragh north-east from Ireland's shore was not Columba. It might have been St Ciaran of Saighir. Often associated with St Patrick as another of the Twelve Apostles of Ireland in the later fifth century, he was a hermit, a wild solitary who reputedly wore animal skins and hid from the world in remote places. Just as John the Baptist had prefigured the Coming of Christ, the trope of Ciaran as a voice in the wilderness praying and preparing the way for the coming of Patrick and the beginning of his mission seems altogether too pat to reflect any historical reality, a construction run up long after memories of the actual events of the time had withered.

Place-name evidence suggests that Ciaran sailed to Kintyre, the closest part of the Scottish landmass to Ireland, only twelve miles across the North Channel and often clearly visible from the Antrim shore. Near Campbeltown is St Ciaran's Cave. At the foot of steep cliffs and only safely accessible at low tide, it is the largest of a cluster of caves around a small headland. An impressive fissure in the rock, the cave is forty metres long and about eight metres wide for much of its length. Chilly and salt-sea washed, it could have been home to more than one hermit, a place where the flesh would certainly have been mortified on stormy winter nights. There are carvings in the rock that might date as early as the seventh century but there is nothing that might certainly associate the cave with Ciaran. More place-names offer a stronger, if circumstantial, link. The original Gaelic version of Campbeltown was Ceann Loch Chille Chiarain, 'the Head of the Loch of the Church [or Chapel] of Ciaran', the sea loch where the town grew into a port. Kilkerran was the name of the surrounding parish and remains in use for the southern part of the town. There are also whispers of reverence for Ciaran on Islay, Lismore and on Lewis but these are likely to be memories of another St Ciaran, the abbot of Clonmacnoise.

For the year 577, the Irish annals note the death of St Brendan. As well as being well travelled, he appears to have been long lived, certainly a generation older than Columba. Even if he did not cross the North Atlantic, Brendan did sail often and to the north, and there are scores of sites dedicated to him on the Atlantic shores of Ireland and Scotland. The earliest life of the saint was written sometime after his death but it insists, as do other sources, that his earliest foundation was amongst the wild islands of the Hebrides: 'He [Brendan] came to a certain island of Britain called Aileach, and there founded a church, proposing to remain there to the end.'

When I reached the watershed summit of Soutra Hill and its wide vista of the drama of Scotland's geography, the green plain of the Lothians, Edinburgh's spires and castle, the Forth and Fife beyond, I could see rain clouds moving through, clustering over the dark heads of the distant mountains of Perthshire. Wind blew from the west and I wondered if I would see the rocky shore of Eileach an Naoimh that day, or any time soon, unless the weather settled. It was only three days after midsummer so at least the Highland days would be at their longest. Perhaps the strength of the wind would be more influential than the rain and only breezes were forecast. If the sun appeared, then there would be a dusky yellow glow in the sky even after midnight as it edged along the rim of the world towards the next morning.

I had packed wet weather clothes for my week amongst the islands, planning each day in turn, adding up what I would need and then packing even more. It could all go wrong, of course, or even have to be abandoned, but my car carried everything I thought I would need – providing I could get back to it from the islands. Two pairs of waterproof walking boots were essential since no boot I have ever pulled on keeps out the wet all day, especially if there is tussocky, uneven grass to be crossed – which there would be on Eileach an Naoimh and elsewhere. Because I had room, I even threw in a pair of wellies – you never know.

When and if I reached these remote islands and found myself clambering ashore, I was determined to do all I could to see them through the eyes of these leathery old saints as they pulled their curraghs above the high tide mark. Like them, I was determined upon solitude and would not seek conversation or company, despite my sociable instincts. In pursuit of an understanding of the lives of solitaries, I would be silent and alone. That meant I had to be self-sufficient, at least on the islands. In a backpack, I crammed a complete change of clothes, a spare mobile phone, fully charged, a compass and maps, a spare hat, two bars of thick chocolate, two pork pies and two small bottles of water. Finally, I squeezed in a thin but waterproof groundsheet in case I got stranded overnight.

I was taking my car rather than public transport and had booked a self-catering cottage near Oban in order to avoid the conversation that staying in a B&B or a hotel might involve. Because the cottage claimed to have Wi-Fi and a mobile phone signal, I also indulged in the luxury of taking my laptop, more maps, three bottles of New Zealand Sauvignon Blanc and some reference books. Hamish Haswell-Smith's sailors' guide to the Scottish Islands is a master-work, comprehensive and indispensible.

Central Scotland is clogged with cars. For long periods in the mornings and early afternoons, the traffic around Edinburgh and Glasgow is slow moving, often stationary. The M8 between the cities is usually little more than a queue. By stark contrast, the M9 to Stirling and the heart of the southern Highlands is gloriously open, fast, the way a motorway should be. As I sped past the belching chimneys of the refineries, the chemical plants of the port at Grangemouth and the vast, stinking refuse dump near Falkirk, I realised that seventy miles an hour would seem like warp-speed when I reached the mountains. Nevertheless, I was making good time and, barring mishap, would arrive at Seil Island at 10.45, where my expensive Rigid Inflatable Boat (RIB) would be waiting.

Passing the sentinel mass of Stirling Castle, dark and dour in the downpour, I turned north-west towards Callander and the mountains. So far as I could see, the rain was on for the day and the sky was an undifferentiated grey. The treetops told me that the wind had eased, and while it might make a crossing to Eileach an Naoimh possible, it would not move the rain through quickly. Beyond the tartan and shortbread shops of Callander's main street, Scotland's geography suddenly looks as though it was devised by children. The flatlands of Flanders Moss, long ago drained and now very fertile, and the farmlands to the north slam abruptly into the Highland Fault Line, a geological divide that sees the mountains rear up as though they had pushed through the crust of the green Earth.

At Kilmahog, kitsch takes over from geology. Near the car park for the Trossachs Woollen Mill, a roadside field was once home to Hamish the Highland Cow. Despite his impressive horn spread and rich, shaggy auburn coat, this old bull seemed at ease with the constant stream of people who came to photograph him and pat his magnificent head. Perhaps it was the treats he was offered that made him so patient and docile. He even had a middle name and a surname. His many friends called him Hamish McKay Denovan. The managers of the woollen mill occasionally arranged holidays for the old boy – 'farm breaks', where he could relax out of the spotlight and recover from all that celebrity.

In 1996 Hamish had a close brush with an unwanted destiny. The BSE epidemic meant that all cattle over three years old in many areas had to be culled. Immediately, a Save Hamish campaign cranked into action and, remarkably, he was spared a visit from the slaughter men. Fortified by love, mercy and many titbits, the old bull went on to live for almost twenty-three years, far outrunning the normal fourteen-year life expectancy of his breed. He became the most venerable, the oldest living Highland cow in Scotland and the second oldest in the world. Strangely, the oldest is a resident of India. Hamish's successors are black Highlands. When I passed, I could see that they had calves. Swaddled in their long, waterproof coats and next to a woollen mill, the symbolism is clear. You are about to enter the land of mountain and flood.

The rain seemed to be easing, becoming a drizzle. Perhaps it would clear. After a series of long, easy straights since Stirling, the A84 began to wind slowly through the Pass of Leny before snaking along the shore of Loch Lubnaig. The mountains crowded around, their summits sheathed in streamers of low cloud, and, as I passed a sign that said *Fàilte don Gaidhealtachd*, 'Welcome to the Highlands', I drove deep into the heart of another Scotland.

More than thirty years ago, it was a Scotland I felt I needed to understand better. It seemed ridiculous to me that as Scots and English-speaking Lowlanders, we could not even pronounce half of our geography far less understand the language and culture of the society that named the mountains, the lochs and the glens. The more immediate prompt was necessity. At that time, I worked in television, gradually moving from presenting to production and management. As part of a wider brief, I was asked to oversee the few Gaelic programmes STV made. And then, a few months later, an interest in learning the language was transformed into an urgent need when, in 1989, the Conservative government surprisingly and inexplicably decided to inject £8m into the production of Gaelic programmes on ITV. And one hour a week was to be broadcast in peak time.

Guided by an enthusiastic and empathetic teacher, I took a course of frequent and long lessons (with a great deal of homework) and within a few months had grasped some of the basics. I amazed an unsuspecting audience of Gaelic speakers by welcoming them to STV in their native tongue. I was told I had the *blas* – 'the right accent'.

But it was difficult to advance beyond simple sentences and ideas. Gaelic is not like English or any of the romance languages. There is no word for yes and none for no. Instead, a question is answered by using the negative or affirmative version of the verb. '*A bheil thu sgith?*' – 'Are you tired?' – prompts the answer '*Tha*' or '*Chan eil*' – 'I am' or 'I am not' – and so on. This means something daunting. In order to have even basic conversational skills, a learner has to be able to conjugate many verbs. And all Gaelic verbs are irregular.

In sentences, word order is different from English, another factor that makes listening comprehension hesitant. 'I am hungry' is a relatively simple example when it is expressed as '*Tha an t'acras orm*', but in the literal translation in the Gaelic sequence it can sound scrambled as 'There is hunger on me' or 'The hunger is on me'. Not a question but a statement. 'Is there hunger on me?' is '*A bheil an t'acras orm?*' – not a question you would ever ask yourself.

More complexity awaits those who are not yet daunted. In English, only tiny traces of the cases of nouns survive, but in Gaelic several are essential to understanding. The genitive case is seen in Eileach an Naoimh and what transforms the nominative of *an Naomh*, 'the saint', is the key addition of 'i', giving *Naoimh*, 'of the saint'. The vocative case is used when addressing an individual and it changes pronunciation. The name *Mairi* is pronounced maari – that is with a long /a:/ – but, if you find yourself talking to Mairi, she needs to be addressed as *a' Mhairi*. The 'mh' is pronounced /v/, resulting in vaari. Patriotic Scots make the common mistake of naming their girls Mhairi – Mairi in the vocative case – when it would be more correct just to call them Mairi. The same is true for *Seumas*, 'James'. The vocative form *Sheumais* is rendered in English as 'Hamish'.

The pronunciation of Gaelic in general can be a challenge for English speakers who are used to a largely phonetic scheme. Some English spellings, such as the vowels in the words 'through' and 'though', suggest they would be pronounced the same, but in the first it's a long zooz sound – /u:/ – like in the Scots pronunciation of 'look', and in the second it's a long zoz sound – /o:/ – like in the Scots pronunciation of 'low'. For some Gaelic consonants, the correlation between spelling and pronunciation is not equivalent to that of English. In addition to 'mh', ['bh' can also be realised as a 'v' sound, but at the end of words, it is usually silent. And sometimes in the middle of a word like *sabhal*, meaning 'a barn', it is also silent. But not always. In the middle of *abhras*, 'wool', it is sounded like a 'v'. Or, just to make matters even more entertainingly complex, it can be pronounced 'aaawraas'. And if that was not sufficiently perplexing, there are many words with terminal syllables that are written but not sounded. And even more confusing is the habit of aspiration, sometimes but not always caused by the use of a preposition before a noun. That alters the sound of an initial letter, usually by adding an '*h*' and sometimes changing the meaning. The vocative case of *Morag* is *a' Mhorag*, changing the sound of the initial consonant from 'm' to 'v', which is straightforward, but when *geas*, 'a spell', is rendered as *gheas*, it means 'spellbound'.

Which I was. A language of such staggering complexity that describes places I thought I knew well fascinated rather than frustrated me. There is a trope often quoted by people who are ignorant of its lexicon that Gaelic lyrics are romantic, even vague, as they swirl around the mountain tops and the shores of the lochs. Nothing could be further from the reality. Good Gaelic can be as lexically tight as Ciceronian Latin and the precision of its vast stock of adjectives, especially those applied to the natural world, is staggering in its subtlety and range. Some Gaels describe English as a thin language and, by comparison, it is. Learning these beautiful phrases and words, even as patchily as I did, turned out to be a key to understanding but certainly not to acceptance.

Worn down by centuries of oppression, much of it violent, and by the steamroller march of English, the Gaelic language is dying. Statistics fiddle on the margins but the speech community has dwindled to about 57,000. More Gaelic speakers die each year than are being born. Against that background, my own efforts to learn the language were sometimes derided, often suspected. Eight million pounds of government money had been devoted to making television in the language and it looked to some as though the Lowlanders were taking over that too. Published on Skye and widely read in Highland Scotland, the *West Highland Free Press* was a welcome addition to the world of Scottish newspapers and it often carried articles and features in Gaelic. My own involvement in Gaelic language television was compared variously to the stench of urine and also likened to the two thieves who were crucified on either side of Christ. And I was called a bully. Lavatorial, apocalyptic and defamatory, the writers of two of these articles failed to realise that I could understand them, albeit with a dictionary at my elbow. I had to look up *mun*, the word for 'pee'. But it was hardly surprising to read such things in the context of historic Lowland oppression of Highland society.

Despite the bile and the pee, we made some very good Gaelic television and dragged it into the late twentieth century, rejecting the radio with pictures of the past. When I finally escaped corporate life in 1999, the language was a welcome legacy. As a historian, I felt I had a firmer grasp of the story of the whole of Scotland and I never forgot the beauty of Gaelic, especially when it is sung by musicians such as Donnie Munro and the great Ishbel MacAskill.

My command of it, such as it was, is fading fast now. The Borders has few Gaelic speakers, being the region of Scotland furthest from the mountains, but I sometimes had the company of an old friend, a native speaker from South Uist. Our conversations awoke old memories and, while I had constantly to ask him to speak more slowly, we had some grand talks in *Canan Mor nan Gaidheal,* 'the Mighty Language of the Gael'. But a few months ago he lay dying from inoperable cancer in the local hospital. Moving in and out of consciousness and drinking only Lucozade, he seemed to be drifting. His wife, also an old friend, thought he might respond to the sound of Gaelic, the tongue of his boyhood in the islands, and I went to speak to him. We had a good half hour, breaking into English to include everyone, but as I left I said, '*Chi mi thu a'rithist, a' charaid*' – 'I'll see you again, my friend.' ''S dòcha,' he whispered. 'Maybe.'

Early Gaelic was brought to Scotland by the saints of the sixth century and by those who colonised the Argyll shore before them. Brendan, Columba and the others described what they saw in the Hebrides and where they settled and set up monasteries in Gaelic. As I drove on through the glens, turning westwards towards the ocean, I wondered if the language would help me see what they saw fourteen centuries ago.

Winding along the eastern shore of Loch Lubnaig, the first of the great lochs to be guarded by steep-sided mountains, like vast troughs in the dramatic folds of the landscape, I noticed a change in the signposts. It was cheering to see that the Gaelic place-names were now set above the English versions – An t-Oban above Oban, Glaschu above Glasgow – everyday symbols of local and national government commitment to the language. I hoped that these were signs of better times to come.

After a famous radio speech by Saunders Lewis in 1961, Welsh language activists began a twenty-year non-violent campaign to have road signs made bilingual. They sabotaged television masts and offices and held many demonstrations. Eventually Plaid Cymru MPs were elected, Sianel Pedwar Cymru (S4C), 'Channel 4 Wales', was created as a Welsh language TV channel and Wales was at last designated as a fully bilingual country. While there are real and pressing concerns about the inclusion of the majority who do speak Welsh, the increase in the number of speakers, particularly amongst young people, is nothing short of a cultural miracle.

Supporters of Gaelic have never been militant – possibly because the speech community was so fragile – but it may be that government support for the language will eventually see numbers creep up.

I stopped at Tyndrum – Taigh an Droma, 'the House on the Ridge' – and, walking to the cafe in the soft drizzle, I was assailed. The instant I left the car, clouds of midges attacked me, the humid conditions perfect for them. A few even followed me into the toilet. It occurred to me that these microscopic pests are an excellent means of mortifying the flesh in the Highlands and Islands. Monks who wished to suffer did not need to stand up to their necks in an ice-cold loch or lie down in a bed of nettles. All they needed to do was expose their sinful flesh to midges. After that torture, a plunge into a loch or the sea would seem like a blessed relief.

Miraculously able to receive a mobile phone signal, I saw that there was a yellow weather warning over much of Scotland. The road to Oban was mostly straight, well made and open, but I seemed to be in the only vehicle travelling west. All of the other traffic was moving east, out of the mountains, towards the cities, into the worst of the weather. Behind me, a sudden shudder of thunder boomed and, in my rear-view mirror, I thought I saw a flash of lightning over the Breadalbane Mountains. From an unseen perch in a roadside wood, an eagle lifted into the air and wheeled away to the north. There is no mistaking an eagle, their size is spectacular, their wingspreads far greater than any other raptor. As I breasted a ridge above Dalmally, I was certain I could see light in the western sky. Were these omens? Were they good or bad?

As the pale sheen of Loch Awe came into view, I passed the turning for the shore road and Ardbrecknish House and glanced at the ghost of my younger self, driving to Edinburgh Airport, to Cannes, an unexpected boat trip to Île Saint-Honorat and a first encounter with an ancient sanctity. It had stopped raining and I decided that I had enough time to pause on my journey to Seil Island and stretch my legs. On the northern shore of the finger of Loch Awe that reaches into the Pass of Brander, there is a church I wanted to see. St Conan's Kirk is dedicated to a contemporary of Columba and Brendan, and he seems to have brought the word of God to the wild interior of Argyll. Innis Chonain is a small islet that might have been his hermitage, and near Dalmally a holy well remembers his name.

These faintest of echoes of a mission of conversion were swept into the background when the wealthy architect Walter Douglas Campbell designed a new kirk for Conan. Begun in 1907, it took until 1930 for it to be completed and consecrated, and it is a splendid building. Gorgeous detail, from the lead rabbit gargoyles to the statuary on the exterior, is everywhere but especially glorious is the chancel. Rounded at its farthest end with an internal semicircle of columns screening a series of high Romanesque windows at the apse, it is flooded with light reflecting off the waters of the loch below it. Richly detailed wood carving adorns the rest of the interior and, incongruously, there is a recumbent tomb sculpture of Robert Bruce with a fragment of bone set below it like a saintly relic. There is a sculpture of Conan on an exterior plinth. He looks very handsome – more early modern than early medieval – and, as far as I could make out from below, he had a full head of hair with no sign of a monastic tonsure. Delightful though it is, this building obliterates the memory of Conan's mission in all but name, and as I drove through the pass I began to think about the sixth century – the time when he, Brendan, Columba and the other white martyrs rowed their curraghs up the Firth of Lorn, strangers in a strange land.

It was a pagan landscape made by a pantheon of gods who were often believed to be vengeful, ill-disposed towards mortals, very different from the focus of the saints' lives – the loving and forgiving Christ. The names of about four hundred pagan gods appear in classical sources linked to Roman Gaul and Britain. Approximately three hundred are noted only once, clearly implying localised, cultic worship, as well as a degree of tolerance. But some pagan gods were clearly more important than others. Lugh is remembered in place-names such as Carlisle, Ludgate Hill in London and perhaps London itself. In pagan Ireland, the saints will have known him as Lugh Chronain, 'Little Stooping Lugh', 'the Trickster' – a name that was eventually anglicised as leprechaun.

Perhaps the Trickster's clearest survival is in the name of the Celtic feast of Lughnasa, held on 1 August or thereabouts. Mistakenly thought to have been a harvest festival, it in fact occurs too early in the calendar, especially in Ireland, Scotland and the north of England. Instead, Lughnasa was originally a rite of propitiation. Little Stooping Lugh and his tricks with the weather needed to be appeased. Great bonfires were lit to attract his attention and, as in Brian Friel's wonderful play and film *Dancing at Lughnasa*, people linked hands and danced around the blaze. Offerings of food and other items were made to the god and, if it pleased Lugh, the year's harvest on which life depended would be brought home safely.

Christian conversion was a process and not an absolute event, even with the defining ritual of baptism. Pagan beliefs took many generations to fade and the white martyrs will have been familiar with these competing, well-established ways of understanding creation. On a visit to Loch Ness, Columba felt the need to behave more like a Christian wizard than a meek and mild man of God. He banished the monster, the first historical outing for the creature that lurks in the depths of Loch Ness, and contended with Broichan, a pagan priest who was probably a druid. Here is Adomnán's description of the contest:

St Columba asked a wizard called Broichan to release an Irish slave-girl, having pity on her as a fellow human being. But Broichan's heart was hard and unbending, so the saint addressed him thus, saying: 'Know this, Broichan. Know that if you will not free this captive exile before I leave Pictland, you will have very little time to live.'

He said this in King Bridei's house in the presence of the king. Then leaving the house, he came to the River Ness, where he picked up a white pebble from the river and said to his companions: 'Mark this white stone,' he said, 'through which the Lord will bring about the healing of many sick people among this heathen race.'

At this point, Columba intensified the struggle, presumably to impress King Bridei with his stronger magic, and the power of Heaven was invoked. An angel broke a glass cup as Broichan was drinking from it. The fragments seemed to choke him or worse, and he 'drew near to death'. Columba was called upon to intervene. Putting the white pebble into some water (where it floated), he advised Broichan to drink it. The druid recovered and God and Columba triumphed. However, this miracle appears to have had little effect, since the druid's master, King Bridei, neither disavowed him nor converted to Christianity. In his visit to the Pictish royal palace, there were more impressive moments of holy magic as the saint forced gates to open and reversed the direction of the wind on Loch Ness. But if these feats persuaded Bridei to be baptised, then Adomnán does not mention it. If the king had indeed become a Christian, he surely would have recorded such an achievement. In reality, the influence of Columba, Brendan and the others who first sailed north from Ireland in the sixth century seems to have been restricted to the shores and islands of the Firth of Lorn.

In the landscape I drove through, a pagan cosmology persisted for many generations. Conan's name may have become attached to a tiny islet in Loch Awe but the towering mass of the mountains above it was once swathed in stories of other worlds. Ben Cruachan is the highest peak in Argyll, and it and the loch at its foot were made not by God but by the Queen of the Winter, Cailleach Bhearach. In modern Gaelic, *na cailleachan* simply means 'the old women', but in the pre-Christian past they were the Storm Hags or the Giant Divine Hags who strode over the mountains and ordered the land. Cailleach nan Cruachan was most powerful and she ruled the winter, made the weather and named the land and the sea. The notorious Corryvreckan whirlpool swirls between the northern tip of Jura and the small island of Scarba, not far from where I hoped to be sailing later that morning. The name derives from An Coire Bhreacain. It means 'the Cauldron of the Plaid' and the plaid or cloak belonged to An Cailleach nan Cruachan. Before her realm of winter came each year, its queen washed her great plaid in the whirlpool until it was snow white and then the snow covered the land.

This is not an ancient myth lost in the darkness of myth history. The tales of Na Cailleachan can be dated to the time when Irish Gaelic began to absorb loan words from Latin. This is likely to have been in the period when the Roman Empire began to reach west into Gaul in the first century BC and then later across the Channel and the conquest of Britannia after AD 43. *Cailleach* is a Celticised version of *pallium*, 'a cloak' or 'a veil', and the original meaning might have been 'the veiled one'.

An Cailleach nan Cruachan made Loch Awe by accident. Near the top of her mountain, a spring bubbled out of the screes; at sunset, the hag capped it with a heavy stone lid before removing it in the morning. But one night, warm under the great plaid, she fell into a deep sleep and forgot to lay the slab on. The spring then gushed down the mountainside to create the vast loch.

It was a myth that became an engineering reality. Where the Cailleach's spring overflowed, designers drew plans for a great dam. Cruachan is the most prominent peak in an encircling ring of high mountains, forming a natural basin for the run-off down their steep slopes. The core of the design concept was to use gravity and channel the force of the water behind the dam and make it roar downhill to turn four huge turbines that would then convert this natural energy into electricity. But what made this scheme elegant and different would be an ability to use off-peak electricity, essentially during the night, to pump water back uphill so that the whole cycle could be repeated each day. It was a magically simple cycle – a spell worthy of the Cailleach herself.

A tunnel was driven deep into the mountain so that a turbine hall could be built in its heart and designers were determined that this huge mechanical heart would never miss a beat. They gave the power station what is called a black start capability. If the turbines ever ceased to turn, they could be re-started without the need for electricity from the national grid. This was achieved by the installation of diesel-fired generators that could instantly rumble into action to keep Cruachan in production. They also added what was known as bootstrapping. In the event of a major outage, all of the necessary component devices would be able spontaneously to recreate a communications system that would allow power to flow.

The Second World War produced more than one gifted politician. Using the sweeping powers granted to him as Secretary of State for Scotland, Tom Johnston laid the foundations of the National Health Service and brought into being the Scottish Council of Industry, but he himself reckoned that his most successful initiative was the setting up of the North of Scotland Hydro-Electric Board. The Ben Cruachan scheme was its most famous, spectacular legacy. Very sadly, Johnston did not live to see it open in 1965, death having taken one of Scotland's greatest politicians only five weeks before. It stands as a fitting monument.

Cathedral-like, carved out of Cruachan's granite heart, the Turbine Hall remembers the past as well as modern innovation. Designed by Elizabeth Falconer, a vast relief of inlaid woods includes stylised images of pylons, Celtic crosses, mythical beasts, men of industry and the image of one woman. Asleep next to her overflowing spring lies the Queen of Winter, An Cailleach nan Cruachan, her magic flickering around her.

When I reached Connel Bridge and the shimmer of the Atlantic shore, I could see that the Storm Hags were making devilry in the

black-dark skies behind me, for that day I later heard tales of tremendous downpours, crackling lightning strikes and cold, stiffening
winds. Out to the west, the Firth of Lorn looked calm and even
inviting. Perhaps the old gods were with me as I began my quest to
understand something of the lives of the men who brought the new
belief.

Easdale, on Seil Island, where my boat waited to take me to Eileach
an Naoimh, was sixteen miles beyond Oban, and since the weather
was brightening I wasted no time in the town. If I arrived early, so
much the better, especially if the weather was unsettled. Remembering
that the little island was uninhabited, had no roofed building where
I might shelter and that nothing stood between it and Canada except
the ocean, I took a complete change of clothes in my backpack and,
reckoning that the grass and the ferns would be long and damp,
decided that wellies were preferable to boots. The Eileach was so
small that no great footslogging distances would need to be walked
– in theory. What concerned me most was being stranded there by
storms and these could blow up off the Atlantic in moments.

And so I came to the Bridge Over the Atlantic and the shores of
my first island. More correctly known as Clachan Bridge, it was
built between 1792 and 1793 to link Seil Island to the mainland. All
that isolated Seil was a narrow channel of the ocean, little wider than
thirty or forty feet at high tide. Driving over the bridge turned out
to be a strange sensation. Single track, it is so humpbacked that on
the upslope all that can be seen through the windscreen is the sky,
and it is impossible to see if a car is coming in the opposite direction.
And then, once over the hump, all that fills the windscreen is the
surface of the road. However, it does not do to complain that a
bridge built at the end of the eighteenth century did not anticipate
the invention of the internal combustion engine.

The Bridge Over the Atlantic was designed with more old-fashioned modes of transport in mind. Its humpback was especially
elevated so that at high tides boats could safely pass beneath it.
Incredibly, whales also chose to navigate down the narrow channel.

In 1835 a huge creature, seventy-eight feet in length, was stranded, probably under the bridge. Perhaps it was a humpbacked whale. Two years later a school of 192 pilot whales also chose the wrong time to navigate the sound and they too were trapped. The largest was twenty-six feet in length.

The seaway influenced the design of the roadway because in the eighteenth century it was still the preferred highway around the islands and the sea lochs. Along the jagged Atlantic shore, geography dictates the direction and length of land travel far more radically than the sea. In a car, the long way round is often the only way round. Not for the first time did I reflect that my journeys to this scatter of holy islands, those that look so remote on a map, would have been faster and more easy to manage if I had been sailing a boat rather than driving a car. But since I can neither swim nor sail, or navigate, there was no other option. The fragmented nature of the Atlantic shore was understood from early times, even by those who were not natives. In his biography of his father-in-law, Agricola, the Governor of the Roman province of Britannia, written around AD 100, Tacitus captured perfectly the relationship between the land and the sea in Scotland and how very different it was from the familiar Mediterranean: 'Nowhere is the dominance of the sea more extensive. There are many tidal currents, flowing in different directions. They do not merely rise as far as the shoreline and recede again. They flow far inland, wind around, and push themselves amongst the highlands and mountains, as if in their own realm.'

Warmed by the waters of the Gulf Stream, Seil Island seemed a fertile place. Flowers and decorative shrubs grew tall in many of the gardens I passed, some of them clearly enthusiastically cultivated, others manicured and austere. The winding road led me to a spectacular viewpoint that compelled me to stop and park. It looked out over a wide Atlantic bay. Far away in the ocean, I fancied I could make out the cliffs of Garbh Eileach, the largest island of the archipelago of the Garvellachs. Eileach an Naoimh lay beyond it, perhaps over the horizon. I had used a ruler on the Ordnance Survey Landranger map and I reckoned that I would have eight nautical miles to travel from the harbour at Easdale to reach Brendan's monastery. That is, if the skipper of the boat agreed to sail. What the map did not mark was a place-name that intrigued me. On a gazetteer mounted on the viewpoint, there was an inscription: 'Erected by the people of Kilbrandon to commemorate the coronation of Queen Elizabeth, 2nd June, 1953'. Kilbrandon means the chapel, church or even cell of Brendan, a name not given on the OS. However, I was able to consult my copy of Hamish Haswell-Smith's superb *The Scottish Islands* and found that the parish is named after Brendan and the church at Balvicar, literally 'the township of the vicar', is dedicated to him.

I looked at a second magisterial tome that I had put in the car, *The Celtic Place-Names of Scotland* by W.J. Watson, first published in 1926, and enjoyed the unusual pleasure of consulting scholarship in the landscape it described. He had noted a Kilbrandon in Lorn but did not say where it was. A fluent Gaelic speaker with an intuitive feel for how names change in the pronunciation and spelling over long periods of time as well as being a very great scholar, Watson is an authority always to be trusted and premiated over more modern researchers, especially those who write about the early history of the north of Scotland but who have not troubled to learn Gaelic. He does specify – and the OS agrees – that immediately to the south of where I stood looking out over the ocean there was another church, now gone. It was dedicated to St Bridget of Kildare in Ireland, who may have died in 525, and she has many dedications in the east and the west of Scotland. Beyond the obvious observation that Irish saints were much revered, probably from the sixth century onwards, no narrative can be reliably reconstructed. And Watson is too wise to make more than a series of accurate and acute observations.

6

On Brendan's Isle

Around the bay lay Easdale, my destination at last, and even before I could find the car park I met a young man in seagoing gear, already wearing a life jacket and looking like he was dressed for bad weather. I wound down my window, expecting bad news. 'Are you Mr Moffat?' I agreed that I was and immediately asked if we would be sailing. 'Yes, we should go now, though, since bad weather is forecast to be moving in this afternoon.' I parked at the foot of what might have been a slate quarry. There were several motor homes, the curse of winding Highland roads, and, on the foreshore, the usual clutter of maritime kit, a boat trailer and what looked like an abandoned offshore fishing boat, its blue and white paint peeling.

I went to the boat-hire office to pay the balance of the vast cost of my voyage and the lady said that if the weather shut down and the rain turned stormy I should call her number and the RIB would come out to get me off the island. There should be a mobile signal, no problem. I had two phones, both fully charged and using different networks.

On the jetty, my rigid inflatable boat waited. Bigger than I had imagined, there were five rows of three seats of a curious design. Passengers were invited to sit astride them like saddles and then hold on to a stainless-steel arm set in front, presumably in periods when the sea was rough. The boat was bright orange, had no keel, like a curragh, and it was completely open to the elements, which, at that moment, were benign.

After he had helped me with my life jacket and stowed my backpack, the crewman who greeted me when I arrived told me that he had never been to Eileach an Naoimh. Even though he had worked a few summers at Easdale, taking boatloads of passengers out to see the Corryvreckan whirlpool and on trips as far as Iona, he had never landed on the island. The skipper said he had only been there once, a long time ago. The closest the crewman had been was Garbh Eileach, an occasional destination for groups of birdwatchers and naturalists. A few weeks before, he had been handing out life jackets on the island for the return trip and was surprised when a person on the fringes of the group refused one. 'I live here,' said an older man before disappearing into the trees around the slipway. Apparently, there is a bothy on Garbh Eileach and this man lived there alone, somehow surviving on what he must have brought with him. No one knew how long he had been on the island. I would very much liked to have met him, the hermit of Garbh Eileach, the spiritual descendant of the white martyrs, splendidly alone on his diseart.

The RIB had to wait for the ferry from Easdale Island to disembark its eight passengers. Small, open and cheerily brightly painted, this little boat plied a five-minute course across Easdale Sound, a narrow channel of perhaps three hundred yards. Sixty people live permanently on the island and the population grows in the summer when holiday-home owners arrive. The crewman told me there had been a wedding there last week and the ferry had made twenty trips back and forth. Apparently, passengers had burst into song – in both directions. Easdale is the smallest and most densely populated inhabited island in the Inner Hebrides and its people looked to me like good company. From the late seventeenth until the early twentieth century, more than two hundred and fifty lived on Easdale, most working in the slate quarries. In the Sound, there were the gaunt remains of a large pier where ships docked to load what had been hacked out of the hillsides and the cliffs. In 1825 more than five hundred ships tied up at the pier to be loaded with slate before they sailed through the Crinan Canal and on to Glasgow's building boom.

Once the RIB had glided out of the still and sheltered waters of the Sound, we turned first to the north into the Firth of Lorn. At last I was on the sea road, moving through the same waters where Brendan has steered his curragh, seeing the land and the islands from seaward and as he did, about to make landfall on Eileach an Naoimh, the Rock of the Saint. When we changed course once again, this time to the south-west, to the windward, most of these thoughts fled fast. Suddenly, the skipper pulled on the throttle and the RIB launched itself down the firth – doing twenty knots according to the crewman, shouting above the roar of the engine. It could do fifty, he added. Like me, he was hanging on to one of the stainless-steel arms of the saddle-seats and I felt as though we were not sailing but riding a bucking bronco at a rodeo. As the RIB tore over the choppy sea, its bow rose and then slammed down hard on the rushing water. I gave up trying to record the short voyage on my phone's camera, gave thanks that it would be short, and concentrated on staying in the saddle and avoiding the spray flying over the open deck.

Garbh Eileach reared up fast on my right, what I should have thought of as the starboard side, and the crewman pointed out the bothy where the hermit lived. To avoid contrary currents and perhaps invisible reefs, the skipper steered towards the Black Islands and Lunga and Scarba, not far from where the Corryvreckan was churning – rather like my stomach. That course gave me a view of the Eileach in profile, allowing me to make out its high points and the very rocky nature of its south-eastern shore. I could see the white dots of sheep, some of them grazing like mountain goats on the precipitous screes and cliff edges. There seemed to be no slip or jetty – or indeed any inlet that might let me disembark. I turned to the skipper, who was scanning the shoreline, edging closer so that he could see more clearly. Then he cut the main engine and started to glide towards a high rocky outcrop.

Pulling the tiller around, the skipper pointed to two iron rings that had been hammered into the top of a low cliff-face. This was as much of a harbour, jetty or slipway as Eileach an Naoimh could offer. I suspected Brendan would have smiled at that. With a moor-ing line in one hand, the crewman jumped on to a tiny flat platform no more than a foot or so across and scrambled up the black, jagged rocks. Pulling the rope through one of the rings, he secured the bow end of the RIB, and catching a second mooring line thrown by the skipper he brought the stern around so that the boat was alongside the foot of the low cliff. I wriggled on my backpack and the skipper pointed to the small platform. The slight swell was making the RIB bob up and down a little and so I needed to wait for an up. Taking the skipper's hand, I put one foot on the gunwale and, for a ridiculous moment, I thought of bouncy castles. And then, at the right moment, I stepped ashore.

There was nowhere obvious to make progress, no path, no set of rock-cut steps, just a series of edges, the upended strata of black, very rough and ragged rocks. Crawling rather than climbing, I managed to clamber up to the top of the little cliff, sometimes on all fours, probably looking like a much less agile lower primate. There were no flat surfaces at all. 'We'll be back at about five o'clock to pick you up,' shouted the skipper, 'but if the weather shuts down or you get in trouble, just call the office at Easdale.' With that and a wave, the crewman pulled in his mooring lines, cast off and they turned back into the Firth of Lorn. I watched the RIB suddenly accelerate back up the loch, a wide white bow wave trailing behind them.

And, suddenly, there was silence. Only the whisper of a breeze blew in from the west and the vastness of the Atlantic. Over to the east lay Jura, a scatter of inshore islands and beyond them the wild heart of Argyll, mighty Ben Cruachan, Loch Awe and the endless miles of dense Sitka spruce forest. Bad weather roiled in the skies above them. Riding the thunderheads, the Storm Hags were making mischief. If the breeze freshened into a strengthening wind and backed from the south-east, I could expect a soaking.

The going got no better as I balanced on one edge and tried not to hop too far to another. It occurred to me that Brendan was defending his island and that it would not easily give up its story or its secrets. But then unexpected, delicate miniature beauty began to reveal itself. Between the fissures and even the narrowest cracks in the upended strata that made walking so difficult, I noticed clusters of many sorts of flowers. Perhaps alpine, certainly tenacious, there were white, star-shaped, pink-tinged little bouquets set off against lush green leaves. Stepping unsteadily around an outcrop, I came across a rainwater pond, dark and peaty, and around it grew yellow irises, their long stalks somehow surviving the strong winds that must blow off the ocean. Ferns were everywhere. They softened the starkness of the Rock of the Saint. But despite these unexpected patches of beauty, the island seemed to me like a raw hunk of angry geology, the jagged deposit of elemental violence, a product of the period when the crust of the Earth convulsed, when volcanoes erupted, sending kilotons of ash and ejecta rocketing into the atmosphere, when thunder roared in the red skies.

Near the shoreline, I could see a strange, contorted rock formation. Seven irregularly formed columns of the black rock I was scuffing over seemed to have been stacked upright at extravagant angles, as though they had been carelessly left there. It looked like a corner of a builder's yard where giants worked, the stones waiting to be picked up and set upright, in a circle as at Stonehenge or the Ring of Brodgar. Other stacks punctuated the near horizon, parts of a once-mighty geological rampart. Perhaps Brendan believed that God built it to keep out the world. And then, emerging from the thick carpet of ferns, rose a singular feature, perhaps twice the height of me. Two huge hunks of rock had somehow been conjoined. A lighter coloured base supported a massive, much larger wedge of stone that looked as though it had been placed there by a divine hand reaching down from Heaven. Perfectly balanced, at an angle like a rakishly worn hat, it seemed that it might slide off at any moment. The topmost stone appeared also to be some sort of signpost, and as I walked closer, on easier ground, I turned to see what it was pointing at. And there they were.

Behind a rickety, bent iron fence were two beehive cells, a smaller one built into the shoulder of a larger one. If it had not been for the gaping holes in the roofs, I might have mistaken the cells for cairns. In Irish, they are *clochán* and that simply means 'the stones'. Their English name derives not from modern, wooden beehives but from the older style that were made from straw and known as 'skeps'. I edged around the kissing gate and saw that the two cells had been laid out in a figure-of-eight arrangement. Each had a low, external entrance and there was a passageway connecting them. Trying and failing to avoid scraping my scalp on the rough lintel, I crawled into the larger cell and, to my surprise, found it spacious and mercifully with plenty of headroom. Through the wide hole in the roof, the angry clouds over Argyll were framed. These two cells are thought to be original – the oldest structures on the island, probably dating from the middle of the sixth century and the arrival of Brendan and his community of monks, his fellow white martyrs. That means that they are the oldest surviving ecclesiastical buildings in Britain, and it was both humbling and magical to think that, where I stood on that grey morning, God had been worshipped fourteen centuries ago. And it was also exciting to find solid, concrete relics of a story that is mostly whispered, a legacy of sacred stones rather than the faint, windswept echoes of place-names and dedications.

The cell surprised me because I had expected it to be much lower than its three metres in height and smaller than its six metres across. I imagined that eight to ten monks, maybe more, could have stood there, knelt, prayed and sung psalms. Now open to the skies, the larger cell would have been very dark in the sixth century. There was one small gap in the wall that looked as though it had been deliberately formed as a window. A small lintel and a flat sill framed a rectangular opening that will have admitted only a little light and could easily have been blocked if a severe gale blew. It had been let into the north-eastern curve of the wall, and on fine days the rays of summer morning suns might have shone in the darkness. Candles must have made this silent place very atmospheric. I wondered if it had been a chapel – a communal space where Brendan and his group of solitaries came together to worship and where he talked to them as their abbot. In the darkness, with only the sound of their own breathing, their hands clasped in earnest reverence, these men listened for the voice of God.

Perhaps the oldest church in Britain, older than St Martin's in Canterbury or St Peter's in Jarrow, the cell has its own uncommon beauty. Instead of the lustre of stained glass, rich carving or the vivid colour of fresco or embroidery, this holy place remembered ancient skills, austere, God-given gifts. Built entirely in drystone, blocks of stone bound together without mortar, picked up on Eileach an Naoimh, its internal walls seem to defy gravity as a mosaic of subtle shapes and shades leans overhead, the roof still curving inwards despite serial stone robbery and the elements. Keyed expertly into the overhanging walls, each stone seemed considered; not only fitting into the edges and forms of its neighbours, they looked as though they had become part of each other, a pattern. The monks who made these beehive cells were supremely skilled masons, expert at the art of corbelling, a building method common in their native Ireland. But now the only cells that are as complete as these I stood in are to be found on Skellig Michael.

Scouring the rocks and shorelines of Eileach an Naoimh, the monks found stones they could shape with their iron chisels and wooden *mels* or mallets. Having chosen a site that was well shel-tered from the winds and storms blowing off the Atlantic but had open vistas to the east, the Firth of Lorn and its sea traffic, the monks first dug a circular trench and then laid foundations. Using massive bedding stones, many of them a two-man lift, they formed walls that were more than two metres thick. Sizes varied a good deal, of course, but each stone had to be trimmed in a particular way so that the structure of the corbel could begin to rise. Cut in a rough rectangle and with nothing but gravity to hold them in place, the stones were laid with the shorter ends showing on the outside and inside faces and with the longer sides hidden in the body of the wall. As they rose, the walls of the cell needed to be formed with smaller and smaller stones so that it did not topple under its own weight, and each had to be canted, projecting slightly further inwards, overhanging the circular course below but, crucially, with its centre of gravity kept well within the depth of the stone immediately underlying it. Gradually the rings of stones built up, growing smaller in radius, before the roof was finally closed with a capstone.

What made these remarkable structures stable and able to endure the winds, rains and snows of fourteen hundred winters was an understanding of a particular sort of architectural stress. Instead of a vertical stress created by laying one stone or brick on top of another to make perpendicular walls, the circles of corbelling created horizontal or sideways stress and, when each was closed with its final stone, they all pushed against each other as successive courses were laid. If the capstone had to be removed for any reason, the beehive cell would not collapse. But if the keystone of an arch was removed, the whole structure would fall down.

Buildings of immense and enduring beauty, the cells may have been austere but they were efficient shelters. When stones were laid in the courses of corbelling, the masons made sure that they sloped slightly downward on the outside so that rain would run off. When I walked around the northern and most complete side of the larger cell, I noticed that the first few courses had been built a little more vertically to form what is known as a scarcement. Essentially a ledge in the wall, it may have been built to allow the roof to be covered with turf. Not only will this have made it wind- and weather-tight, it will also have insulated the little building and made it even darker inside. Perhaps there was also a sacred silence – a still place where not even the whistle of the Atlantic wind could be heard.

What puzzled me was the double cell arrangement. Unless it was done for speed in the early and most fragile years of the monastery, reducing time and labour spent on building, like adding an extension to a house, I could not understand why the monks had not wanted separate cells. They were a group of solitaries and there is no shortage of rock on the Rock of the Saint. There were also probably no trees available to make wooden huts. In fact, I found only one tree, a skeletal old elder that had recently lost a main limb. Or perhaps they followed the example of Pachomius's early monasteries where several monks shared the same cell. It may be that the community dispersed instead to natural caves, fissures and overhangs around the mile-long island – places where they could gaze out over the eternities of the ocean and be alone to pray, fast and try to bring themselves closer to God. The double cells might simply have been the core of the first monastery – the meeting place where these leathery ascetics came to worship, eat in common and listen to their abbot.

After I had crawled back out under the low lintel, remembering to keep my head down this time, I looked up to see that the clouds seemed to be lifting. A breeze kept the midges from gathering and out to the east, over Argyll, the Storm Hags had relented, at least for the morning. Before the RIB had sped back to Easdale, the skipper had warned that the expected rain might come in at about 2 p.m. On the corner post of the iron fence that kept the sheep away from the beehive cells, I found a souvenir that remembered better weather. The modern equivalent of a monastic habit, a hoodie, had been left behind. When I climbed up to the top of the bank that sheltered the cells, I immediately understood why Brendan had chosen that site. It looked down to the shore and a small, hidden inlet where a curragh could be pulled up over the shingles and above the tideline. Too shallow for the RIB, it was perfect for the skin boats and their draught of only a few inches.

I found a path, little more than a sheep-walk hidden by ferns, that led down to the curragh inlet. Its name was first noted in 1824 in *Description of the Western Islands of Scotland* by Dr John MacCulloch. Born in Guernsey in 1773, he developed a consuming interest in geology and visited Eileach an Naoimh at some point in the early nineteenth century. Although he probably did not have Gaelic, he certainly had local, well-informed help. Those who knew the island told him that the traditional name for the inlet was Port Chaluim Chille, 'the place where Saint Columba landed'. Above the shingles, MacCulloch noted another name associated with the saint, Tobair Chaluim Chille, 'the well of Saint Columba', but, despite searching in what I thought was the right place, I could find no trace of it, not even the flow of a spring hidden under the dense cover of ferns.

So that I might have a sense of what Brendan saw and perhaps intuit some insight into the reasons why he chose to found his monastery on Eileach an Naoimh, I decided to walk around the shores of the island. It must have been immediately attractive for a very simple reason. All of the early monasteries, from the deserts of Egypt to the green interior of Ireland, defined the margins of sanctity. They created a sacred precinct, a *sanctum sanctorum*, a holy of holies, a place apart from the temporal world. That was the resort of evil, of devils and sinners, whereas inside the monastic precinct, prayers, the sacrifices of white martyrdom, fasting and the mortification of the flesh had purified the ground itself.

This was an ancient and powerful instinct, one that animated pre-Christian belief. No evidence exists for the nature of the rituals enacted inside the Ring of Brodgar, Stonehenge and the many stone circles that were raised in the landscape of Britain, but one aspect of pagan worship seems certain. Inside the circles lay sacred ground, a place where only an elite may go; priests, priest-kings, powerful people. When the earliest ditches and banks of the first henges were dug, the upcast was used to create a screen between the world of the gods and the world of mortals, a strong sense of insiders and outsiders, of a *sanctum sanctorum*.

When the monks at Marmoutier, at Old Melrose and in many other early monasteries wanted to create a sacred precinct, a clear frontier between the men of faith and the sinfulness of the world, they dug a ditch, just as the henge-builders had done millennia before. Often known as the monastic vallum, it probably also acted as a screen with a palisade of stakes rammed into the soft upcast. Having almost certainly sailed his curragh around the island to find a good landing place, Brendan could see the obvious. There was no need to define Eileach an Naoimh in the traditional way. It was entire unto itself and the depths of the sea were protection enough, a divinely created version of the monastic vallum. Except for Port Chaluim Chille, there were no strands, sandy beaches or even shingle beds where a boat could be pulled up. And for good measure, in places, God had built a monumental rampart against the rest of the world, for He had raised up the stones themselves.

Walking was very difficult. The shoreline was unremittingly rocky and sometimes sheer and, inland, the dense coverage of ferns and other tangles of vegetation could hide ankle-breaking holes and declivities. Where there were sheep walks, I followed them gratefully and carefully. Many erratics sit on the landscape of the island – large, individual rocks deposited by the rumble of the glaciers twelve thousand years ago as the last Ice Age was ending. In the lee of one of these huge stones, where its angle of deposit had created a low overhang, someone had built a semicircle of drystone walling, much of it tumbled, overgrown and hidden. It looked recent, showing none of the mason skills of the builders of the beehive cells, and I wondered who had made it. Perhaps a visitor had become stranded for some time by storms and sought makeshift shelter. As that thought occurred, I looked up at the grey skies.

Beyond the erratic rose more geological drama – a huge, reddish rock formation reared up out of one of the few patches of grass and it was very different from the dark, black strata I had seen elsewhere. And beneath it, just audible, was the trickle of a natural spring. Having run over stone, the water was clear and pure, as I found when I tasted it. Old Testament allusions will have been difficult for Brendan to resist, steeped as he must have been in its stories. If God had indeed guided him and his fellow martyrs to this blessed isle, then analogies with the Exodus, the flight from Egypt and the quest for the Promised Land would be easily drawn. And Brendan could have taken the flow of the spring from the rock as a sign.

In the Book of Numbers, God commanded Moses to tell the rock to bring forth water for his people and their cattle. But instead, God's messenger 'struck the rock with his staff twice', did not speak to it as instructed and did not give thanks to God for this deliverance. The divine response was immediate and harsh – 'Because you did not believe in me, to uphold me as holy in the eyes of the people of Israel, therefore you shall not bring this assembly into the land that I have given them' (Numbers 20:12). When Brendan saw the spring that already flowed from the rock, he knew that his exodus from Ireland was over, that God had delivered him and his companions from the dangers of the ocean to their Promised Land, to the Rock of the Saint.

For me, the timelessness of that moment was brutally short-lived. The twenty-first century crashed into view when I walked around the base of the reddish rock and came to a V-shaped fissure. In it were crammed many pieces of rubbish – plastic milk flagons, a wine bottle, some tubing, a metal pipe and part of a plastic bucket. At least someone had picked up all this litter, much of it no doubt washed ashore. For only an hour or two, I had seen the island as pristine, wild and jagged rather than Edenic, but not defiled.

As if to continue the link with the story of Moses and the Exodus, I came upon a boggy place where bulrushes had grown. Tall, brittle canes covered a flattish area, and on its margins yellow irises grew. From the RIB, I had seen that on the south-west tip of the Eileach there stood a small lighthouse, its beam no doubt seen some distance out in the Atlantic. Thrashing through the rushes, I began to climb up the rock on which the little white tower stood. When I reached the foot of the metal ladder up the sheer face, access had been deliberately blocked. The bottom rungs had been blocked off by a long metal sheet that had been bolted and padlocked to them, making ascent impossible. Beyond where the ladder had been set in concrete, there seemed to be another way up to the summit of the rock. But when I inched around the bottom of it to a ledge, my heart suddenly missed a beat. Falling away abruptly and without warning was a sheer cliff face. About a hundred feet below, the sea crashed against several reefs. I managed to stop before my momentum took me any further but I almost overbalanced, rocking for a terrifying moment on the balls of my feet, the weight of my rucksack swinging round, gravity tugging at me.

Winded by that near misstep, I sat down on the concrete moorings of the lighthouse ladder. The sea terrifies me and heights can make me dizzy. Teetering on the edge of sheer cliffs dropping down to the deeps of the ocean made me promise myself to be more careful and not allow curiosity to become a cause of grave mishap. This island was a dramatic but dangerous and uncomfortable place.

Having drunk some water and eaten some chocolate, sensing that it was somehow inappropriate to picnic in this place but needing something to settle myself, I pulled out my map and my transcription of the list of Dr MacCulloch's place-names. I wanted to plot the rest of my perambulation a little more carefully.

Across the valley of the bulrushes I saw a remarkable natural gateway. Somehow the glaciers had gouged out a wide gap between two massive upright stones and then placed a lintel on top of them. It looked to me like something I had seen fifty years before – the Lion Gate at Mycenae in Greece, the entrance to the palace of Agamemnon – except there was a gap where the lions should have been. The Homeric epics and the siege of Troy will certainly have meant much less to Brendan than yet more clear evidence of the hand of God at work on his holy island.

Keeping well back from the edge, I made my way along the north-western cliffs. Where I could look down safely, I saw wide fields of yellow lichen covering much of their surface. From seaward in the sun, that must look very beautiful. Elsewhere the strata had been twisted like gigantic sticks of barley sugar and it occurred to me that Zeus's thunderbolts might be a better metaphor than the gentle hand of God when it came to making the Rock of the Saint. Where the strata folded up to the cliff edge, there were several caves. Not large enough to stand up in, they were sufficiently recessed to provide shelter. When I crawled into one, the stony earth on its floor was dry and the breeze did not penetrate. Perhaps during the months of building work at the beehive cells, the monks used these natural features as places to sleep and keep out of the weather. And perhaps they were also places of solitary retreat. In the low cliff below the Heugh on Lindisfarne, there are recesses in the rock known as prayer holes where the monks could find solitude. There they shivered, gazing out across the eternities of the sea, listening to the rhythmic wash of the waves and whispering their devotions.

Beyond the cave lay a large freshwater pond. The water was clear, only tinged a little by the brown peat, but I could see no signs of fish in it. Nothing was rising to take flies and there were no telltale ripples. Near it was the low rectangle of the founds of what might have been a building. It seemed to be a much later structure than the beehive cells, resembling the ruined blackhouses of long-deserted crofting townships. Near it, what looked like some small gravestone peeped up through the bracken and around these was the outline of a low wall. An excavation by the Glasgow Archaeological Society in 1927 discovered the remains of two rectangular buildings as well as the wall. Four slab-lined graves were also found and it seemed that the site had once been an old burial ground. Eileach an Naoimh was only intermittently inhabited in the medieval and modern periods and the two buildings may have been the houses of farmers and shepherds, people who scratched a meagre harvest from amongst the rocks.

The graveyard seemed much older, long abandoned. Sanctity fades, holy places are forgotten, ignored, and they soon become neglected and overgrown, almost invisible, like this one near the freshwater pond. But until the Reformation of the sixteenth century, holy ground mattered very much because its soil was thought to have great power. Being buried inside a sacred precinct or even under the floor of a church, the closer to the altar the better, was something those with sufficient wealth or influence greatly desired. As they grew old and sensed they were near to death, some medieval noble-men and -women gave great gifts to monasteries in return for becoming novice monks or nuns. Their new status would guarantee burial inside the sacred precinct.

This was considered a great privilege, the first steps on the path to salvation, because the soil that had been walked by saints for centuries, constantly sanctified by prayer and psalm, and purified by sacrifice was thought to have the power to cleanse sin. And not in a metaphorical sense. Once a corpse was interred and began to decompose, the holy soil would begin its work of cleansing it of mortal sin and thereby reducing the time that would be spent in the wastes of Purgatory. Sacred precincts were reliable portals to Heaven and those who were buried in the slab-lined graves by the pond will have believed absolutely that the blessed ground of Eileach an Naoimh would speed their journey to eternal life with God and His angels. It was a chosen place and not only by Brendan. God's guiding hand had filled the sails of the curraghs and blown them to that rocky shore. That simple fact, believed absolutely to be true, meant that the island was different – a place set apart from the temporal world.

Looking at Dr MacCulloch's description of the island and the place-names he listed, I noted an unusual word, one I had not seen on any map. *Geodha* derives from Old Norse (as do the vast majority of place-names in the Western Isles) and it means 'a narrow creek between rocks'. Near the old graveyard and along the south-western shore of the island were Geodha Bhreanain, 'St Brendan's Creek', Geodha Bhride, 'St Bridget's Creek', and Geodha na h'Aithne, possibly a reference to the saintly Eithne, an Irish princess and mother of Columba. As I was to discover, all of these names had significance in the shadowy story of the monastery on Eileach an Naoimh.

7

The Place of Penance

At eighty metres, Dun Bhreanain, 'St Brendan's Fort', is the highest point on the island and, moving diagonally up its flanks, at first wading through waist-high ferns, my legs burning at the steepness of the gradient, I began to climb it. The increasing exposure to the wind thinned the ferns, made them shorter, and eventually the walking became easier. When I reached the long summit, I had hoped to be able to see An Clarsach, 'the Harp'. Dr MacCulloch's enthusiasm and his geological knowledge had encouraged me to make the effort:

> The principal constituent rock of the island, owing to a large admixture of calcareous material, weathers very unequally, resulting in many curious and fantastic shapes. One peculiar effect is to be noted at the north end of the island, where a magnificent arch many feet in height has been left abutting the face of a cliff. The arch has a striking resemblance to a harp, and has consequently received its Gaelic title, An Clarsach.

Sadly, the fall of the ground did not allow me to see this feature from Dun Bhreanain, but I was determined not to be defeated by the difficult terrain. Each time I gained the top of a rise, invariably with cliffs falling sheer to the sea below, I could see that I was nearer the north-west tip of the island but still, maddeningly, unable to see the Harp. However, the breath-catching drama of the geology was worth all the effort. Several of the deep declivities between extravagantly upended strata were very striking. Framed by a perfectly V-shaped gap in the cliffs, I caught a distant view of the coast of

Mull and the mountains beyond. And at the foot of the cliff there was a brilliant, bright pink beach made from shells washed and crushed against the rocks by the relentless waves.

Once again, I had to climb down to climb up. The island's fractured, awkward geology was teaching me patience and, after the moment at the lighthouse, very definitely counselling against bravado. Often I was forced to retrace my steps and look for a better way. Nothing seemed to be easy on Brendan's rock. I crossed a quaking bog, rocking back and forth to make it billow like a clean sheet being spread on a bed. I was making my way to the south-eastern shore to see if there was another route to the Harp but the ground looked very uncertain amongst the scattered rocks and there were no sheep walks to follow.

From below the bog, lying between Eileach an Naoimh and Garbh Eileach, I could see A' Chuli. Hamish Haswell-Smith notes that on old maps it is plotted as Culbrandon. The initial element of the name is from Gaelic *cuilidh* and it gives the meaning as 'Brendan's Retreat'. If this islet was where the saint sought solitude, a retreat from the communal life of his monastery, then it followed a well-established tradition. On the northern peak of Skellig Michael, a vertiginous retreat was built, and on Lindisfarne, St Cuthbert first began to withdraw from the community of monks to Hobthrush, a tidal skerry off the south coast of the main island. Perhaps these devout men were pursuing the goal of *unitio,* the final stage of John Cassian's approach to understanding the mind of God.

Four times I tried to find a way to a place where I could see An Clarsach, having resolutely borne in mind the Old Testament example of Job. I finally decided to give up and climb Dun Bhreanain once again. I wanted to find another vantage point, the best place to comprehend the layout of Brendan's monastery. At the foot of the hill, cradled between the rocky ends of the island, on the only large area of flattish ground, it is miraculously preserved.

Circling around by the beehive cells, which stand a little way apart from the ruins, I decided to take a long way round so that I could approach from Port Chaluim Chille – the place where curraghs could safely approach – and immediately found the spring for his well! Perhaps the trials I had endured persuaded the saint to reveal it to me. It must have been a blessing for those who had rowed long voyages in their curraghs to drink the sweet water the moment they pulled the boat over the shingle at the head of the creek. Or maybe it was used as a font of holy water for blessing those arriving on the sacred island.

To my surprise, I saw the remains of an outer wall around the ruins and, from Dun Bhreanain, what might have been part of a monastic vallum. The double beehive huts lay well outside this perimeter, on the far side of a low outcrop, and I wondered if the wall and the ditch had been formed later, perhaps to keep increasing numbers of pilgrims and visitors from approaching too close. The sheep that grazed the only wide area of good pasture certainly thought I was much too close and they scattered, probably not used to people wandering around.

Between two large gatepost stones, a path led towards what seemed to be a smaller, inner precinct. Dominating it were the squat, roofless ruins of a small chapel. It too seemed to be younger than the beehive cells. Its walls were tremendously thick and beautifully made. I could find no traces of more beehive cells in or around the precinct, but the ferns may have hidden whatever remained. To the south-east lay the shell of a fourteenth-century church that had been built using mortar and sandstone imported from Mull. And, to create another layer of the palimpsest on the Rock, there were the ruins of some farm buildings, probably dating to the seventeenth or eighteenth century.

Even amidst all of this confusion, there was nevertheless a palpable sense of sanctity – the monastic precinct was like the calm heart of a wild, elemental island set in a turbulent sea that crashed around its shores. Dr John MacCulloch had a very different overall impression. He visited Eileach an Naoimh in the early nineteenth century when the island was grazed by cattle as well as sheep. Their appetites seemed to have tamed it:

On traversing Ilachanu [his transliteration of the Gaelic name], I was surprised at the singularity and beauty of a spot which seemed at a distance to be a bare hill, and of which, even from the creek where our boat was drawn up, no conjecture could have been formed. Surmounting one ridge after another, a succession of secluded valleys appeared, which, although without other wood than a few scattered bushes, were beautifully disposed, and were rendered interesting no less by their silence and seclusion than by the intermixture of rock and green pasture, amongst which were wandering the cattle of the adjoining farm of Garvelloch.

At the south-western edge of the precinct ran a line of low ruins, the wall around the monks' graveyard. In one corner cowered the only tree on the island, the dogged, very elderly elder, its white blossom a faint scent even in the freshening breeze. Beyond it was a row of small tombstones, some leaning at perilous angles, others having fallen and sunk into the grass. On one I could make out a simple incised cross. In its simplicity and scale, it looked ancient, perhaps the grave of a nameless monk who had ended his days on the Rock. In the early nineteenth century, this area of sacred soil was much grander, more heavily populated. Here is a surprised Dr MacCulloch coming across the ruins of the monastery:

While I was amusing myself with imagining a hermit here retired from the world and its cares, I came, most unexpectedly, on a heap of ruins accompanied by characters which left no doubt of their original design. I had no great cause for surprise perhaps, after my experience at Inch Cormac [between Jura and the Mull of Kintyre, the site of St Cormac's Chapel], to find that no account of this establishment should exist either in the legendary or antiquarian lore of Scotland. It had not even been mentioned to us in the islands which we had left; and appeared, indeed, utterly unknown except to the tenant, and to the very few fishermen who occasionally touched at this place.

The ruins of that which must have formed the monastery are sufficiently extensive to show that the establishment must have been considerable; at a small distance from these ruins was the burying-ground, containing many ornamental stones, with remains of crosses – apparently votive, as most of those on Iona probably were. On some of the tombs are carved the usual objects: ships, arms, and the cognizances [heraldic devices] of MacDonalds, MacLeans, and Mackinnons. But all is quiet about their graves, and the turbulent chiefs now sleep below, in that peace which, when living, they never knew.

Even though Iona lies not far to the north and the abbey and the famous graveyard of the Reilig Odhrain are filled with the graves of Hebridean noblemen, this list of tombstones shows that Eileach an Naoimh had lost none of its aura of sanctity in the Middle Ages. A later visitor, probably at the end of the nineteenth century, commented on MacCulloch's account, supplying a melancholy update:

MacCulloch speaks of many ornamental stones and crosses. If this be true, then, with the exception of one broken carved stone, all have disappeared; some may be buried, but the majority were undoubtedly stolen. In 1879 the Rev. Dr Hugh MacMillan of Greenock visited the island, and, by probing with an iron rod in the graveyard, discovered lying about two inches below the surface a perfect specimen of an Irish cross miniature in size. The stone was raised and placed at the head of its grave, but within a year, it too was gone and no trace could be found.

Crosses were more than elaborate gravestones. The approaches and bounds of sacred places were often marked by crosses set up at places where pilgrims and visitors could kneel in prayer and be made aware that they were passing from the temporal to the spiritual realm. Around the ancient monastery at Coldingham in Berwickshire, place-names remember where they once stood – Applin Cross, Whitecross, and Cairncross – and on Iona, at least one of many ancient crosses, that of St Martin of Tours, remains where it was originally raised.

Such scant records as exist show only intermittent occupation of Eileach an Naoimh in the modern era. In 1637, two tenants of the Duke of Argyll lived on the island, grazing both sheep and cattle as well as growing some grain. Beyond the graveyard, an area deeply overgrown with ferns nevertheless still shows evidence of runrig cultivation, the lines of ditching just discernible. On the north-eastern side of the monastery are the substantial ruins of a corn kiln, essentially a drier for the limited but vital crops of oats that ripened on the runrig. Most of the stones used to build the kiln will have been robbed from the ruins of Brendan's monastery. By the nine-teenth century, when Dr MacCulloch visited, Eileach an Naoimh was uninhabited, making it easy for its antiquities to be stolen. Stock was grazed and run from the farm on Garbh Eileach. Without a quay of any sort, moving sheep and especially cattle off the island must have been awkward and animals will have to have been hobbled to prevent them from panicking and capsizing the boat. In the 1890s, a sheepfold was built, using more stone from the monastery buildings, and as the workmen dug a shallow foundation trench they came across a rickle of bones just below the surface.

Near the entrance to the monastic precinct, there is a strange, discordant survival. The official sign reads: 'Underground Cell, probably used for storage of food'. That interpretation is probably influenced by a type of prehistoric excavation known as a souterrain. Found all down the Atlantic coasts of Britain and Ireland, these were underground passageways that were thought to have been used to store food, places where it would be cool in the summer months. Butter, cheese, grain and suchlike were stored in sealed pots that kept out rodents and insects. But researchers and archaeologists have begun to offer other interpretations. Particularly in those discovered on Orkney and Shetland, souterrains also contained the remains of bodies or body parts as well as objects that seem to have been depos-ited there deliberately. In the first millennium BC and before, ritual deposit was clearly an important feature of pagan worship. Objects of great value, especially those made from metal, such as weapons and war gear, were thrown into lakes and rivers with no intent to retrieve them. This was done as a sacrifice of some sort, almost certainly born of a wish to propitiate the gods. Were similar deposits and burials, however partial, in souterrains part of the same pattern of pagan beliefs?

In 2010 I spent a week on Orkney looking at the magnificent prehistoric landscape and its monuments, marvelling at the Ness of Brodgar, Maeshowe and other survivals. On an industrial estate in Kirkwall, a very well-preserved souterrain had been discovered and I decided, despite more than a touch of claustrophobia, to visit what was called the Grain Earth House, a name attached to an assumption. With its roof supported by short pillars and the walls expertly lined with stones, it felt utilitarian – a good place for food storage. I could not sniff the odour of any sort of sanctity, not even a whiff of ancient cheese. Afterwards I spoke to a local archaeologist who suggested I visit a very different underground space, a place called Mine Howe.

Much less well looked after, this turned out to be an otherworldly, disconcerting, unforgettable place. Only about two thousand years old, built inside a mound was what felt to me like a corkscrewed stairway into the bowels of the Earth. Mine Howe has a set of twenty-nine stone steps that lead down to a small underground chamber with a high, corbelled ceiling. When I reached it, after a careful, slippery descent, it was at least twice my height but very narrow, perhaps only four feet in diameter. The silence was absolute, any noise coming from inside my head, and the darkness was total, stifling. Gradually, I began to feel dizzy, as though I was drifting from my moorings even though I stood on solid earth and could touch the damp walls on every side. It occurred to me that Mine Howe was a sensory deprivation chamber, an ancient version of an abhorrent method used by modern torturers.

All my instincts screamed at me to climb back up the twenty-nine steps, back to the light and the fresh air. But something anchored me in the black-dark chamber. It was certainly not peace – more of a light-headedness, a sense of transcendence, of otherness of some kind. Language frankly fails me in describing what I felt and all I can claim is that it was unique, as well as utterly disorienting, certainly mysterious.

When, at last, I gathered myself and climbed back up the steps, pulling on the handrail, fearful I would fall backwards, I thought the light would split my head. Rather than clambering up from its depths, I felt as though I had come back down to earth hard. For a long time, I sat on the passenger seat of my car, the door wide open to the ever-present Orcadian breeze, trying to make notes. The only coherent comment was a question. What was Mine Howe for? Was the effect it had on me intended? Did everyone who climbed down into the darkness feel themselves moved in the same way? I thought at the time that they must have, that this was a machine for shifting perceptions out of the everyday, a journey to another consciousness, perhaps even a rehearsal for death. Even writing the last few paragraphs brought back the headache-y disorientation of that morning almost ten years ago.

While the underground cell on Eileach an Naoimh has little of the drama of Mine Howe, there is nevertheless an atmosphere of strangeness. Down a few grassy steps lies the entrance to a small chamber. More like a window than a door, it is difficult to climb through. Peering inside, I could see that it was low, almost circular, and opposite the entrance there was a shelf recessed into the opposite wall. The stubs of two candles sat there, looking somehow forlorn. Ferns grew out of the gaps in the lower courses of the stonework and the floor shone with damp. Once I had squeezed through the square doorway, I realised there was room for only one or two people – or three if they knew each other very well. I waited for a time, trying to settle and be still. This cramped, very damp little cell did not seem to be sinister but it was certainly uncomfortable.

Early medieval cosmologies followed classical examples that located Heaven or Olympus in the sky and Hell or Hades in the depths of the earth and I wondered if that was the purpose of where I found myself. Was this also a rehearsal for death, a version of Hell on Earth? Some archaeologists wonder if the underground cell was designed for penitents and one source claimed that the Gaelic name was Am Priosan, 'the Prison'. It would have been a simple matter to close the entrance by placing a large stone in front of it and wedging it so that it could not be moved. Another tradition spoke of punishment – a large stone at the bottom of the cell with a V-shaped depression in it. A prisoner or perhaps a penitent was made to place his clasped hands in the depression and then another stone was set on top so that it was impossible to pull them out. This was known as A' Ghlas Laimh, 'the Hand Lock'. Such an odd story might recall a distant reality. It may be that monks who were guilty of sin went into the underground cell as a penance and the hand lock is a garbled memory of forced perpetual prayer, the *laus perennis*.

Here is a passage from Adomnán's *Life of St Columba* that adds a little to this interpretation:

> Once the saint came to the island of Hinba, and the same day he granted a relaxation of the rules about diet even for those living in penance. Among these penitents was a man called Neman mac Cathair, who disobeyed the saint and refused. The saint berated him with these words: 'Neman, Baithene and I have allowed a relaxation in the diet, and you refuse it. But the time will come when in the company of thieves in the forest you will eat the flesh of a stolen mare.'

Like Atlantis or Tír na nÓg, the island of Hinba is shrouded in the mists of myth-history or its location has been submerged by the tides of cultural change that washed over the Hebrides in the early Middle Ages. But it was certainly real for Adomnán when he wrote of Columba sending 'his elderly uncle, Ernan, a priest, to be prior on the monastery he had founded before on the island of Hinba'. And later, another more substantial reference:

> Once, when the praiseworthy man was living in the island of Hinba, he saw one night in a mental trance an angel of the Lord

sent to him. He had in his hand a glass book of the ordination of kings, which St Columba received from him, and which at the angel's bidding he began to read. In the book the command was given him that he should ordain Aedan as king, which St Columba refused to do because he held Aedan's brother Eoganan in higher regard. Whereupon the angel reached out and struck the saint with a whip, the scar from which remained with him for the rest of his life. The angel addressed him sternly: 'Know then as a certain truth, I am sent to you by God with the glass book in order that you should ordain Aedan to the kingship according to the words you have read in it. But if you refuse to obey this command, I shall strike you again.'

Clearly an Old Testament sort of an angel. And, needless to say, Columba did as he was told.

What these and other references make clear is that Hinba was a dependency of some kind of Iona and a place of occasional retreat for Columba. But the name has disappeared off the map and this has led to a merry-go-round of controversy that still spins.

As ever, a common-sense solution to the puzzle is to be found in the pages of W.J. Watson's *The Celtic Place-Names of Scotland*. Associated with the geography of Hinba was *muirbolc mar*, which translates literally as 'great sea-bag' and sensibly as 'great bay'. Some scholars have opted for Eileach an Naoimh – clearly without ever having been there. It has only small, rocky inlets – nothing that could be described as a bay. There is also a clear implication that Hinba lay on the sea road from Northern Ireland and Watson reckons that narrows the field to two options, either Jura or Colonsay and Oronsay, which are linked by a tidal bay. With his extraordinary ear for the derivation of geographical terms in Gaelic, the great philologist makes a link between Hinba and *inbe*, an Irish term for 'an incision'. This 'suggests the deeply indented isle of Jura'. So Hinba is Jura. Mystery solved.

And now, something I never imagined I would write. With a trembling hand, I offer a contradictory suggestion to Watson's reasoning. It is not clear from the context that *muirbolc mar* is a feature of Hinba itself. It might equally be a description of its setting. The wide mouth of the Firth of Lorn might be seen as a great sea-bag or bay into which traffic from Ireland might sail. And at its mouth lies Eileach an Naoimh, a perfect place for a retreat and easy for an angel with a whip to find. On the other hand, Watson might be right.

Whether you opt for Hinba being another name for Eileach an Naoimh or you think Jura or Colonsay and Oronsay are more likely candidates, Adomnán shows that Columba had a close association with Hinba, sometimes using it as a retreat, and he certainly saw its monastery as subordinate to Iona. It may be that, after its foundation in 542 and after Brendan's death in 577, the monastery on Eileach an Naoimh was drawn into the orbit of Iona. The two islands lie close to each other, no more than twenty-five nautical miles separate them – a few hours in a curragh, depending on wind and weather.

Adomnán wrote of 'those living in penance' and, by this, he was referring to communities of monks who had undertaken long-term mortification as a consequence of sin and rule breaking. These men lived a very austere existence, subsisting on a meagre diet (which appealed to Neman, apparently) and were required to recite many prayers and psalms as well as mortifying their flesh regularly. Sometimes long sentences were handed down by abbots – one is recorded as stretching to seven years. Irish sources listed tariffs of punishment and one notes 'the penance for eating horseflesh, four years bread and water'. After Brendan's death, a community of penitents may have eked out a harsh existence on the Rock and the underground cell may be a memory of their suffering. When I clambered out of Am Priosan, it occurred to me that this raw, awkward island might have suited that purpose well.

The huge Highland sky seemed to be lifting, the light brightening and all around me the coasts of the Firth of Lorn seemed more graphic. On the eastern horizons there were no signs of the mischief of the Storm Hags and the tops of the Argyll mountains were clear.

Beyond the monastic precinct, high above the low walls of the grave-yard, there rises a steep-sided mound. It dominates the near horizon and silhouetted against the sky was a small gravestone. Set up inside a small, circular enclosure, it had a rough cross incised on one side. Its arms were all the same length, and at the end of each the mason had chiselled small round terminals. Close by there was a scatter of other stones that might have been grave markers or perhaps they marked the edge of the enclosure.

Archaeological investigation suggests that this little graveyard was an artificial creation. Soil had been piled on to the sloping bedrock so that burials could be made possible on the rock of the outcrop. What prompted this significant effort is not clear but it must be the case that the monks filled their baskets with precious earth and climbed up the steep mound to create a grave enclosure for an important person, someone whose remains would look out over the monastery below, someone who deserved to be literally exalted. Apparently the site was excavated many years ago and the bones of a woman were found but no record of this dig was kept.

By the side of the path that winds up to the mound, another Historic Scotland sign reads:

Eithne's Grave
Traditionally identified as the grave of St Columba's mother.
This round enclosure seems to have been intended for burials,
as the early Christian cross-marked stone indicates.
Who was buried here remains unknown.

Eithne was an Irish princess who belonged to the Ui Neill, an extended kindred of dynasts descended from Niall Noigiallach – 'King Niall of the Nine Hostages', probably the first High King of Ireland. They proved to be very influential and resilient and Columba was born into their web of privilege and status. Indeed, if the gene-alogies are to be trusted, both his parents were noble born and Iona's founder was the great-grandson of Niall Noigiallach. His given name was Crimthann, 'the Fox', but once it became clear that his life would be lived in the Church it was changed to Columba. In Latin, it means 'the Dove' and it had a biblical antecedent. St Jonah's name – he who was swallowed by a whale – is from the Hebrew word for a dove. And, as is often the case, a Gaelic diminutive is tied to the word for church – here to give Columcille, 'the Dove of the Church'.

Columba was blessed in another way because his kindred network was wide and well populated. This came about in a somewhat un-Christian fashion. As Ireland emerged from a pagan past, old habits withered slowly. One of these was polygamy, especially amongst powerful men who could afford to maintain several wives. Indeed, kings like Niall Noigiallach were in the habit of siring children with many different women beyond their wives, thereby giving themselves many descendants. This is not historical guesswork but solid scientific fact. Geneticists have been able to demonstrate that millions of men, almost all of them Irish, in the past and now, are descended from Niall Noigiallach, for they carry his Y chromosome marker.

If Columba was only three generations distant from his prolific great-grandfather, the numbers of his genetic cousins would be considerable but not yet astronomic. It is very likely that, when he and his twelve companions set sail from Ireland in 563, he was not a true white martyr and all of the myth-making about the wrench of leaving home and finding a place from which it was impossible to see Ireland – it is, in any case, possible from Iona – was somewhat disingenuous. His course northwards led him into friendly territory – to Argyll, the Coast of the Gaels – for, between 558 and 574, the king of Dalriada was Conall mac Comgaill, his Ui Neill kinsman. And it is likely that the king made a gift of the little island off the west coast of Mull to the saint.

In his *Life of St Columba*, Adomnán supports the idea of Columba's royal roots in the second preface: 'Saint Columba was born of a noble lineage. His father was Fedelmid mac Ferguso, his mother was called Eithne.' A cluster of small kingdoms was controlled by a dynasty of high kings whose lives and deeds straddle the grey area between myth and history. Niall Noigiallach was the most renowned of them and royal families of sub-kings who acknowledged his primacy were bound to send family members to live in Niall's household. Their continued good health was contingent on good behaviour and unquestioning loyalty. Beyond the evidence supplied by Adomnán and the early genealogies, little is known about Eithne, except that she seems to have been much revered and was made a saint.

Book Three of the *Life of St Columba* is different from the other two, being 'concerned with angelic apparitions'. One of the first was a revelation to Eithne:

An angel of the Lord appeared in a dream to St Columba's mother one night after his conception but before his birth. He seemed to stand beside her and to give her a robe of marvellous beauty with what looked like the colours of every flower. After a little time, he asked for it back and took it from her hands. Then he raised the robe and spread it out, letting go of it on the empty air. She was disappointed that it was taken away from her and spoke to the man of holy appearance: 'Why do you take away from me so quickly this delightful mantle?' she said.

'Because,' he answered, 'this is a cloak of such glorious honour that you will no longer be able to keep it with you.'

Then the woman saw the robe moving further and further from her as if in flight, growing greater and greater so that it seemed to be broader than the plains and to exceed in measure the mountains and the forests. Then she heard a voice which said: 'Woman, do not be distressed, for you shall bear to the man to whom you are joined in marriage a son of such flower that he shall be reckoned as one of the prophets. He is destined by God to lead innumerable souls to the heavenly kingdom.'

As she heard these words, his mother woke up.

The biblical trope is blindingly obvious. Columba is made to seem more Christ-like by his hagiographer because, just as happened to the Virgin Mary, an angel appeared to his mother to enact a version of the Annunciation. The metaphor of the robe floating over the mountains, plains and forests suggests conquest, perhaps conversion, and at the same time protection. It may be that the monks on Eileach an Naoimh wanted Mother Eithne to be buried on the rocky outcrop so that she could watch over their monastery in an eternal vigil.

This is, of course, no more than a hypothesis, a flimsy construction built on little more than tradition. But Eithne is a fascinating figure. In Irish Gaelic her name derives from the word for a kernel, and the association with seeds and fertility are attractive. The princess may have been born into a largely pagan society. Despite the efforts of Patrick and the overblown claims of later hagiographers, the north of Ireland may have remained in thrall to a pre-Christian pantheon and its particular set of beliefs and rituals at the beginning of the sixth century. Indeed, Eithne was the name of a significant pagan goddess and the mother of Lugh, Little Stooping Lugh, the Trickster.

On the coast below where I stood lies Geodha na h'Aithne, 'Eithne's Creek' and nearby is Geodha Bhride, 'St Bridget's Creek'. The latter also remembers the recent pagan past. Brig or Briga was a mother goddess and some scholars believe that she was simply translated into Christian form as St Bridget of Kildare. With Columba and Patrick, she completes the triad of Ireland's patron saints. Her feast day is 1 February, also the Celtic festival of Imbolc, the time when first fruits appear after winter and ewes begin to lactate. Paganism was not swept away in a series of cathartic events of mass conversion, as the hagiographers suggest. It must have lingered for a long time, its powers and beliefs fading only slowly. Perhaps it is significant that the successors of two goddesses left their names on an island monastery of motherless monks.

Up beside Eithne's grave, I was startled out of my reveries. I had been looking at something without realising the significance of what I was looking at. Pulled up on the shingle above Port Chaluim Chille was a large white RIB, with its oars clipped to the sides. It had not been there when I finally found Columba's Well an hour or so before. It looked brand new and there was a small outboard engine attached to the stern. Although I had only been alone on the island for five or six hours and not twenty-five years, I felt like Robinson Crusoe finding the footprints of Man Friday on the beach. Except I had no idea where Friday was – or if there were more Fridays. From the vantage point of Eithne's grave, I could see a good deal of the island and there was no sign of anyone and no voices I could make out on the wind. And yet someone had beached the RIB on the shingle in the past hour. They were not visitors because no one had approached the ruins of Brendan's monastery, the only reason people come to Eileach an Naoimh. I was no longer alone on the island. But I could not see who had joined me. All sorts of cheap paperback plots played in my head – even some lurid titles like *Murder on the Rock of the Saint* or *Death on the Rock*.

Much more seriously, I had recently read a sinister story in a Scottish newspaper about ghost ships in the Hebrides. Over a period of about five years, more than three hundred vessels had sailed into the waters around the islands off the Atlantic coast and then suddenly gone dark – all of their tracking devices switched off – sometimes for long periods of twelve or thirteen hours. This meant that, in essence, they disappeared. Their courses could not be observed on coastguard screens and other means of observing seagoing traffic. Some sailed under Russian flags, others were registered in African countries. Police suspect that they wanted to go dark so that they could stop to unload drugs and sometimes human cargo to smaller boats that can navigate the shallower, inshore waters. It struck me that, as an easily reachable, uninhabited island, Eileach an Naoimh was the perfect place to conceal large packages of cocaine or heroine and be completely unobserved doing it. Except by me. It also struck me that if I was spotted by a drug-running gang I would quickly find myself at the foot of the cliffs by accident – something I had almost achieved all by myself.

To get out of sight, I quickly sat down behind Eithne's gravestone, praying that I would not be joining her any time soon, and tried to think what to do. I could just hide and hope whoever owned the RIB just returned to it, fired up the outboard and left without seeing me. After wriggling off my backpack and pulling out both mobile phones, I decided to call the office where I had paid for my passage to the island. The young woman had given me both the landline number and her mobile and I switched on both of my phones. Good, all the bars were showing. Excellent reception. And it was the same for my backup phone. But, when I dialled, there was no connection – nothing whatsoever – on both phones, which used different networks. So, no help there. All I did get was a flicker of Three Ireland, an Irish mobile network. Even as I wondered what to do, the irony of that was not lost on me.

Lying flat on my stomach, I peeped around the side of Eithne's headstone and risked looking down to the site of the monastery. I reasoned that if those who had left their RIB at Port Chaluim Chille were concealing caches of drugs, then they would not consider leaving them anywhere near the precinct. I was sure that I would not be the only visitor that summer and that was where everyone who came to the island went. And still I could hear nothing; no voices or the sound of any engines.

After a time, I decided to creep down through the fern-covered area of runrig to the monastery, believing I would be safer behind its ancient walls, perhaps in the chapel. I could always dive down into the ferns if anyone appeared. No one did and I quickly ducked inside the chapel walls, which were easily high enough to hide me. Immediately I was confronted by an upright grave slab with a plaque below it that read: 'Resting in Peace'. Great.

There was still no connection on my phones, but as I stuffed them in my pockets I heard a voice, loud, clear and close. 'Dad! Dad! Wait, Dad!' When I stepped out of the chapel, feeling both foolish and very relieved, I saw two young children, one in a nappy, following Dad up the path to the precinct. 'My God! What a fright!' I apologised for startling him, and in a moment three other adults appeared, two of them much older. Granny explained that they lived on the island of Luing, which lies immediately to the south of Seil

Island, and they had come to Eileach an Naoimh for a day out with the wee ones. Looking behind her, I could see a much larger boat moored on the iron rings where my RIB had tied up. 'My great-grandfather used to come here to check the sheep,' said Granny. I reflected that instead of a run in the car, islanders were more likely to cast off from a quay or a jetty.

These unlikely drug smugglers spent only half an hour wandering around the ruins, making a point of showing the children the under-ground cell. At 2.30, almost exactly the time when the skipper of the RIB said it would rain, the sun came out and a butter-coloured light rolled over the island. As the three generations walked down to Port Chaluim Chille to take turns to be ferried out to the larger boat, I took off my anorak and laid it on the downy, well-grazed grass by the south-west-facing wall of the chapel. I sat down, probably with much grunting, pulled off my wellies, found the rest of my chocolate in the backpack and washed it down with some bottled water. Laughing at my daftness, spooking myself with melodrama, I began to relax, my back against the smooth old stonework.

Even though I had left home at 5 a.m. and then driven for five hours before making a bumpy crossing to the island, I was not tired. I began to notice how much the sunshine changed this raw, elemental place, softening its jagged lines, making its subtle colours glow. Perhaps Brendan and his monks saw this often in the summer – the beauty of Creation amidst the shining sea, God's bounty and the grace of all His works. In my notebook, I noticed that I had scribbled earlier that morning, 'No comfort here.' But in the silence I saw the clumps of colourful wildflowers much more clearly and watched with pleasure the little birds that flitted upwards for moments from the long grass before disappearing back into it.

After a long journey, scrambling around the island, failing to reach An Clarsach and then flapping over the sudden appearance of a RIB, I was beginning to calm down and to feel a peace begin to settle. I sensed I could see what Brendan saw as I sat quiet by the chapel wall. For two hours, I thought of nothing much and remembered what a friend once said about the common ridings that are held each summer in the Borders. Emotional, often ancient celebrations of a town's identity, they revolve around unchanging rituals, many of them to do with horse riding, all of them about a deep sense of community. When trying to explain what the attraction was, my friend gave up, saying, 'It's better felt than told.' Something like that was floating around my head as I watched the white clouds, the blue sky and the sea. The tiny white triangle of a yacht was moving gently, almost imperceptibly up the coast of Jura, about three or four miles away. Almost hypnotic, its slow progress seemed to lull me into thinking while not thinking, something like meditating. It is not an experience I have had often but I realised that I was discovering another reason Brendan chose Eileach an Naoimh. It has an undoubted identity that I had discovered as I scrambled around its rocks, but it also has a *genius loci* – it is a place of spirits.

I had originally intended to spend the night on the island, but my wife forbade that on the basis that if an accident was going to happen it would happen to me. And remembering the incident on the edge of the cliff by the lighthouse, I had to agree that she had a point. In fact, her view remains that I should not be allowed out alone. Hamish Haswell-Smith had anchored his boat off Eileach an Naoimh and considered staying overnight but he felt there were too many ghosts swirling in the air. Perhaps he was wise.

When I stood up and stretched, I turned to look up the firth. It was early evening and around the time I had agreed with the skipper of the RIB that I would be picked up. In the distance but closing fast, I could see the orange hull of the boat and the wide, white wake behind it. I reckoned they were about ten minutes away. I passed the beehive huts, retracing my steps beyond the freshwater pond and climbing back up on to the upended strata. I found the walking even more awkward and only managed to get to the tiny platform by the iron rings with some difficulty and a cut on my left hand.

'Did you find what you were looking for?' asked the crewman.

'I don't know,' I said. 'Maybe.'

PART THREE

THE GREAT
GARDEN

Lismore

8

On the Feast of St Moluag

Clinging to the curve of its bay, with high ground to the landward and the long island of Kerrera sheltering it from Atlantic storms, Oban seems a safe harbour. All of its windows appear to look seaward, the one-sided esplanade turns the town outwards, embracing its reason for being there. In Gaelic, An t-Oban means 'the Little Bay' and it is on the busy waters of this haven that life thrives. There is one steep, winding road leading north out of the town and another going south, while difficult, precipitate upcountry had to be cut through in order to connect the town to the railway network. Every day, thousands cross the Little Bay bound for or returning from Lismore, Colonsay, Islay, Coll, Tiree, Mull, Barra and South Uist. The great ferries pull gently alongside to allow cars to load and unload. People stream on and off constantly. Once they are ready to depart, the ferries' mouths close and the vessels must then steer a cautious course through the sound between the tip of Kerrera and the ancient ruin of Dunollie Castle on a mainland promontory. From the safe anchorages in the Sound of Kerrera, hundreds of yachts make many voyages, taking care not to get tangled in the comings and goings of the ferry traffic. Oban is the hub of the southern Hebrides.

Having parked close by, I walked over to the Caledonian MacBrayne terminal building to buy a return ticket for the ferry to Lismore. At only £5.70 – just a little cheaper than the £640 I had paid for my trip to Eileach an Naoimh – the cost is subsidised from the public purse, as it should be, and low fares keep the island economy ticking, with more than five and a half million journeys made in 2018 on CalMac ferries.

The early morning summer sun and the windless day made the bay shimmer. When I left the ticket office to walk to the quayside, all of the familiar sounds and scents of the sea filled the crystal air – the stink of fish, the acrid reek of diesel, the squawk of wheeling gulls and the echoic rumble of the turbines. Rounding a corner into a narrow street of low buildings, a fish shop, a chandlery, I was stopped in my tracks by the sight of the huge ferry for Mull heaving to at the quay. Its bright red funnel, white superstructure and dark blue hull seemed enormous, towering over me. It was as though a skyscraper had appeared in a street of bungalows. And then the behemoth opened its vast maw. The bow of the ferry began to raise itself so that cars and lorries could rattle and clatter over the metal ramps, appearing one by one from its bowels. It was a wonderful start to the day.

I knew that the ferry for Lismore would be much smaller and that it was about to leave the island and bring people to work and shop in Oban. It was not due to depart for another hour. I decided to have a wander around the town, find some coffee and sit somewhere to enjoy the warmth of a clear West Highland morning.

Oban has changed a great deal. I first came to the town many years ago as a young television presenter to help make an hour-long documentary about the National Mòd. Modelled on the Welsh Eisteddfod and intended to be a celebration of Gaelic music and poetry, the first Mòd was held in Oban in 1892 on a Saturday afternoon when ten competitors turned up. Numbers have expanded enormously and the range of classes is very wide and very specifically framed: Choral Two Part Harmony Under 19, or Solo Singing Boys Ages 9 to 10, or Bible Reading Ages 9 to 12. Before the film crew arrived, I spent a day watching young children perform the same piece many times, sometimes to tiny audiences of what seemed to be parents, teachers and other competitors. Occasionally, there was only one person in a class. I found myself at a loss as to how to structure a film based on what I saw. In fact, the Mòd seemed to me to be a dismal, disappointing Victorian version of a culture and I struggled to make any sense of it.

The evenings were no better. In Oban's staid and determinedly old-fashioned hotels, different competitions seemed to be taking place. In packed, smoke-filled bars, people appeared to be vying to drink as much whisky as possible before closing time. Every night seemed to be Hogmanay but without any sense of celebration. Indeed, resentment was definitely in the air. As filmmakers from Glasgow, Lowlanders (in fact, worse, my director was English) with no Gaelic, we were not exactly welcomed and the organisers, when they could be found, were not helpful. Having shot a great deal of footage, we left Oban, in the rain, very uncertain about what story we could tell – or should tell. Instead, a cheerful, superficial film was made – one that ruffled no feathers.

Almost forty years later, the atmosphere around Gaelic culture has changed radically. It has modernised itself out of a Victorian time warp and become bright, optimistic and forward looking – the result of a great deal of hard work from a handful of dedicated people. Gaelic seems much more open now and not the closed preserve of a dwindling minority – it's what those who fought so hard for the language wanted. Learners are the future, the sole route to survival.

Oban has also emerged into the twenty-first century. Not only was I able to buy some coffee, I noticed a string of attractive restaurants, many of them cooking locally caught seafood. The town recognises that it lives on tourism and has embraced it. Gone are the surly staff and the bad food. Even though tourists are the target market, some of the shops have avoided stocking the usual tat and their window displays looked very attractive. Remembering the Mòd of many years ago, I had anticipated simply passing through Oban, but on that bright morning it looked like a place to linger and enjoy a good lunch. Maybe another time. In my backpack I had cheese sandwiches, more chocolate, bottles of water and a hunger to explore the island of Lismore. It was the green and fertile heart of a lost kingdom, one that has long faded from the map of Scotland.

At the head of Loch Lomond, by the side of the A82 that leads north to Crianlarich, Breadalbane and the Drumalban Mountains, there is a massive, very striking rock. An erratic deposited on a mound of smaller rocks by the glacier that rumbled down the slopes of Ben Lomond about ten thousand years ago, it has a fascinating name. Clach nam Breatann means 'the Stone of the Britons' and it was conferred by the Gaelic speakers of the west and north of Loch Lomond. The big boulder was once a frontier marker between the ancient kingdom of Strathclyde and the territories of the Irish invaders known as the Dalriadans. Because the Strathclyders spoke dialects of Old Welsh, the language of the indigenous peoples whose kingdoms emerged after the departure of Rome in the early fifth century, they were called the Britons, the British.

From the head of Loch Lomond, the frontier ran south-west to Loch Goil, where another great stone, Clach a' Breatannach, marks it and then it turns south to the tip of the Toward Peninsula. Place-names that include *crioche* or *criche*, Gaelic for 'a border', mark its course down to the shores of the Firth of Clyde. On Bute and the Cumbraes, archaeologists have discovered a network of coastal fortresses that once guarded the approaches to the firth. Cumbrae is cognate to *Cymry*, the Welsh word for 'the Welsh'. It is a memory of Rome and derives from *Combrogi*, those who share a common border, something like 'the Citizens'. These island fortresses expected naval attacks, flotillas of large curraghs carrying many warriors, led by the sea lords of Dalriada.

At the beginning of the sixth century, Irish warbands sailed the North Channel and began to colonise Kintyre and part of the southern Hebrides. The origins of the name of Argyll remember conquest and settlement, for it derives from Earra Ghaidheal, 'the Coast of the Gaels', those who spoke Gaelic, not Old Welsh. By the middle of the seventh century, the *Senchus Fer n-Alban*, the *History of the Men of Scotland*, listed three sub-kingdoms. They were Cenel nOengusa, 'the Kindred of Angus' based on Islay, the Cenel nGabrain, 'the Kindred of Gabran' in Kintyre, and the Cenel Loairn, 'the Kindred of Loarn' in Lorn and Appin. In the wake of the warriors and their curraghs, the word of God also set sail from Ireland and it was in the territories controlled by the Irish kindreds that Brendan,

Columba and others began to found monasteries. They also supported and helped to legitimise the Dalriadan kings and evangelised their peoples.

As a safe, natural harbour, Oban lay at the heart of the kingdom of the Cenel Loairn. When I walked down to the quays to wait for the Lismore ferry, I knew I would soon see the ancient remains of the capital place of their kings. Dunollie Castle's ruined tower on the rocky promontory at the entrance to Oban Bay is substantially a late medieval survival but its origins as a fortress are much older. It was the principal sea castle of the Loairn kings because it stood at the heart of a dominion that stretched down either shore of the great firth, from Appin, beyond Benderloch and Oban Bay down to Loch Melfort, across to Morvern in the north-west and the south coast of Mull, and all the islands of Lorn. Principal amongst these was Lismore, Lios Mor in Gaelic, meaning 'the Great Garden or Enclosure'. Dunollie watched the traffic around this sea kingdom and archaeologists date its fortification to the seventh century and almost certainly earlier, to times when Dalriada was forming, as the colonists from Ulster stopped raiding and began settling.

The morning had grown warm by the time I saw the little ferry from Lismore sail below the ramparts of Dunollie. Passengers had begun to gather around the glass-sided waiting room, welcome enough on a wet day but too warm this morning. Off came my jumper to join the redundant anorak in my backpack. I wondered about melting chocolate and cheese and wrapped my sandwiches and Cadbury's bar tight in all of the unwanted clothing. My bottles of water would just have to get warm. In any case, I was not bound for an uninhabited island like Eileach an Naoimh. There were shops and at least one cafe on Lismore – and no drug smugglers to worry about, I assumed. Nor was I the sole passenger that morning. Several cyclists waited at the top of the slipway, having no doubt worked up a sweat under those odd crash hats that look like toasters. Most conspicuous was a couple who stood close together, with linked arms, the woman talking incessantly in an estuarine whine, a voice that cut through the west Highland air like fingernails down a blackboard. But when I turned to look at her again, I had to reproach myself for selfish thoughtlessness and jumping to unpleasant conclusions. The reason she had folded her arm though her partner's was because the man was blind. I had not noticed the telescoped white stick and thought the black Labrador was a pet. Her incessant descriptions of the quay, the town, the bay and the sky were his eyes.

As it chugged slowly towards us, I could see that the Lismore ferry was not on the scale of the leviathans that took passengers and vehicles to Mull and the larger islands. It had ramps at both ends and sailed like a rectangular box. The vehicle deck was open and the passenger lounges long and narrow on either side. Still, it was not likely to do twenty knots like yesterday's RIB and bang down hard on the waves as it raced across the sea. The much more stately crossing would take only fifty minutes. To my cheerful surprise, passengers were welcomed aboard in Gaelic before having the safety instructions repeated in English. The male voice was certainly that of a native speaker who had a lovely lilting *blas,* possibly from the Isle of Lewis. On the larger ferries, the Gaelic welcome is done, I am certain, by Cathy MacDonald, an excellent radio and TV presenter in any language, someone I used to know and work with. These announcements and their beautiful language could not have been understood by many of the passengers but their coming first, before the English, was an elegant reminder to visitors that they were moving through a very different part of Britain.

I had arranged my diary so that I would set sail for the island on 25 June. It is the feast day of St Moluag, a white martyr who came from Ireland with twelve companions to found a monastery on Lismore in 562, twenty years after Brendan's monks rowed their curraghs to Eileach an Naoimh. Moluag was hailed as the patron saint of Argyll in a charter of 1544 issued by the Earl of Argyll. It begins, 'In honour of God the Omnipotent, the Blessed Virgin, and St Moloc, our patron.' The reforming Benedictine abbot, Bernard of Clairvaux, wrote that the saint 'is said himself alone to have been the founder of a hundred monasteries'. It is very likely that the Earl's charter records an ancient tradition that Moluag was also patron of the Kings of Lorn. Their dynasty eventually ruled over all of Dalriada and, in the ninth century, claimed the kingship of Alba, that part of Scotland that lies north of the Forth–Clyde line. Moluag may well have been the earliest patron saint of Scotland, more favoured than Columba or Andrew.

And yet, until recently, he has been almost entirely forgotten. I was on the Lismore ferry on 25th June only because Moluag's feast day had been revived by Pope Leo XIII in 1898. For centuries, history has been very unkind to this man and I wanted not only to walk where he had walked, to see what he had seen on his island, but also to understand why his mission and virtually all of the details of his life had all but disappeared.

Moving slowly across the turquoise waters of Oban Bay, the ferry was steered carefully between the marker buoys on either side of the safe channel and the tower of Dunollie came into view. There was no prow where I could stand and find a panoramic view of the Firth of Lorn as we passed the stubby rock of Maiden Island. Instead, I stood on the open deck above the passenger lounge, as far forward as possible. But when we reached the open water of the firth and the ferry picked up speed, high plumes of spray washed over the ramp and forced a retreat into the lounge.

The sea roads were busy. Out in the Firth of Lorn, one of the big CalMac ferries from Mull was making its way towards us, to dock at Oban, while another was sailing west, probably to Islay and Kennacraig on Kintyre. It was a magnificent morning, the sea deep blue, the coasts of Lorn grey-green and the sky cerulean with puffs of brilliant white cloud to set it off. St Moluag's feast day had dawned bright and clear.

9

Walking to the Cathedral

Like Brendan, Moluag had taken holy orders in Ireland, appearing to have been ordained as a bishop in the north. One of the many, later, mysterious texts that weave legends around Patrick, the *Life* written by Jocelyn of Furness in the early thirteenth century, lists Moluag as destined for greatness. Patrick further prophesied that he would become a bishop. Included as one of the First Order of Celtic Saints in another devotional work, the *Martyrology of Oengus*, Moluag is described as 'the Clear and Brilliant, the Sun of Lismore in Alba . . . most holy, shining like the sun'. The value of these references is not in any historical details they might supply but in the language and the ranking. They show how revered this forgotten saint once was. And, importantly, he is not described as an ascetic hermit or an abbot. Like Patrick, Moluag was seen as a bishop and, in what I was about to discover, that distinction would turn out to be eloquent.

Like Columba, Moluag was noble born, a son of Dal n'Araide, a confederation of kindreds in what is now County Antrim in Northern Ireland, the part of the Ulster coast closest to Scotland. According to a *Life of St Patrick* composed in the ninth century, the kings of the Dal n'Araide had granted land so that churches could be built and supported. It seems likely that Moluag was raised in a Christian family. In the sixth century, it appears that Dalriada existed as a sea kingdom on both sides of the North Channel. Indeed, the name may derive from Dal n'Araide. The Antrim kindred was almost certainly one of its constituent territories, a fourth province linked to the three kindreds on Kintyre, Islay and Lorn. Such links will have made it much easier for churchmen like Moluag and Columba to settle in the southern Hebrides and found new monasteries.

His name also hints at the affection in which the saint was held, to say nothing of a remarkable paradox. Various versions appear in lists and references but most agree that his given name was Lughaidh. This was transformed into the modern rendering by a prefix and a suffix – *mo* simply means 'my' and it is seen as a term of endearment, while *oc* is a diminutive best translated as the Scots 'wee'. Moluag might therefore be read as 'My Wee Lughaidh'. This sort of embellishment happened to other saints such as Mo-Bhi and Mo-Lua. But what is surprising is the given name. Lughaidh is clearly from Lugh, the pagan god, the Little Stooping Trickster. As with Bridget, there seems to have been some sort of unblushing transfer from the pre-Christian world to Christian belief.

When the shores of Lismore drew close and the ferry slowed to begin its manoeuvres to meet the slipway square on, the spray abated and I climbed up to the observation deck for a closer view of the island from the seaward. We were about to dock at Achnacroish – appropriately in Gaelic Achadh na Croise, 'the Field of the Cross'. There is a Port Moluag further up the coast, but I suspected that the little harbour had long been a landing place on the holy island of Lismore and that a high cross had once marked the boundary between the secular and spiritual realms. Parked on the slipway was a red Post Office van, its back doors open, waiting for letters, parcels and newspapers. White haired and white bearded, the postman seemed even older than I am. Perhaps no one else wanted the job or perhaps, like many folk in the west of Scotland, it was only one of his jobs. As the blind man, his helpfully garrulous partner and their guide dog made their way up the concrete slipway, they were passed by a mum with a child in a buggy and two other women who looked to be on their way to Oban and its supermarkets. Where else on Earth could a shopping run be done on such a staggeringly beautiful route?

Gaelic once more came first, this time on the sign by the side of the road, *Failte gu Eilean Liosmor* was above 'Welcome to the Isle of

Lismore'. It occurred to me that the day before I had scuffed and scraped over the jagged edges of the Rock of the Saint, and here I was entering the Garden of Eden. The contrast could not have been more profound. About eight miles long and rarely more than about a mile wide, Lismore, the Great Garden, was just that, green, lush and apparently fertile. The steep road up from the slipway was shaded by an avenue of mature trees, and once past a colourful primary school it went through grass parks that were well grazed. Rock sills and outcrops sometimes broke through the greenery, but the immediate impression I had was of good, well-drained stock-rearing country.

My plan was to walk up to the road that runs down the spine of the island and make my way to the remains of St Moluag's Cathedral. The sixth-century monastery was reckoned to have been built next to it but I had been unable to discover much information about what still might be seen. On the way, I wanted to visit Ionad Naomh Moluag or maybe Aonad Naomh Moluag. Either way, whatever the spelling, it was also known as the Lismore Gaelic Heritage Centre and it housed an exhibition about the history of the island as well as a library of archive material. Perhaps I could discover more of the life and work of Wee Lugh amongst the material held there.

It was good to see Gaelic used to name the centre which opened in 2007 but odd that the name varied. *Ionad* simply means 'place' but *Aonad*, usually written with a terminal *h*, means something like 'unity, one-ness'. Perhaps it is also used colloquially to mean a meeting place. But also the spelling of *naomh* for saint jarred. As in Eileach an Naoimh, it should have taken the genitive case. But I am a learner whose Gaelic is fading through disuse, as well as being a natural pedant. No doubt the usage and the orthography were both checked by a scholarly native speaker.

On the Ordnance Survey Explorer map, I saw that there might be a path that led from Achnacroish a little way up the coast before turning inland to the Heritage Centre. But my track record for taking the wrong track is strong and I decided that I would follow the tarmac road from the slipway until it joined the long, spinal road that went past St Moluag's Cathedral. After the scrapes of Eileach an Naoimh, perhaps I felt I deserved a day of easy walking. And not having constantly to look where I was putting my feet meant that, for the three or four miles to the centre and then the church, I could look around myself, see something of what Moluag and his companions had seen when they had rowed their curraghs to the garden island from the north of Ireland.

Such as they are, sources for the history of the sixth century in Northern Ireland and western Scotland are scant and sometimes contradictory. The consensus is that Moluag was born between 500 and 520. A firmer date of 552 saw him ordain Comgall, a close kinsman from the Dal n'Araide, as a deacon and later as a priest. If accurate, this episode echoes the events of Patrick's early life and the story of his family. His father, Calpurnius, was a deacon and Potitus, his grandfather, was ordained as a priest. This episode assumes that Moluag was, at that time, a bishop and had the authority to ordain. The office of deacon was familiar in the episcopal organisation of early Carlisle and also understood as a preliminary to the priesthood.

Soon after these ceremonies were concluded, Comgall is said to have expressed a wish to become a white martyr and 'to go to Britain' but Moluag dissuaded him. Instead, he suggested to Comgall that he found a monastery at Bangor on the southern shore of Belfast Lough. The first monks may have been admitted in 555 or 559. Perhaps under the influence of the teachings of the Desert Fathers and his own experience as a hermit on an island in Lough Erne near Enniskillen, the regime at Bangor was famously severe. There was only one meal a day, taken in the evening, an austere collation of bread, water and perhaps some herbs. Milk was thought a luxury. The *laus perennis* was made sustainable on a grand scale by the huge numbers of monks who flocked to Bangor, despite the menu. Irish annalists reckoned that, by his death in 602, more than three thousand looked to Comgall for spiritual guidance. Also known as 'the Perpetual Harmonies', Bangor's choral psalmody became famous throughout Europe.

Columbanus, one of Comgall's most famous disciples, founded the Abbey of Bobbio in Italy, in the Apennine Mountains behind Genoa. In the early seventeenth century, a scholar discovered a fascinating manuscript, the *Antiphonary of Bangor*, a codex that contained *ymnum sancti Congilli abbatis nostri*. Compiled at the abbey at Bangor, it is a unique musical and devotional record, listing six canticles, twelve longer hymns, many collects or short prayers that were recited at particular times of the monastic day, short choral pieces or anthems, a version of the Creed and the Pater Noster, the Lord's Prayer. Much of this music was used in the *laus perennis* and St Bernard of Clairvaux much admired Bangor's practices and described how the perpetual praise was arranged: 'The solemnisation of divine offices was kept up by companies, who relieved each other in succession, so that not for one moment day and night was there an intermission of their devotion.'

When the referee blows his whistle at 3 p.m. on a winter's afternoon and a game kicks off at a stadium in Paisley, the players remember a white martyr who sailed from Ireland in the seventh century and the crowd roar his name. St Mirren Football Club is named after Mirin, another monk who left Comgall's community at Bangor. He and his companions rowed their curraghs up the River Clyde until they came to its confluence with the White Cart Water. On the eastern bank, they founded a diseart. The lands around the White Cart and the Black Cart seem to have been subject to regular flooding – literally isolating the place where the monks built their cells with water. But here they began to pray and to search the skies for their God and His angels.

Their little church prospered and provided its location with a very distinctive name, a clear memory of Mirin's foundation. Paisley is rendered as Paislig in Gaelic and hidden inside it is a fascinating derivation. It comes from *basilica*, a Latin word originally applied to a colonnaded building usually at the centre of a town or city where courts were held and business transacted. Later, it came to mean an important church. In Mirin's native Ireland, there is a village of Baslick in Roscommon and a Baslickane in County Kerry. Related to Paisley, these names signify that once there were great churches there.

In 1163, Walter fitz Alan, the first High Steward of Scotland and the progenitor of the Stewart dynasty, founded a Cluniac monastery on the site of Mirin's diseart. He was the son of a Breton knight known as Alan fitz Flaald, a mercenary who had come to England to enter the service of Henry I. Walter had the new church dedicated to saints Mary, James, Mirin and Milburga, the Abbess of Wenlock Priory, where the Cluniacs had a house. In 1245, Paisley had become so wealthy and grand that it was raised to the status of an abbey and all six of the line of High Stewards of Scotland are buried there.

This magnificent church, surely one of the greatest in Scotland, was also the scene of an emergency and some pioneering surgery. In 1316, when heavily pregnant, Marjorie Stewart, the daughter of King Robert Bruce, fell from her horse. Rushed to the abbey, no doubt in pain and possibly bleeding, she was cared for by the monks who saved her life and her baby by performing a caesarean section – without anaesthetic. The monks also ensured the succession of a dynasty of kings and queens that would rule Scotland and Great Britain and last into the early eighteenth century because the baby would become Robert II, the first Stewart king.

When they pull on their distinctive strip in the dressing rooms, the footballers of St Mirren remember these medically skilled monks. Their jerseys' black and white stripes preserve the sombre colours worn by the Cluniacs in the Middle Ages, a black habit over a white shirt.

Paisley Abbey is a beautiful, atmospheric church but its rich fabric shares only its location with Mirin. Nothing survives of the old diseart except its name. But there is a link that bridges between the seventh and twelfth centuries. Now sheltered by the roof of the abbey after standing through a thousand winters on a low hill to the north, the Barochan Cross was carved in the ninth or tenth century. While it is a fine example of a Celtic cross that can match St Martin's on Iona, the shaft carries carvings that are not scenes from the Bible but look entirely military. Very reminiscent of the tableau on the

Aberlemno Stone that commemorates a battle at Dun Nechtain in 685 between the Picts and the Angles, a horseman with a spear rides above a group of robed men who seem to be blowing battle horns. The Barochan Cross used to stand out in all weathers – and the carving is much faded as a result – on a knoll near the town of Houston, not far from a ford across the Clyde. Those who splashed over at low tide arrived on the northern shore, close to Dumbarton Rock, the great citadel of the kings of Strathclyde. Place-name evidence suggests that the cross may have been a muster point for warbands or armies.

Persistent tradition associates the Barochan Cross with the Battle of Renfrew in 1164. Somerled, Lord of the Isles – known by some as King of the Isles – had led a fleet of birlinns up the Clyde to challenge the kings of Scotland. He was killed and his army of Gaelic-speaking westerners were defeated by the forces of Walter fitz Alan. It was a moment when destiny turned, when different versions of Scotland clashed and two languages collided. The Celtic west was driven back to the islands and mountains by an army of Lowlanders. And ultimately the legacy of Columba, Moluag, Maelrubha – and Mirin – was overlaid by the monastic orders who came north from Western Europe.

What complicates the neat chronology of who influenced, ordained or trained whom is a competing tradition that Moluag was in fact a monk at Bangor under Comgall's abbacy. Having decided to leave, he embarked on the journey of white martyrdom to the northern kindreds of Dalriada and founded his own monastery on Lismore. To pile confusion on contradiction, yet more wispy evidence suggests that Comgall either accompanied him or came later to Moluag's island. In at least one sense, he may have been returning to his ancestral homeland, for at least one of the annalists records that Comgall's father was Setna, a Pictish warrior from northern or eastern Scotland. Perhaps Comgall understood his father's language.

What might draw all of this together is an alternative interpretation of Columba's visit to the fortress of the Pictish king, Bridei, near Inverness. Recent studies suggest that Moluag and Comgall led what might be seen as a deputation to pagan Pictland. Both may have spoken Pictish and, unlike Columba, they were not closely politically aligned with the Dalriadan kings, something that might have softened Bridei's attitude. Far from being its leader, as Adomnán asserts, Columba may have accompanied his Ulster countrymen as an exiled penitent. His influence did not extend beyond the bounds of Lorn and, contrary to what some scholars have argued, he was almost certainly not the Apostle of the Picts. As I was to discover, Moluag probably has a far stronger claim to that accolade.

Walking through Lismore's green pastures, enjoying the day, setting one foot metronomically in front of the other, but in no hurry, I realised more and more what a prize the island was. Compared to the barren rocks of Eileach, the Great Garden would have been bountiful, even comfortable. And in the middle of the sixth century it must have been heavily populated. Only a hundred years ago, more than a thousand people lived permanently on the island. Now it is home to two hundred. Unlike Brendan, Moluag will have been apportioned only a small part of Lismore on which to build his monastery and sustain his monks.

When I reached the junction with the road running up the middle of the island, I was struck by how shaded it was, some of the mature trees on either side reaching right over to form a canopy. And the gardens of the houses by the roadside were lush, some with exotic plants. The Gulf Stream warms Lismore and it seemed to be watered by generous rainfall. I passed two wayside springs and one had been made into a trough where thirsty horses could stop and drink. Until the decade after the Second World War, Clydesdales and other horses were the main source of traction for farmers, pulling ploughs, harrows, carts and other sorts of farm gear. On an island such as this, these noble animals were to be preferred to expensive machinery that might break down. But all of that began to change in the later 1940s. Parked outside an old stone barn stood an antique example of what eventually supplanted these faithful equine servants and, like Moluag, it came originally from Northern Ireland.

Splendid in the noonday sun was a red Massey Ferguson 240. I have a great affection for, perhaps a borderline obsession with, these little tractors. Brilliantly designed, inexpensive to buy, cheap to run and easy to maintain, they improved the lives of farmers and farm workers all over Britain enormously. Harry Ferguson was an Ulsterman who had the breakthrough idea to manufacture a small tractor with what is known as a three-point linkage at the back end. This allowed the power of the tractor's engine to be transferred to whatever implement was attached to it. Earlier tractors had merely pulled implements like ploughs with more power but less precision than a Clydesdale. Now harrows, reapers and other implements that needed to be dynamic could be.

In addition, the Standard Motor Company of Coventry achieved tremendous economies of scale, turning out more than half a million tractors before they were technically superseded. One of the economies was colour. It had to be grey but no one cared – the Wee Grey Fergies were a godsend. The Massey Ferguson 240 (so called because an American company merged with Ferguson Tractors) I was looking at was perfect for island work. With a small three-cylinder engine and a tank that needed only eight gallons of fuel, it was still powerful at 45 horsepower. It was small, easily housed and, here is a confession, beautiful. When I did more around our farm and needed more tug than a quad bike, I could never find a Wee Grey Fergie that was in good condition and did not cost a fortune. They are highly collectable. But I did buy a 1960 Fordson Super Major. Bright blue, with an upright exhaust and red wheel trims, I loved it. When I eventually and sadly sold it to a collector, I got more than I paid, not because it was in excellent condition but because it had a rare set of wheel weights that kept me from getting stuck in deep mud many times.

Undulating rather than hilly, the central road made for good, steady walking. Its rhythm inevitably attracted a soundtrack as tapes played in my head as I remembered music, irritatingly often the last thing I listened to, often inappropriate. But on that bright morning, I had the perfect accompaniment, a piece of music that has stayed with me for many decades.

In the late 1950s and 1960s, when I was allowed to go to Saturday matinees with my sister, the main features in the cinema were always preceded by shorts. The Pathé News and its extraordinarily ringing, patriotic, quintessentially British voice-overs from Bob Danvers-Walker were regulars, only dying out with the coming of cheap TV rentals and the BBC and ITV news bulletins. His baritone delivery, in impeccable received pronunciation, certainly stern, almost severe, always authoritative, is printed indelibly on my memory. It seemed to many to represent continuity. Danvers-Walker voiced over wartime footage – the suffering of London in the Blitz given dignity by his superb delivery and the D-Day landings made even more dramatic by the steel and determination of his tone. This extraordinary, unseen icon of British culture retired as late as 1970 and the last Pathé bulletin voiced by him was, I think, Winston Churchill's state funeral on 30 January 1965. It seemed and, indeed, was the end of an old Britain, the last flicker of empire, of wartime glory and spirit.

What sparked these memories on sunlit Lismore was another sort of glory, the vast panoramas and the music that played while I walked. When I reached a rise in the road, I could see all of the shores of Lorn and I fancied I could make out the Nevis ranges to the north-east. Whenever Pathé News ran a story from the Hebrides or, for that matter, anywhere in the Scottish Highlands, it seemed to me that they always used the same music. Over shots of sparkling water, high mountains and heather-clad glens, the soaring strings of Felix Mendelssohn's *Hebrides* overture filled the cinema. Long before I had ever seen the Atlantic shore, I knew what it would sound like.

Even though Mendelssohn was German and dedicated the piece to Frederick William IV, the Crown Prince of Prussia, it was a genuinely inspired composition. As was much of early nineteenth-century Europe, the Prussian court and its composer were bewitched by 'the Wizard of the North', the great Walter Scott, and, in 1829, Mendelssohn travelled to romantic, dramatic Scotland, the land of the mountain and the flood. On a boat trip around the southern

Hebrides, he visited Staffa and the remarkable Fingal's Cave (named after an invented Celtic hero) and the music for the opening of the overture sprang immediately into his head. Making hurried notes on the boat, he sketched out the melodies that grew into a full-blown, magnificent work. In a letter to his sister, Mendelssohn wrote how the sight of Staffa had made an immense, unforgettable impression. That is why, I think, it was this unlikely manmade music that the film editors at Pathé used again and again. It was genuinely inspired, it fitted the pictures perfectly and it was impossible for me to get it out of my head on that crystal morning.

When Moluag and his companions pulled their curraghs above the tideline, there was no orchestral score playing in their heads. Instead, they had something that may have been more awe inspiring – the choral music of the *Antiphonary of Bangor*. Sometimes it is forgotten how much monks sang and chanted at their devotions, how the beauty of these canticles and anthems was in itself a simple means of praising God, as much a form of worship as a prayer or the recital of the Creed. It seems very likely that these holy men marked impor-tant moments with prayer and with music. When they first gained the shores of Lismore, I think they would have fallen to their knees to thank their Lord for safe passage and to seek His blessing on the new monastery. And when they stood and looked about themselves at the unchanging glories of His Creation, they may have chanted the *Te Deum Laudamus*, 'Thee, O God, we praise'. It is one of the oldest pieces of choral music in the world and scribes wrote its words into the pages of the *Antiphonary of Bangor*.

When the *Te Deum* rings around a cathedral now, often an open-ing note is sounded with a bell. One of only a handful of surviving objects from the early ecclesiastical history of Argyll is a monastic handbell found at Kilmichael Glassary near Lochgilphead. It once formed part of a small shrine and its casing had a hole through which a finger could be poked. This was important – a tangible link to sanctity – for the bell was closely associated with Moluag. Those who were permitted to touch his bell are thought to have prayed to him to intercede with God to help heal their wounds, both physical and mental. In the first book to be printed in Scotland, the early sixteenth-century *Aberdeen Breviary*, a link is made with Moluag; apparently, the bell shrine was kept on Lismore in what later became the Cathedral Church of St Moluag. Whatever the truth of that tradition, it is very likely that the monks who came in 562 had stowed a handbell in one of their curraghs.

As Mendelssohn's *Hebrides* overture played its closing chords, I came at last to the Ionad Naomh Moluag. Hoping the centre would prove a source of locally gleaned knowledge about the saint and his monastery that was unavailable elsewhere, I had brought a note-book, my phone with its camera and a long list of questions. Set on a low ridge, the centre is attractive – a single-storey wooden building with a grass roof and a decking terrace outside a cafe that looked towards the Appin shore of the Firth of Lorn. Beside it stands a thatched stone building. A reconstruction of a crofter's cottage, its walls are beautifully made. To keep the thatch secure in the bitter winter winds, a lattice of rope work had been set on it and weighted with large stones attached that dangled over the edges of the roof. Pushing open the door, I was stopped in my tracks. Sitting on either side of the fire were the life-like figures of a crofter and his wife and playing from hidden speakers was their conversation. For a moment, I felt I should have knocked. Naturally, the couple spoke to each other in Gaelic, but I found it difficult to make out more than a fragment or two. But it turned out that this recorded exchange was the only time I would hear Gaelic spoken on Lismore. Encouraged by the many signs and information boards in the language, I had developed the notion that Gaelic would be readily spoken, and I was disappointed to find no one who had any. Perhaps, if I had, it would have been an excruciating experience for them.

In one part of the Ionad Naomh Moluag was a permanent exhibition that was well laid out and explained. Especially helpful was an aerial photograph of St Moluag's Cathedral and an explanatory diagrammatic map that showed the site of the original sixth-century monastery in the open ground behind the church. It looked as though there was nothing upstanding, unlike Eileach an Naoimh, only humps, bumps and ridges that might remember the ditch and bank of the monastic enclosure. One area was plotted as the site of a building but there was no accompanying photograph of any founds or extant stonework.

Apart from the bell shrine (and that may be contentious since some believe it to be associated with Columba), the sole remaining relic for St Moluag is his staff or crozier. Known as '*Bachuil Mor*', 'the Great Staff or Shepherd's Crook', its etymological history led me, in my early experiences of learning Gaelic, to Edward Dwelly and his *Illustrated Gaelic–English Dictionary*. A towering figure, Dwelly's introduction to the language consoled me when I found it impenetrable. I also found his discussion about the complex relationship between native speakers and learners interesting. His magisterial dictionary was compiled between 1901 and 1911 and Edward Dwelly clearly knew of the *Bachuil Mor* and its story. Appended to the entry for *bachall* is this: 'By virtue of an ancient grant from an Earl of Argyll, a piece of land in the island of Lismore was held on condition that the holder kept and took care of the crozier of St. Maluag, from whom its church is named. Hence the holder is known as Baran a' Bhachaill [the Baron of the Crozier].'

It is entirely and delightfully typical of Dwelly's dictionary that detailed historical information, often available nowhere else, can be found. And it is also very surprising. Edward Dwelly was an Englishman born in Twickenham, now a suburb of London, in 1864. He came to Gaelic as a learner after having been stationed in Scotland while he was in the army. Fearful that his work might not be accepted by the Gaelic speech community, he worked under the nom de plume of Eoghann MacDhomhnaill, Ewan MacDonald. With the help of his wife, Mary McDougall, a native speaker from Perthshire, and his children, Dwelly illustrated, printed, bound and, essentially, self-published his definitive dictionary. When he reached the halfway mark, welcome help arrived from an unexpected source when King Edward VII awarded Dwelly a civil list pension. Someone at the royal court had recognised that a very significant initiative was underway. For the first time, an exhaustive vocabulary of the language, with all its variations and combinations, was being captured. More than seventy thousand entries also standardised orthography (as well as recording variants) and, therefore, made the dictionary absolutely definitive. Between 1911 and 2011, there were twelve editions of this beautiful, meticulous lexicon. Thesaurus is derived from the Greek word for 'treasure' and that is what Dwelly bequeathed to Scotland.

This mighty work of scholarship lies at the core of the Gaelic language, but its making was enormously complicated and very difficult. In his preface, the lexicographer explained why:

No-one who has always spoken a language like Gaelic from the cradle can ever realize the extraordinary difficulties presented to a stranger who wishes to acquire it. First, the majority of Gaelic speakers only a very few years ago could neither read nor write it, so when one heard an unfamiliar word or phrase and the first instinct was of course to write it down lest it should be forgotten, the question was how to spell it – of course the speaker could not tell! I was baulked in this way times without number, and my progress with the language immensely retarded in consequence.

Next the great difficulty of inducing a Gael to engage in a Gaelic conversation if he thinks he can make himself understood at all by means of indifferent English, or even if there is anyone present who cannot understand Gaelic, makes the acquisition of a knowledge of colloquial Gaelic much more difficult than is the case with other modern tongues, for it is only by posing as a Highlander and one who knows Gaelic that one can ever hope to hear it spoken habitually and without restraint. These are real difficulties, but they may be overcome by scheming and persever-ance as I have proved.

Very sadly, Edward Dwelly's love affair with the Gaelic language ended in bitterness. Ignored as well as frequently hindered in his great enterprise, he felt himself alienated by some of the native speech community and even those without the language. He felt himself forced to leave Scotland, despite the fact that he had given the nation a rich, comprehensive means of describing and understanding its Highlands and Islands and the lives of the communities who lived there. In 1939, this extraordinary, devoted man died in Fleet in Hampshire, almost as far from the Gaidhealtachd as it is possible to live.

I spent a long time looking at the permanent exhibition at the Ionad Naomh Moluag. There seemed to be no detailed brochure I could buy, which was a pity because the information boards next to the exhibits were informative. With the permission of the helpful lady at reception, I photographed everything with my phone and made several pages of notes. But I was still groping for a sense of Moluag, his mission and the establishment of a monastery on Lismore. Perhaps that would become clearer when I visited the humps and bumps behind it. Places often speak of those who made them, even across many centuries of absence. Eileach an Naoimh had certainly been eloquent. Meanwhile I bought a copy of a new history of the island, several booklets on place-names, archaeological trails and something that sounded intriguingly detailed – *Survey of Sandstone Blocks in Drystone Walls in the Vicinity of Lismore Parish Church*. And why not?

After reading Dwelly's entry for *bachall*, perhaps I should not have been surprised that it was not in the exhibition. The staff or crozier is kept by the Livingstone family at Bachuil House near the cathedral and can be seen by appointment. Made from blackthorn it is apparently studded with nails that once kept a metal sheath in place. Niall Livingstone is currently the chief of Clan Livingstone. Their surname used to be MacLea but, for some reason, Livingstone was adopted. It comes from the place-name in West Lothian. He is styled Niall Livingstone of Bachuil, Baron of the Bachuil, Coarb of St Moluag, Abbot of Lismore and his full title claims fifteen centuries of continuity since the time of St Moluag. Coarb is listed in Dwelly as *comharba* and it means 'a successor or heir' or sometimes 'a partner in church lands'. This title is reckoned to be the most enduring ecclesiastical office in British history – older even than the archbishopric of Canterbury. And, in a formula shared only with the Queen, Niall Livingstone holds these titles 'by the grace of God'.

But his family's hold on the hereditary guardianship of the Crozier of St Moluag has been shaky. In the late nineteenth century, the Duke of Argyll asked if he might borrow the ancient staff since he had some friends who would be interested in seeing it. Despite many, no doubt respectful, requests, it was not returned to the Livingstones for almost a century. Perhaps that is why the crozier has not been loaned to the Ionad Naomh Moluag. And it seems that another link with the long past was in danger of being severed. Bachuil House was put on the market because it had become too difficult for two people – Niall and his wife, Anita – to run and maintain. Beside a news story about the sale sat a photograph of Niall Livingstone holding the *bachuil mor*. He wears a white monastic habit and a pectoral cross and appears to be giving a blessing. However, the house was not sold and was run by Niall and Anita as a country house hotel. Sadly, a recent click on the hotel's website told me that 'Bachuil Country House is now closed' and the Livingstones wanted 'to thank [their] past guests for their support and kind reviews'.

Not even the heads of the Nevis range on the mainland attracted cloud on that glorious morning as I walked from the centre to the cathedral and the site of the old monastery. There was only the merest whisper of a breeze – what might best be described in that lovely example of onomatopoeia a zephyr, from the name of the Greek god of the west wind. It was enough to keep the midges at bay. On Lismore, I saw few damp, peaty places where they might multiply. The knowledgeable Hamish Haswell-Smith pointed out that the island was largely formed from Dalriadan limestone, creating an environment where midges do not thrive. Which was a blessing, and it was lovely to have a warm West Highland day without being pursued by these little fiends. When I passed the fire station, several sensible sheep were enjoying the shade by the main doors.

St Moluag's turned out to be a modest sort of cathedral, no bigger than a small parish church. Box-like, harled and painted white with a small bell tower perched on the east gable, it sits foursquare by the central road. On one side, there is an old graveyard that seemed no longer to be in use, and on the far side rows of new headstones stood in a well-kept area that had left plenty of room for the generations to come. But appearances can be misleading. Behind the unpretentious facade of this little cathedral lies a story of great pretension, of ambitions that threatened the Scottish state, that created a powerful sea kingdom down the Atlantic shore and beyond and that inspired myth, music and the praise of bards.

In the early twelfth century, a hero sailed out of the sea mists and made himself a king. Only a few miles from where I stood, around the Morvern coast, just across the Firth of Lorn, mythical tales of his origins swirled, some of them remembering the coming of the holy men from Ireland. Sometime in the early years of the twelfth century, Somerled was fishing a pool in a stream that spills into the Sound of Mull near the castle at Ardtornish. Outwitted by a wily, old salmon, *Am Bradan Mor*, 'the great fish', he was determined not to give up until he had hooked it. But the young man was suddenly interrupted by a deputation of people from Morvern who had lost their chief to raiding Vikings. Would Somerled lead their warriors? Only if they waited until he caught his fish.

The importance of this episode lies in its location. Somerled seems to have been a man of Lorn and he became the greatest warrior-king of the medieval Gaidhealtachd. And yet his name speaks of a different genesis. *Sumarliði* is Norse and it means 'Summer Raider', in other words, 'the Viking'. Popular history has produced a traditional tautology that reinforces that, for he was hailed as 'Somerled the Viking'. Much later, when bards recited the hero's genealogy and sang that his father was GilleBride, the Servant of St Bridget, and his grandfather was Gille Adomnán, the Servant of St Adomnán, they remember the saints and a Gaelic heritage.

Leaving aside the story of the salmon and the symbolism around that, it seems likely that Somerled's family did not suddenly appear out of nowhere. They were probably landed, powerful and perhaps linked to the royal houses of Dalriada and Kenneth macAlpin. Not only do the genealogies recall St Bridget and St Adomnán, they also record that Somerled's father and grandfather married women with Norse names. The most reliable conclusion is that this young warrior was a Gaelic-speaking, Celto-Norse chieftain from Morvern who began to push back against the Norse takeover of the southern Hebrides and the Atlantic coastlands.

Somerled was a sea lord. His soldiers were marines, oarsmen who crewed highly manoeuvrable little galleys known as birlinns. Fitted with a hinged rudder rather than a steering oar, fast and with a shallow draught, a fleet of birlinns could deliver an army to fight on land or could take part in naval engagements. A sense of the look of these warriors can be seen in the small figures of the famous Lewis chessmen. They were carved in the early twelfth century. By 1140, Somerled had made himself master of Knapdale, Lorn and much of mainland Argyll and Kintyre. These possessions were tied together and protected by a network of sea castles at Dunollie, Dunstaffnage, Duart on Mull, Ardtornish in Morvern and Achinduin on Lismore. But Somerled's ambition was not sated. On the night of 5–6 January 1156, off the island of Colonsay, he expanded his Atlantic principality when his fleet of birlinns engaged with and defeated the navy of Godred, King of Man. The islands of Islay, Jura and Mull were added and Somerled began to style himself in Gaelic *Ri Innse Gall* or the Latin equivalent *Rex Insularum*, 'the King of the Isles'. In 1158, he expelled Godred from Man and took over the island and also annexed the Manx-held islands of Lewis, Harris, the Uists, Benbecula and Barra. His empire of the islands now stretched down the Atlantic shore for three hundred and fifty miles.

A place-name recalls a naval headquarters. Dunyvaig on Islay means 'the Fort of the Little Ships' and it was one of the places where Somerled moored his fleet. The harbour was guarded by skerries and hidden reefs that larger ships might not have risked but which presented no dangers to the birlinns. Although the details of the great sea battles won by Somerled are lost, there is no doubt that his

sea lords knew the inshore waters of the islands and the coast inti-
mately, and used them to great tactical advantage when he attacked
the Vikings and their descendants on the Isle of Man.

As often happens, those who rise like meteors crash suddenly to
Earth when they overreach themselves. In 1164, Somerled chal-
lenged for the throne of Scotland. Having led a huge fleet of birlinns
up the River Clyde to attack the Stewart possessions at Renfrew, he
was confronted by the army of King Malcolm IV and was undone
by treachery. Somerled was betrayed by a kinsman and stabbed to
death in his tent. Shattered by the sudden loss of their charismatic
admiral, the Islesmen did not offer battle but, instead, pushed their
birlinns into the firth and set sail for the west and the kingdom of
the islands.

According to custom, Somerled's legacy was partible and was to
be divided between his three sons – Ragnall, Dugald and Angus.
Their branches of the ruling family eventually became known as the
MacDonalds, the MacDougalls and the MacRuaris. And Lismore,
along with much of Lorn and the centre of Somerled's patrimony,
fell to the MacDougalls. At the end of the twelfth century, they
decided they needed to have a cathedral built – one that was dedicated to St Moluag. But before work could begin, they needed a
bishop – one of their own.

At that time, Argyll and most of the southern Hebrides were
included in the vast diocese of Dunkeld, its centre lying far to the
east. Paradoxically, Dunkeld's distance from the Atlantic fostered its
pre-eminence in the west because, in 849, Kenneth macAlpin
brought some of the relics of Columba over the mountains and into
the safekeeping of the abbot of the monastery near the confluence of
the Tay and the Tummel. Since the turn of the ninth century, Viking
raiders had savagely despoiled Iona, occasionally massacring monks,
and, while Columba's monastery was probably never completely
abandoned, the relics had to be removed and placed far from danger.

Sometime between 1183 and 1193, John Scotus, the Bishop of
Dunkeld, sought papal approval for the detachment of Argyll and its
elevation as a separate diocese. John Scotus's name implies his ethnic

origins were either Irish or Gaelic Scots but one of the reasons given for his wish to relinquish Argyll was that he could not speak Gaelic. That seems unlikely. John Scotus had form as an ecclesiastical politician and he attempted to have himself consecrated Bishop of St Andrews, only later accepting Dunkeld as a consolation prize when his intrigues at the papal court failed. A twelfth-century rent roll listed the relative incomes of Scotland's bishoprics: St Andrews led the rankings by some distance with revenue of £8,018 per annum, while Argyll languished at the bottom of the table with a paltry £281. John Scotus may simply have decided that it was too far away, too poor and simply not worth the trouble. In any case, the MacDougalls were probably agitating for their own bishopric. It may be that, for a price, Scotus obliged.

Moluag's ancient sanctity meant that the cathedral should be on Lismore, on the site of the holy ground of his monastery at Kilmoluag. The new bishops often styled themselves Bishops of Lismore. Recorded by the annalists, Harald appears to be the name of the first Bishop of Argyll. Records are imprecise and patchy but he probably based himself at Moluag's monastery on Lismore between 1200 and 1230. In the absence of anything more grand and episcopal, Harald may have used a small chapel in the ancient precinct. There is a tradition that the cathedral was eventually built on its footprint. It is certain that by 1225 Harald had succeeded in establishing some sort of diocesan centre on the island.

The bounds of his authority are also shrouded in mist. Despite Somerled's conquests of the twelfth century, the Hebrides appear to have remained part of the vast see of Sodor and (the Isle of) Man. The name Sodor derives from Sudreyjar, what Norse lords and kings knew as 'the Southern Isles' – the Northern Isles, or Nordreyjar, being Orkney and Shetland. Nominally, Sodor and Man were subject to the Archbishop of Nidaros – the medieval name for Trondheim – in Norway. Argyll, at that time, extended far further than it does now; when Dunkeld allowed the bishopric's creation, it comprised only the mainland, but it stretched from Kintyre and the Firth of Clyde in the south to as far north as Loch Broom and the old diseart on Eilean Mhartainn. Iona had passed into the possession of Ragnall, the second son of Somerled, and he brought a community of Benedictine monks to build its abbey. A nunnery was founded on Iona at the same time, with Ragnall's sister, Beathag, at its head. After these new communities had been set up on Iona and the MacDougall bishops were established on Lismore, the reach of Trondheim began to slacken.

Building did not begin at Kilmoluag until long after the time of Harald – not until 1250 – and the cathedral was not completed until the early fourteenth century. It was approximately twice as large as the existing parish church. In the 1950s, archaeologists discovered that the nave of the old church extended to the west and that a tower was raised to house its bells. When I went into the church, it was good to see that some of the early stonework had survived. To my left there were three arched alcoves set into the wall, places where clergy could sit during worship. And there was also a piscina, a small basin where the communion cups could be washed. Behind the altar table stood an arch that must have led to the nave beyond it. Lit by a brilliant sun, a beautifully made stained-glass window showed Moluag, the Sun of Lismore, holding the *bachuil mor* and an open psalter inscribed with 'Thine is the Kingdom'. Behind him the multicoloured sail of what might be a birlinn has been unfurled and a man pulls on the oars. In the thirteenth and fourteenth centuries, the bishopric and its little cathedral appear to have become a MacDougall family heirloom. At least three bishops, Laurence, Aonghas and Martin, were styled *de Ergadia*, 'of Argyll', a kind of surname that the MacDougalls used especially in Latin contexts.

10

The Apostle of the Picts

Outside the church stood a sturdy and very handy bench, slightly shaded by a vigorous shrub that cascaded over the wall head in front of the vestibule. A good place to sit down and ease my backpack off my shoulders. Unwrapping my sandwiches and bar of chocolate from unneeded clothing, I enjoyed an excellent lunch, washed down by warm, fizzy water. How good even a humble cheese sandwich tastes when one is very hungry. Having made some notes, I sat back, stretched my legs and, in that peaceful, warm place, felt myself slipping into a pleasant doze.

Sometime later, I'm not sure how much, I realised I was not alone. In the tarmacked space in front of the church, a car drew up and an old lady emerged. As she opened the boot, she looked up at me and smiled.

'Feasgar math,' I said and she smiled again, straightening her back and having a good look at me. When she returned my 'Good afternoon' in Gaelic with the usual 'Cò às a tha sibh?', I explained that I was a learner. Her question asks not only where you are from but, more precisely, who are your people – meaning 'Are you from Lewis, the Uists or Islay or wherever?' and, if you tell me your name, I might know someone who knows you or is related to you and be able to place you. It is a far better question than simply asking where you are from or, even less interesting, what do you do. That is why I explained immediately that I was a learner. There was no likelihood that she could know my people.

As we spoke in the afternoon sunshine, the old lady gathered up flowers, a plastic bag and a pair of secateurs. 'Airson an duine agam

[For my husband],' she said and she pushed open the gate to the new graveyard. I sat back down on the bench, not wishing to intrude on private moments. The diagrammatic map I had photographed on my phone at the Ionad Naomh Moluag showed that the site of his monastery probably lay beyond the parish church and the graveyard. So, I waited. With an unpretentious, everyday dignity, the woman was setting fresh flowers on her husband's grave and perhaps remembering something of what I hoped had been a long life together. Sometime later, I went into the graveyard. There were vases of flowers by several headstones and one of them had '*Gus am Bris an Latha*', 'Until the Break of Day', inscribed on it.

The little cathedral and its dedication kept the memory of Moluag alive for, in essence, it was all that remained of him in that place. Beyond the new graveyard, all I could see were undulations in a wide grass park pastured by sheep. Halfway up the slope were the founds of a later lateral dyke but, under the glare of a sun, it was difficult to make anything of the lines on the diagrammatic map from Ionad Naomh Moluag. Unlike on Eileach an Naoimh, there was no sense of the presence of the old monks and their community. All I had was tradition and even the old lady with the flowers had little idea of the location of the ancient monastery, despite having lived on Lismore for more than seventy years.

I walked up to the top of the ridge to be sure I had missed nothing and was rewarded with panoramic views over the Firth of Lorn to the Morvern coast. All too easily, I could make out the great gash of the Glensanda Quarry. Several yachts were making headway to the south-west, perhaps running before the wind. It was a timeless image.

From the sketchy and provisional evidence that exists, it seems that Moluag spent a great deal of time in his curragh, travelling widely in the north-east of Scotland. As Bernard of Clairvaux wrote, 'the Sun of Lismore' was the founder of a hundred monasteries. It may be that some of the surviving dedications of churches chart a course that he followed. Lismore lies at the south-western end of a dramatic geological fault-line, the Great Glen that runs from the

Atlantic and the Firth of Lorn up to the Moray Firth and the North Sea. Lochs Lochy, Oich and Ness are deep ribbons of water that almost make the north-west Highlands an island. And throughout Scotland's history, they acted as a busy highway with ideas, beliefs, armies and merchandise travelling in both directions for millennia. Certainly by the beginning of the ninth century and probably much earlier, the kings of the Cenel Loairn began to extend their reach up the Great Glen into the heart of Pictland. And with their warriors in their seven-bench curraghs came the Word of God. And it seems at first to have come out of the mouth of Moluag.

The chain of the three lochs made travel easy and rapid. The River Lochy drains into the sea where Loch Linnhe turns west to become Loch Eil, the place where Fort William now stands. Although it is wide and very shallow in places, especially in summer, the season when most journeys were undertaken, there would have been enough water for the draught of a curragh. And, where there was a danger of boats running aground, they could be emptied and dragged upstream.

Beyond Loch Lochy and Loch Oich lies Fort Augustus at the south-western end of Loch Ness. Nearby is Auchterawe, now a country house but once an ancient burial ground that was known as Kilmalomaig, 'the Cell or Chapel of Moluag'. Less than a day's journey from Lismore, it may have been an early foundation – what later used to be known as a 'daughter house' of the monastery. Further up Loch Ness, on its eastern shore is another memory on the map, a place where God was worshipped, psalms were sung and prayers murmured. At Ballagan, near Inverfarigaig, aerial photography has revealed crop marks of earthworks that might be the banks and ditches of a monastery. Its old name was Cill Moluag.

On the opposite shore of the great loch stands the romantic ruin of Castle Urquhart, its medieval keep still rising to its full height above the bay where birlinns dropped anchor. In the 1950s, excavations revealed the remains of a much earlier fortress, very extensive and dating from the fifth century onwards. In his *Life of St Columba*,

Adomnán claimed that on his way to the court of the Pictish king, Bridei, the saint did have some success when he converted a nobleman called Emchath. The earlier fort at Castle Urquhart may have been his main residence.

However, it is difficult to reconcile Adomnán's story with the dedication of a church to Moluag on the opposite shore of Loch Ness, a place that was close and easy for Emchath to reach and probably belonged to him. It seems much more likely that, on this expedition into Pictland or another, perhaps with Comgall of Bangor, Moluag was a leader and that is why the foundation at Ballagan was built in his name. Diplomacy almost certainly travelled with the Word of God and if the Cenel Loairn were expanding up the Great Glen, likely a slow process rather than an event such as a decisive battle, it made sense for them to bring their holy man with them. A process of assimilation may have been underway as early as the late sixth century.

Dates and events can only be guessed at but the most significant initiative undertaken by Moluag himself, or in his name, was at Rosemarkie on the southern shore of the Black Isle. It too could be easily and quickly reached by curragh, lying only a few nautical miles into the Moray Firth from the mouth of the River Ness. A monastery was established and a church dedicated to Moluag. Intricately carved Pictish stones with crosses incised have survived and they suggest a rich and vibrant community. Very quickly the diocese of Ross was set up, and in 697 Bishop Curetan witnessed a famous document at the Synod of Birr in County Offaly in Ireland. At the request of Adomnán, as Abbot of Iona, Irish, Pictish and Dalriadan noblemen gathered because he wanted them to support his Law of Innocents, an agreement that women and non-combatants should not be harmed in warfare.

Down the Atlantic shore and amongst the islands of the Hebrides, cells, chapels and perhaps monasteries were either founded by or dedicated to Moluag. The most northerly is perhaps the most evocative. On the Butt of Lewis at Eoropaidh near the village of Ness stands Teampull Mholuaidh, a later, small church that has been beautifully restored. No electricity reaches it and so its stone-faced interior is made even more atmospheric by candlelight. Furthest south lies Kilmalu, near Inverary, and between it and the Butt there are many more dedications – at Kilmaluag on Skye, Raasay, Mull, Tiree, Pabbay and in Knapdale.

Given the speed of travel by sea, it is conceivable that the Sun of Lismore could have shone brightly and personally brought all of these foundations into being. All are accessible by water. And, even if his mission to Pictland is too early to have been supported by the expansion of the power of the Cenel Loairn, the Word of God did not always need to be heard at the point of a sword.

Carved on the Newton Stone near Insch in Aberdeenshire is a strange inscription. At six foot eight inches, it is an impressive Pictish stone and, as on some others, down one edge run the rune-like marks of the ancient Irish language known as Ogham. But inscribed on its face is something even more enigmatic – and unique: *Ette Cunanmain Maolouoeg. Un. Rofiis, I. H. Innsi Loaoaruin.* Brilliantly transcribed and identified as very early Gaelic by Dr William Bannerman in the late nineteenth century, it translates as: Draw near to the soul of Moluag [from whom came knowledge of the faith.] He was of the island of Lorn.'

Deep in rural Aberdeenshire, this unique inscription sounds vale-dictory, as though Moluag is a revered memory. Nevertheless, it is startling to see a tangible record of his mission, more than a place-name or a tradition. Insch finds itself close to a clutch of dedications to St Moluag. There were ancient churches at Tarland, Migvie and Durris, and in the nearby Correen Hills at Clatt and Rhynie. The presence of Pictish stones in many of these places, as at Rosemarkie, with crosses incised on them, attests to great antiquity. All of these churches were in the old diocese of Mortlach (now Dufftown, famed for its distillery) and its cathedral church was dedicated to Moluag. In the 1130s, its centre moved and became the bishopric of Aberdeen.

In the east of Scotland, three medieval fairs were held each year in the saint's honour: in Aberdeenshire, there were St Mallock's Fair in Clatt and Luoch Fair in Tarland; and in Perthshire, Simmalogue Fair in Alyth. Two – those held at Tarland and Alyth – still continue as local agricultural shows. And, as a postscript to all of these whispers of the fame and influence of this half-forgotten holy man, W. J. Watson noted in his magisterial *The Celtic Place-Names of Scotland* that Gillemelooc was an Aberdeenshire surname. Its original meaning was 'the Servant of Moluag'.

Fired with the fervour of piety and energetic though he may have been, it seems very unlikely that Moluag could have achieved all of these foundations in person, especially those far inland in rural Aberdeenshire. Much more plausible is to see him as the patron saint of the expanding Cenel Loairn. Probably because of pressure from successful Pictish kings, Nechtan and Oengus in particular, this kindred disappeared from Lorn and began to migrate up the Great Glen before fanning out to take over the old Pictish provinces north of the Mounth, where the Grampian Mountains almost reach the sea at Stonehaven. After 736, no mention is made of them in Argyll. Having established the kingdom of Moray, which encompassed Aberdeenshire as well as the southern shores of the Moray Firth, they then founded churches and dedicated them to Moluag, their own patron saint. Columba was championed by the Dalriadan kings, most famously Kenneth macAlpin. This rivalry mattered because, through their links to the Cenel Loairn, the kings of Moray claimed the high kingship of Scotland, and in the person of Macbeth they briefly succeeded.

What is striking about the spread of Moluag's dedications is their nature. Like Patrick, he appeared to found bishoprics, first at Lismore, then Rosemarkie and Mortlach. Unlike Brendan and others, he did not seek to retreat from the world in a remote diseart but to be part of it, involving himself in dynastic politics. He resembled Patrick more than Martin. And far more than Columba, despite Adomnán's claims, Moluag does appear to have been the Apostle of the Picts, both in person and in name. But, unlike Columba, he did not have a promoter, a powerful churchman who could use his authority to write his *Life* and have his interpretation believed – to the exclusion of others. Christianity is a religion of the Word, of the

Book, and Columba's fame spread because Adomnán's work was copied and recopied, read and reread. Contemporary churchmen undoubtedly understood that a *Life* of a saint was essential to the promotion of his cult. In Northumbria, there was a clear contest at the end of the seventh and the beginning of the eighth centuries between Bede, the writer of the *Life of St Cuthbert*, and Stephen of Ripon, the writer of the *Life of St Wilfrid*. There surely must have been something written about Moluag, but little survives to remember him and his exemplary life by apart from traditions, dedications, place-names and an obscure Pictish stone.

11

Waiting for the Ferry

I walked back down the central road to the Ionad Naomh Moluag to collect the books and leaflets I had bought and thank the lady on reception who had looked after them for me. My plan was not to retrace my morning steps but to get back to Achnacroish and the evening ferry by walking down the coastal path – if I could find it. Given my limitless talent for getting lost, I made exhaustive enquiries as to the correct directions. Having visited the toilet, I also discovered that the bardic arts of Lismore are alive and thriving, adapted to the modern age:

> Those of us with septic tanks,
> Would like to give a word of thanks,
> For putting nothing in the pot
> That isn't guaranteed to rot.
> Kleenex is bad,
> Paper towels too,
> With your co-operation,
> We'll keep our drains in operation.

From Ionad Naomh Moluag, the single-track road to the coast was lined with mature trees, the dappled shade allowing me to walk without the need for a hat. By the side of the road was an old pile of straw that had been banked up against a series of large stones for some reason. In and out of it flew honeybees, the little ones with the rust-coloured rear ends. The legs of those incoming were stuck with pollen, like saddlebags.

I had allowed two hours to get to the slipway for the Oban ferry and was able to stop and look as often as I wanted. But when I reached the farm steading at Balnagowan, the idyll began to unravel. There were no signs for the coastal path; I had assumed that if I kept going east I was bound to reach it – the coast, if not the path. But where the single-track tarmac ended, I thought it wise to follow an uphill track that led to a metal gate. Beyond it I could see a half-built structure, perhaps a barn. What did eventually become clear, because it ran out, was that I had taken the wrong track. Glancing at my watch, anxious not to miss the ferry, I doubled back down to the farm. There was no one about to ask, but after thrashing around I finally found a path that led downhill to the shore. Several stiles reassured me . . . temporarily. I passed a sign leaning to one side that announced 'BROCH'. The map told me that there was a broch at Tirefour Castle, some way up the coast – a lot more distant from Achnacroish and the ferry. Oh, dear. I quickened my pace.

Into view came a tall monument in the form of a Celtic cross. And on the map, south-west of Balnagowan Farm, marked clearly, was 'Monument'. When I reached it, my sweaty anxieties slackened immediately. Perhaps only a mile or so along the shore, I could clearly see the slipway at Achnacroish jutting out into the sea. It was easy walking and, beside a row of cottages in the tiny hamlet, I found a welcome bench where I could wait for the ferry that I was not going to miss.

It was good to be still, good to have time to gather my thoughts and make something of my impressions. Unlike Eileach an Naoimh, with its harshness and its ruined monastery, there was virtually nothing on Lismore that offered a sense of Moluag. But his mission did begin to become clearer. Brendan chose his Rock because it seemed an elemental place of suffering, where the truly pious might endure the bitter winds whistling off the bleak eternities of the ocean, shiver in the crash of the waves and endure all their privations, natural and self-imposed. As they huddled in the beehive cells and murmured through their prayers, counting the repetitions on their prayer ropes, these men felt themselves moving closer to God. Present suffering would earn eternal glory on the sunlit plains of Heaven.

Gazing over Lorn to the Appin shore, it struck me that Moluag may have interpreted his own godly purpose very differently. Whether or not it was carried along on the tides of politics by the kings of the Cenel Loairn and their migration up the Great Glen to northern Pictland, I had the strong impression that the saint's mission of conversion was, literally, more outward going than the personal struggles of the monks on Eileach an Naoimh, with their demons and their own sinfulness. To persuade pagans and, more importantly, their chieftains and kings to lay down their ancient beliefs and allow themselves to be baptised, Moluag and his followers had to paint a picture of a better alternative, offer a more positive message.

On that soft, warm evening, Lismore seemed Edenic to me – a great garden and also a metaphor. God had smiled on this green and fecund place and the beauties of His Creation will have struck those who came to talk with Moluag. It may be that, rather than making a diseart, he had in mind the great monastic towns of Ireland when he began building on Lismore.

The Second Coming was much on the mind of early Christians, perhaps for the obvious reason that Christ's first ministry and the establishment of His Church were close to them in time. In addition to what can be found in the gospels of the New Testament about Jesus's own prophecies of His return, there was much in the apocrypha, books and testaments that are no longer believed to be canonical but were thought to be authentic in the sixth century. After the Apocalypse and the Second Coming, Christians were certain that there would be a Second Creation, that the world would be remade anew. Saints were thought to share the gift of prophecy, and their lives, decisions and actions could prefigure what the Second Creation might be like. Perhaps that was the power of Moluag's great garden on Lismore. It could be seen as a second Eden – a place apart because it was a place of harmony and peace.

The sight of the CalMac ferry sailing out of Oban Bay, still far in the distance, jolted me back to the twenty-first century, but some powerful links did seem to linger. The busy sea traffic out of Oban Bay and between the islands has been unceasing over the centuries since these sixth-century monasteries were founded. Indeed, their creation and maintenance could only be managed from the sea.

The principal purpose of Adomnán's *Life of St Columba* is as a hagiography but folded into this are many incidental references to sea traffic. One of Columba's special powers was particularly handy and that was the ability to change the direction of the wind so that it helped the crews of seagoing curraghs. Like the CalMac ferries, some of these carried or towed cargo as well as people. Here is a fascinating passage from 'Book II' of Adomnán's account, dealing with the practicalities of life on the islands:

[P]ine trees and oaks had been felled and dragged overland. Some were to be used in the making of a longship, and besides ships' timbers there were also the beams for a great house to be brought here to Iona. It was decided that we should lay the saint's vestments and books on the altar, and that by fasting and singing psalms and invoking his name, we should ask St Columba to obtain for us from the Lord that we should have favourable winds. So it turned out that God had granted to him; for on the day when our sailors had got everything ready and meant to take the boats and curraghs and tow the timbers to the island by sea, the wind, which had blown in the wrong direction for several days, changed and became favourable. Though the route was long and indirect, by God's favour the wind remained favourable all day and the whole convoy sailed with their sails full so that they reached Iona without delay.

The second time was several years later. Again, oak trees were being towed by a group of twelve curraghs from the mouth of the River Shiel to be used here in repairs to the monastery. On a dead calm day, when the sailors were having to use the oars, a wind suddenly sprang up from the west, blowing head on against them.

Hardly a minute had passed when the west wind dropped and, strange to say, a wind immediately blew from the north-east.

Then I told the sailors to hoist the yards cross-wise, spread the sails and draw the sheets taut. In this way we were carried by a fair, gentle breeze, all the way to our island in one day quite effort-lessly, and all who were with me in the boats, helping to tow the timbers, were greatly pleased.

As I sat waiting for the ferry, it occurred to me that there were other connections across the centuries. When Moluag walked with his God in the great garden and wondered if His form would be made flesh soon, he expected an apocalypse but also a second and more perfect creation. With the present turmoil in the western democracies made more acute with every passing month as populists, even proto-fascists, come to power or are listened to, the pace of the coming apocalypse of climate change accelerates. And no policy change seems likely, as it is ignored by leaders who are more anxious about their own political futures than the future of the planet.

The yucca tree near where I sat was casting long shadows by the time the ferry began its final approach to the slipway. Aiming off, allowing for the force of the tide, the skipper manoeuvred skilfully so that the ramp was square-on and, as his turbines worked hard to keep the boat in place, he started to lower it. A few cars drove off and the two women I had seen in the morning walked up to where they had parked, carrying bulging supermarket bags. The grey-haired postman handed over what he had brought from the island shop and post boxes and we were allowed to board.

I was reminded of these appropriate lines of poetry:

> The earth belongs unto the Lord
> And all that it contains,
> Except the Western Islands,
> And they are David MacBrayne's.

Moluag and his monks certainly would not have recognised the words but perhaps the cadences would have sounded familiar because it is a parody of the first verse of Psalm 24. It is ancient, believed to have been the work of King David, and it is quoted in the New Testament. And it is also apposite. After its merger with the Caledonian Steam Packet Company in 1973, MacBrayne's became Caledonian MacBrayne or CalMac and its ferries bind together the communities of the west Highlands and the Western Isles and connect them to the rest of Britain.

Literary romance first brought steamships to the Hebrides. The boat that took Felix Mendelssohn to Staffa was only one of many that carried visitors inspired by the work of James Macpherson from 1760 onwards. His faux heroic epic poems that he allegedly translated from Gaelic originals were enormously popular and clearly influential. They featured heroes such as Ossian and Fingal and were, at first, thought to be authentic discoveries. They made Highland and Island scenery heroic in itself, a fitting stage for ancient drama. Some of that geography, like Fingal's Cave, was even named after one of Macpherson's inventions. Walter Scott's immense success with *Waverley*, his novel about the Jacobite Rebellion of 1745, and *Rob Roy*, the dashing clansman and cattle thief, added to the stream of early tourism. Cruises from the Glasgow quays on the *Highland Chieftain* or the *Highlander* were very popular.

In 1830, the great English landscape painter J.M.W. Turner boarded the *Maid of Morven* at Tobermory, bound for Staffa and Iona. He had come north at the suggestion of Robert Cadell, a publisher who thought that a complete edition of Scott's poems would be much enhanced by Turner's illustrations. Like my trip to Eileach an Naoimh, landing on Staffa and getting back aboard were far from straightforward for Turner. In a letter to the New York art collector James Lenox, he wrote: 'After scrambling over the rocks on the lee side of the island, some got into Fingal's cave, others would not. It is not very pleasant or safe when the wave rolls right in. One hour was given to meet on the rock we landed on.' The result of the trip was, in fact, a strange painting. The *Maid of Morven* sails towards a setting sun, belching smoke under a threatening sky, while Fingal's Cave, strangely lit, barely creeps on to the edge of the canvas.

What revolutionised sea travel in the Hebrides was the coming of the railways. In the second half of the nineteenth century, having traversed the difficult terrain of the Highlands, coastal railheads arrived. At Strome Ferry (then onwards to Kyle of Lochalsh), Oban and Mallaig, passengers, goods and the mail could be transferred to ferries that took them to the islands. David Hutcheson & Co. was one of the most active of these carriers, and in 1878 the company was taken over and rebranded by a dynamic young businessman, David MacBrayne. By 1902 he had built up a fleet of thirty ferries plying between the mainland and the islands. At its greatest extent, there were more than sixty destinations on the MacBrayne network. Because they brought island communities into much closer contact with the mainland than ever before, these ships were sometimes much loved. Here is what the Rev. Donald Lamont wrote in the Gaelic supplement of the Church of Scotland magazine, *Life and Work*. The article looks back on the world of the MacBrayne ferries in its pomp:

> It was a fine sight to see *The Claymore* leaving Tobermory on a summer evening, resplendent in paint and every inch of her copper and brass polished as clean as a new shilling, and a row of English folk standing at her gunwale, with a telescope in the hand or at the eye of each one, gaping at the seagulls of the shoreline and other wonders which they came to see in the Highlands.
>
> . . .
>
> If you have never seen one of MacBrayne's boats loading or unloading cargo, you have missed a spectacle as interesting as any in this world: bags of meal and boxes and baskets of bread, kebbucks of cheese and cement, wood and clay jars of whisky, calves and barrels of tar, all thrown on top of one another, and all the time pigs squealing so loudly and so angrily that men pushing them cannot hear their own bad language.

It is a fine evocation of a singular way of life whose essentials have not changed for millennia despite the advances of technology and the enormous increased speed of travel.

During the depression and the strikes of the 1920s, MacBrayne's found itself near to collapse as revenue dried up and, because of the miners' strike, coal to fire its boilers was either in short supply or completely lacking. The company was rescued by another shipping concern, Coast Lines, and by the London, Midland and Scottish Railway. Governments realised that subsidies were needed so that island communities could be properly and reliably served. But, despite continuing intervention, service could be patchy, even capricious. Here is a passage from Alasdair Maclean's beautiful memoir, *Night Falls on Ardnamurchan*:

For most of the [1950s], however, anyone bound for Ardnamurchan came via Oban rather than Fort William, boarding at Oban a steamer which took him through the Sound of Mull to Tobermory. Disembarking at Tobermory he took a ferry back across to the mainland – if mainland be the right word for Ardnamurchan – stepping ashore at Mingary Pier, Kilchoan.

The main potential trouble spot in this itinerary was the Tobermory–Kilchoan ferry, which was actually a small launch. If the Sound of Mull were at all stormy – and the sound here is more or less at an end and has widened into open Atlantic – the launch crew generally refused to make the run. It did not matter if the crossing, though rough, was yet possible; if they did not feel like it they did not stir and there was nothing one could do about it. Though supposedly tied in with the national transport network, they had in practice a good deal of autonomy. Naturally too, the launch skipper had – or adopted – a sea captain's authority in regard to his vessel and claimed to be the sole arbiter in all decisions affecting her daily running and risk.

Once in a great while, on the other hand – I think when complaints became too loud and too prevalent even for those conveniently deaf to ignore – the same crew would display all the seafaring enterprise that one could wish, and perhaps a little more to boot. I have made the crossing on days when all was noise and welter, when the launch went from crest to trough like a bobsleigh and from trough to crest like a badly overloaded lift, when I had to wedge myself between bulkheads to avoid being hurled about the cabin and had to leap for my life when the vessel at last made a flying pass at Mingary Pier. But derring-do of that order was very much the exception rather than the rule.

Maclean went on to complain about the poor conditions on board MacBrayne's ferries – 'scarcely an advance on the emigrant ships of the nineteenth-century Clearances'. But standards began to rise when a demand for car ferries led to new purpose-built ships in the 1960s and a new company called Western Ferries began to compete on the route from Islay to Kennacraig in Kintyre. In 1973, Caledonian MacBrayne came into being and the Steam Packet Company added its device of the lion rampant to the red funnel.

When I boarded the evening ferry at Lismore and listened to the welcome and safety announcement in Gaelic, it struck me that it was not only a recent reaction to the decline of the language but also an echo of the history of CalMac. Many of the skippers were native speakers from the islands and some became legendary.

When one captain announced to passengers that his ship had completed a very fast crossing, one of them asked, 'Is it a record?'

'No, it is not a record,' replied the captain in the lovely sibilant accent of the Hebrides, 'it is myself who is telling you.'

PART FOUR

THE ISLE OF THE YEW TREE

Iona

12

Founders

The life, the character and the sense of moral purpose of Iona's founder are unusually well documented. As a young man, he fought in war but later softened his views on conflict and devoted himself not only to spreading the Word of God but also the principles of Christian peace. Nevertheless, he lost none of his aristocratic bearing and he could be an autocratic leader intolerant of the views of others, quick-tempered but always ready to forgive. With those who had suffered great misfortune, the meek and damaged, his human kindness knew no bounds.

The founder's learning was prodigious and, for much of his later life, he wielded the pen rather than the sword. Prayers, hymns and what amounted to a form of poetry flowed from his writing room near the abbey of Iona. His power as a preacher was very great, persuasive and authoritative. Many who heard his words were much moved. A simple, almost child-like but charismatic faith moved many closer to Christ and closer to an examination of their immortal souls. Following the example and the precepts of St Martin of Tours, whom he much admired, the founder and the men who followed him saw themselves as soldiers of Christ. Just as at Marmoutier, they lived communally, frugally, working together to build a monastery – a place apart from the world where the virtues of prayer, physical labour and abstinence were conjoined in God's name.

The founder also performed miracles. When work on the monastery was halted because of a lack of timber, he prayed and God answered him. A vast quantity of wood, ready to use for building, was washed up on Iona's shores and the work continued. Laying hands on the head of a blind woman, the founder restored her sight, and then turned to all who witnessed this and swore them to silence. When St Cuthbert wrought miracles, he also told those who saw them to say nothing until after his death. And, like all holy men upon whom God smiles, the founder met an angel. Sitting alone on a hillside on Iona, the cares and the tumult of the world weighing heavy, anxious about his weakness, his inability to do God's work, he looked up when a stranger approached.

'Are you successful yet?' said this man.

The founder replied, 'It depends on what you mean by success.'

The stranger asked, 'Do you not know what success is? Success is hearing the voice of God no louder than thunder in distant hills on a summer's day.'

The stranger left and the founder never saw him again.

It was said that he also had the power of prophesy.

> *An I mo chridhe, I mo ghraidh*
> *An aite guth manaich bidh geum ba*
> *Ach mun tig an saoghal gu crich*
> *Bidh I mar a bha.*

> In Iona of my heart, Iona of my love
> In place of monks' voices will be lowing of cattle
> But ere the world shall come to an end
> Iona shall be as it was.

This stanza reaches across many centuries to make a very powerful link. Probably composed much later than the time of Columba, it is quoted in *George MacLeod: Founder of the Iona Community*. All of the stories and characteristics related above are culled from Ron Ferguson's excellent biography of MacLeod, first published in 1990, and not from Adomnán's *Life of St Columba*, composed twelve hundred years earlier – although they could have been. The parallels are unmistakable and they were recognised at the time.

When MacLeod died in 1991, the Moderator of the General Assembly of the Church of Scotland, the Rev. Bill Macmillan, wrote, 'He was a noble spirit in the mould of Columba, both men being associated with Iona and a source of inspiration for the Church. This man has gone from our midst but his dynamic influence remains as a light from God in the Church and in our land.'

Others also made the connection but were much less charitable. When George MacLeod's plans to complete the restoration of the conventual buildings around the Benedictine abbey on Iona survived the outbreak of war in 1939 and he had wooden huts put up for masons and labourers, an anonymous letter writer urged the islanders to start a petition against his 'strange new stunt' and went on to attack the 'self-appointed successor to St Columba'. Another objected to the workers' washing being hung out to dry on clothes lines near the abbey – and on a Sunday!

In response, George MacLeod summed up his attitude to the past, to Columba and to Iona and outlined his hopes for the future. It is a fascinating insight that illustrates the hold that this remarkable little island had even on radical thinkers and how its power brought the light of God to the Hebrides in the sixth century but also helped shape a new vision of Christianity in Scotland. This extract comes from Ron Ferguson's book:

Folk must make up their minds about a prior question. If what they are looking for in Iona is a dream of the past; some place apart where, amidst mouldering stones and wild grasses, they may let their mind wander back to days 'when Christianity once was great'; a setting in which to indulge a suitable melancholy – if that is what they seek, then, of course, the wooden house will irritate. But we dare to suggest that, were that Iona's destiny, it would have been far better not to have re-roofed the Abbey (as was done some years ago) so that the whole scene might have responded to an atmosphere of ruined glory. Now that it is re-roofed and a potential centre for most enthralling worship, the whole environment cries out for life again . . . Do men want

Iona as a memory of the past, or as an inspiration for days of difficulty ahead?

In 1899 the Duke of Argyll had gifted the site of Iona Abbey to a group of trustees drawn from the hierarchy of the Church of Scotland, and soon afterwards an appeal for funds to restore the church was launched. It was successful, as Iona's magic persuaded many to give substantial sums. Rebuilding work began in 1904 and by the following year the east end of the abbey church had been reroofed. A service of dedication was held on 14 July. By 1910, the whole of the church had been restored and declared wind- and watertight. It was the beginning of a revival as Iona emerged from centuries of neglect, a half-forgotten, remote backwater restored if not to greatness than certainly to pre-eminence.

When Samuel Johnson visited Iona in 1779, he found its atmosphere intensely attractive but mourned its fall from grace: 'The Island, which was once the metropolis of learning and piety, has now no school for education, nor temple for worship, only two inhabitants that can speak English, and not one that can write or read.' But the great lexicographer was also optimistic, prophetic, perhaps prefiguring George MacLeod's intervention in the history of Iona: 'It may be that in the revolution of time, Iona will again become the instructress of the western regions.'

After the rebuilding of the abbey church, work continued but only sporadically. New church furnishings were installed and internal repairs made. On 10 June 1931, a service of dedication was held for the hanging of a new bell in the church tower. Services began to be celebrated regularly and, once more, the little island became a focus, its *genius loci*, its singular magic acting on any who made the long journey.

However, the buildings around the cloister walk, the chapter house, the monks' old refectory, dormitory and *reredorter* (the communal latrine) remained in ruins. With the restoration of the abbey church, pilgrimage had revived and some who came to worship in the restored Benedictine church wished to stay, to go on retreat on Iona. Perhaps the conventual buildings could be made whole again to house a retreat centre? Ambitious plans with estimated costs of £47,000 were proposed to the trustees of the abbey in 1933 and essentially rejected. The world economy was in the grip of the Great Depression and it was decided to shelve these proposals since public donations were unlikely to be forthcoming.

Two years later, attitudes shifted dramatically. Without any prior warning, the trustees were amazed to receive a letter from the American Iona Society that offered to restore the ruined buildings entirely at their expense. Founded by a group of emigrants from the Scottish Highlands, some of whom had been cleared off the land by a brutal aristocracy little more than fifty years before, they wished to give back something to their Gaelic-speaking heritage. The ruins should be used to house a Celtic College, a centre for the study of the Gaelic language and the culture of the Gaidhealtachd. The trustees were both astonished at such sweeping generosity and also suspicious. Perhaps the offer seemed to them too good to be true. How much influence, even control, would the Americans expect to have in return for their money? Perhaps something less ambitious, something that might be done under the aegis and control of the Church of Scotland would be more suitable. George MacLeod certainly thought so.

Sparked into life by the American offer, his lingering love of Iona became something more concrete. By the mid 1930s, MacLeod was a parish minister in the Glasgow neighbourhood of Govan, a place of great deprivation but with a powerful sense of community. He felt that new housing developments around Scotland's cities would endanger social cohesion and that the church's place at the heart of communities would wither because of demographic changes that began to take place after the Great War. In 1919, the government legislated to stimulate the building of Lloyd George's 'homes fit for heroes'. With the help of generous subsidies, local authorities were compelled to build new housing stock to replace the inner-city slums in places like MacLeod's parish of Govan. On the fringes of Glasgow, at Mosspark, Carntyne, Knightswood and Blackhill, sprawling council estates were built on green field sites and communities were quickly evacuated from the slums to homes they were at first delighted with.

George MacLeod realised that, if the Church of Scotland was to find a place in the lives of folk living in these big estates, the traditional approach to ministry would have to change. Middle-class divinity graduates would need to understand how ordinary working people lived better and would have to find better ways of communicating with them than from the pulpit. The Church could not remain aloof or apart and expect to maintain its relevance in the midst of these great social upheavals. Teams of ministers who could bring God's message in new ways would need to come together to create a new, less formal version of the Kirk.

In MacLeod's view, divinity colleges in Scotland's four ancient universities would struggle to supply any realistic grounding for young ministers to deal with these new challenges and so he proposed a new and radical role for Iona. While the trustees of the abbey swithered over the offer from the American Iona Society and worried about how much control they might expect to exert over a Celtic College, George MacLeod came up with a competing scheme. His letter suggested something very innovative but something that was also very much in sympathy with the communal life established by Columba thirteen centuries before. Rather than a cultural initiative that might sustain interest in the Gaidhealtachd, he wanted to restore the chapter house and all the other buildings for a religious purpose – a new element in the mission of the Church of Scotland.

Like Columba, Macleod had well-honed political instincts and, to help his scheme gain acceptance, he was not above stoking ancient Protestant prejudices. Here is an extract from the paper he sent to the Iona trustees on 15 November 1935:

If Christianity is the only answer to Communism, Christianity must become more concerned with its Corporate Witness (or shall we say its Collective Witness), and if the Church of Rome is not to be allowed to be the only purveyor of this Witness, the

Protestant Churches must play their part in developing this emphasis within their own field: or else we deserve to perish by default.

Each summer, a group of licentiate young ministers would come to Iona to work on the restoration of the ruins. Rolling up their sleeves, they would labour for a group of volunteer tradesmen, mainly masons and joiners, under the supervision of an architect. Fully worked out and detailed plans to restore the conventual buildings had been pulled together in 1935. All of the men would live communally in the notorious wooden huts, in a disciplined regime, both monastic and more than a little military in its tone. Captain George MacLeod had served in the Argyll and Sutherland Highlanders in the Great War, winning the Military Cross and the Croix de Guerre for gallantry, and he never lost his taste for command. Later, his style of leadership was criticised by a young minister with a taste for a verbal flourish. MacLeod was so overwhelming, he said, that the Iona Community should be renamed 'I own a Community'.

As the young ministers and the tradesmen worked together on the conventual buildings, their commanding officer hoped that they would learn how to talk meaningfully to each other and the ministers might understand something of lives they could know little about. Each man agreed to spend two summers on the island.

The trustees eventually accepted MacLeod's proposal, and in June 1938 the first group of workers made their way to the island. Both the Gaelic prophecy that 'Iona shall be as it was' and Samuel Johnson's hope that the island and its abbey would once 'again become the instructress of the western regions' appeared to be coming true. But dark clouds were gathering to the east. As the workers boarded the ferry at Fionnphort to make the short crossing to the island, Hitler's Germany was growing increasingly bellicose and increasingly confident. The *Anschluss*, the forced union with Austria, had been pushed through in March, and in the autumn Neville Chamberlain's meetings with Hitler would conclude with capitulation over his demands that his forces occupy the German-speaking parts of Czechoslovakia known as the Sudetenland. Despite the Prime Minister's proclamation of 'Peace in our time', it was clear to many that war in Europe was imminent.

Perhaps it was appropriate that George MacLeod's 'soldiers of Christ' wore something close to uniforms. At his insistence, both tradesmen and young ministers were kitted out in Guernseys – thick, navy-blue fishermen's sweaters – and navy trousers. Stout work boots were standard. For services in the abbey, suits, shirts and ties were worn. Each soldier was paid the same – £1 a week – and, in the phrase of the times, their stay was 'all found', meaning that they did not have to pay anything for their accommodation and food. They dined on homely fare such as porridge, eggs and bread and butter, a substantial lunch and, at the end of the working day, a version of high tea was served – cakes, scones and jam. It was followed at suppertime with cocoa and biscuits. Hard work amongst the ruins in what turned out to be a very wet summer will have burned off all those carbohydrates.

Despite initial awkwardness, disagreements and cultural misunderstandings, the group of tradesmen and ministers, working men and middle-class graduates, began to cohere. What further bonded the men and their autocratic leader was external criticism, some of it from close at hand. Mr MacRae, the parish minister on Iona, was 'not enthusiastic' about what he called 'ritualistic innovations' in the worship in the abbey. Because there was no electricity, candles were lit during services and they perhaps reeked of what some in the Church of Scotland felt they could call 'popishness'. The Apostles' Creed was recited and responses encouraged from the congregation, and communicants were encouraged to kneel in prayer if that was what they preferred. MacCuish and others were happy about none of this.

A gifted orator, journalist and pamphleteer, MacLeod launched *The Coracle*, an occasional magazine (still published three times a year) that included news of developments on Iona and of the activities of what had become known as the Iona Community. The magazine was also a means of raising funds. And it was a useful platform. In its pages MacLeod could defend his people and their work against what he saw as unfair criticism as well as promote the principles behind what they were doing. Christianity would triumph over Fascism as well as Communism, he wrote, and from Iona its particular message would radiate around the world. After his experiences in the Great War, George MacLeod had become a committed pacifist and in *The Coracle*, written in the shadow of St Martin's Cross, he used the example of the saint's life. In the fourth century, Columba too had abandoned a military career and come to the love of God. It is also fair to add that, at a time when a second European war was coming and after it began, MacLeod's pacifism made him suspect in many people's eyes. Having been a popular and successful radio broadcaster for many years, the BBC dropped him.

The Iona Community was itself also an example, a way of communal and cooperative life sustained by a simple Christian faith and mission. A broad set of monastic rules developed. To raise funds and spread their message, MacLeod had established the Friends of the Iona Community with a subscription of five shillings a year. Even if these people were distant from the island, they could be linked. The rule stated that at a specific time of day members and friends would pray and read from the Bible, and that, if they broke off from their routine to do that, wherever they were at that time, then a sense of a spiritual community could form. Members also agreed that their rule should include accounting for resources and time spent and that, in general, their actions should be directed towards securing social justice and peace in society. The current website for the Iona Community expands on these beginnings but adheres to the same basic principles.

These were idealistic, even vague aspirations, but George MacLeod saw them as a beginning – a fresh and new way to approach God and build faith amidst the turbulence of the mid twentieth century. When Columba came to Iona in 563 with his followers, they too established a new community against a background of paganism, on one hand, and the more established set of beliefs they left behind in

Ireland. Over time, these were developed and adapted. The same process has seen the Iona Community change and modernise. In spite of MacLeod's opposition, the first female member was admitted in 1965. In 1976, the first Catholic members were admitted and, in 2003, the Rev. Kathy Galloway became Leader.

13

Beyond the Corncrake Meadow

Before I made my way to Iona, I had read as much as I could about George MacLeod and the community he founded. The story fascinated me, particularly against our contemporary background, as we see the rise of fascism in Europe and in the USA, as well as the accelerating destruction of our environment and our planet as it burns and melts. We may be at a turning point in our history, one that might welcome, of necessity, a much less consumerist society, one that may have to return to simple precepts, much more cooperation and a much sharper sense of social justice. Like MacLeod's contemporaries, we may once more be obliged to fight fascism and the wanton destruction of our planet with a new and renewing version of Christianity – and one that has attractions and connections for non-Christians like myself.

The model of the Iona Community seemed not only to look to the present and the future, it also harked back to the past. These half-formed notions, little more than instincts, would, I felt, come into focus when I reached the island. Iona had inspired Columba and his successor, George MacLeod, and I wanted to understand something of why and how. The spirit of this place must be powerful but how did it work its magic, what made it different, a place apart? Eileach an Naoimh and Lismore spoke to me of the long past, of the remains of the missions of Brendan and Moluag. Would Iona whisper something of the future?

I almost missed the early morning ferry from Oban. Having booked myself and my car on the 7.30 sailing to Craignure on Mull, I had to arrive at the parking lanes an hour beforehand. I was only five minutes late but the dour wee man at the kiosk refused to allow me through. The best I could hope for was to go on the stand-by list. If there was a cancellation or a no-show, I would get on. Restraining my tone and limiting my vocabulary, I apologised for my lack of precise punctuality and explained as best I could that, if he removed me from the list of vehicles that had booked, then that would create a no-show or even a cancellation, an empty space. And so what was to be gained from putting me on stand-by? Apart from a slap on the wrist for being five minutes late. Just as I felt my patience beginning to crack, a colleague, whose lapel identified him as the kiosk man's supervisor, appeared as if from nowhere. Somehow, he had heard what I was saying and summarily overruled this un-Christian judgement. A bad start turned into a good omen as the spirit of Iona reached across the Firth of Lorn as far as Oban.

One of the very largest in the CalMac fleet, our ferry seemed majestic to me as its bow began to open like the jaws of a giant shark. All sorts of satisfying hydraulic groans, clanks and squeals were the soundtrack for this awe-inspiring sight. The ferry's maw opened wide enough to swallow articulated lorries and buses as big as buildings as well as cars. Guided by the crew I edged within inches of the vehicle in front, deep in the belly of the monster. Klaxons sounded and all passengers were directed to leave their vehicles immediately and move up the companionways to the upper decks. It was not the soft, sibilant Gaelic of Cathy MacDonald that encouraged us to leave the car deck but a voice that sounded as though it came from an angry Dalek. Shuffling sideways between the crammed vehicles, I joined those climbing up. The companionways are so steep that one finds oneself not looking at the back of the person in front but their backside. Too early in the morning for that. Eventually I emerged on to the restaurant deck. A long and hungry queue had already formed and so I went outside to look at the glorious view.

It was a perfectly still morning with barely a ripple on the turquoise waters of Oban Bay and there was not even a wisp of cloud in the skies over Lorn. As the ferry's turbines gurgled and we turned to sail out of the harbour, the great ship glided past the stumpy tower of

Dunollie Castle. Like the smaller birlinns of the Lords of the Isles, CalMac follows the ancient sea roads and soon another sentinel fortress would come into view – Duart Castle on the southern shore of Mull. And then, at last, Cathy welcomed us all on board. Out in the firth, there was little more than a whisper of a breeze. A perfect morning waited.

Fried food and a sea voyage might not immediately seem like a good combination, but we would take only fifty minutes to cross the Firth of Lorn and dock at Craignure. My bacon roll was excellent, the coffee unbelievably dreadful – so bad, so chemical that I abandoned it for some flat fizzy water from my backpack. The ferry was packed to the gunnels – from 'gunwale', the uppermost course of planking on the side of a ship where its guns were located. The car deck was full and I wondered how many were stand-bys. The upper decks were thronged with the occupants of several buses as well as many foot passengers with their packs and walking gear. On the starboard side, we quickly sailed past the lighthouse on the southern tip of Lismore before altering course for the Sound of Mull. Beyond the low, green island where I had spent such a happy day, I could see the Nevis ranges against the glowing clarity of the blue, blue sky. Some mornings are so perfect, so full of possibility that they defy description.

Craignure is little more than a hamlet, a row of houses, a cafe and a shop on the shoreline with a massive jetty attached. Almost all who disembark at Craignure are bound for somewhere else. There are no beaches to detain them, only a rocky foreshore. After another even louder klaxon sounded, I drove up the slipway and turned left for Fionnphort, thirty-seven miles to the west, where I would catch another much smaller ferry, this time to Iona and on foot. With no klaxon.

Very quickly, I found myself on a single-track road behind a large bus and its exhaust fumes. After a few miles, it obligingly pulled into a passing place, where it just managed to fit in, to allow me and the queue that had built up behind me to overtake. But the open road soon ran out and I joined another slow procession. Eventually, I stopped at a parking place in Glen More and hauled out the road atlas. The black and yellow line that snaked across the Ross of Mull apparently signified that I was travelling on a 'Narrow A Road'. Narrow! All that was wide was the vistas. Leading to one of the great pilgrimage sites of Western Europe was a single-track road regularly travelled by very large buses carrying many tens of thousands of visitors each year. It is a scandal. Where else would such a thing be tolerated? Eastern Europe? Maybe.

Most drivers have no experience of single-track roads and do not understand the etiquette of passing places. One who came barrelling towards me ignored my signal that I was about to pull into one on my left and cut across me to occupy it. My brakes are good and they needed to be. Others drive far too fast and I met several racing around blind corners, so many that I began to slow to third or even second gear as I approached them, expecting to have to brake sharply. Pilgrimage is not supposed to be easy and a taxing journey was part of the experience in times gone past, but it should not be fatal.

Some of the buses, especially those as big as houses with the blacked-out windows, only just fit on the single track; where they don't, their huge tyres fray the tarmac on the edges. The sharp, blind corner at Bunessan is frankly lethal and I was fortunate to meet a slow bus rather than a speeding car. When John Keats visited Iona in 1818, he complained that he had endured the 'most wretched walk of thirty-seven miles across the Island of Mull, and then we crossed to Iona or Icolmkill'. Footsore and damp he might have been, but at least Keats lived to tell the tale.

It took almost an hour and a half to drive from Craignure to Fionnphort. When I was skidding over to Eileach an Naoimh in the orange RIB, the crewman told me that they did day trips to Iona from Seil Island. How I wished I had changed my plans and taken up his offer. It was not so much that I had paid £30 or so for the car ferry from Oban as the fact that I had not been thinking like a native Hebridean. Allowing travel by road to govern my plans was a mistake in this shattered coastline of sea lochs, sounds and rocky islands. The sea was the fastest highway, not the road. It was a lesson from history I should have remembered.

Twisting around the last turn after pulling out of the last passing place, I breasted the last ridge and came to Fionnphort. Beyond it, lying quiet in the sunshine, was Iona, my first sight of the island. Its houses, many of them white, are strung along the shore and the abbey seems deliberately to have been placed in the most prominent position. Not nestled against the rocky shelter of Dun I, the low hill that dominates the island, or sheltered by trees or the folds of the land, the church and its clustered buildings seem like the centre of a composition. Its placing embraces openness. It is open to the heavens above, close to the highways of the inner sea and on the edge of the eternal horizons of the ocean. Many great churches and cathedrals are to be found in the centre of towns and cities, their holiness hemmed in by the secular world, surrounded by its noise, bustle and traffic. Iona is different – it is meant to be understood as a place apart from the world, requiring effort to reach its shore.

Of course, the Benedictine abbey of the thirteenth century is not what those who came to Columba's monastery saw. Built from the bounty of the land, from wood, wattle and daub, roofed with rushes, heather and grass sods, the first monastery might have been all but invisible to those who stood on the Mull shore at Fionnphort. Only the spiralling smoke of cooking fires on a still day will have drawn the eye. But gradually it changed. The first stone crosses were raised to punctuate the horizon and reach up to the heavens, the first stone church added solidity. As more and more monks came, they cultivated, shaped and altered the landscape. Revealed by the shadows cast by a low sun or under a rare sugar dusting of snow, the bank and ditch of the monastic vallum around the sacred ground will have been revealed.

On the long and tortured drive from Craignure, John Bunyan's famous hymn had been playing in my head and I resolved 'to be a pilgrim'. If Iona's magic, its spiritual power, was to work on me, this could not be a visit, a daytrip. It had to be more than a wander around points of interest – what, in the tourist trade, are known as 'visitor attractions'. First and most important, I was travelling alone and, although I am told that I am naturally gregarious and curious about others, I redoubled my resolve to keep silent, not to seek conversation. Thinking, looking, even listening but not talking, walking not sitting with a cup of coffee in a cafe or browsing the shelves of a visitor centre. In fact, I resolved to ignore all of the information on offer, the guided tours, the information boards, any experience of Iona mediated by others. Only if I did that could I hope to reach back across the fourteen centuries that separated us from any fleeting, whispering sense of how Columba saw the island when he and his companions dragged their curraghs ashore in 563. It is impossible to know where the saint walked, if he led his monks or lay people on pilgrimages to stations of particular piety on the island or where he might have hidden himself to spend solitary hours or days in prayer or contemplation. Iona is small, no more than a mile in width and about four miles long from north to south, and Columba will have known all of it, each path, knoll, crag and rock pool.

George MacLeod walked on Iona. He understood how the business of putting one foot in front of another could act like a balm in troubled times. Suffering from depression, sometimes deep and debilitating, MacLeod was open about his struggles, often talking about them with friends. He wrote to Harry Whitley, the minister of the High Kirk of St Giles in Edinburgh, about his low spirits, seeing his efforts on the island as a sort of pilgrimage: 'True, my brain has ceased to function; my heart is sore; my feet are leaden; but are these things incompatible with the recorded experience of Christian pilgrimage? Is not the Church's real malaise the fact that so few hearts are heavy and so few feet leaden?'

Having left my car in the overflowing car park, I walked down the brae, past the ranks of emptying buses to the Iona ferry. The quayside was thronged with hundreds of visitors, backpacked, colourfully dressed in waterproofs and windcheaters, athletically shod and busy joining queues. From Fionnphort, the ferry more resembles a shuttle, traversing the sound as soon as it is full. There are no set sailing times during the middle part of the day and it simply keeps chugging back and forth, the gunnels full. Apart from vehicles belonging to islanders or those with special permission to cross, the ferry takes only foot passengers. There were also RIBs filling with sightseers for trips around Staffa and Fingal's Cave, only a few nautical miles north of Iona. Chatter filled the clear sea air. Ice creams were bought at the cafe and, as a stately American lady held forth, it struck me that medieval pilgrimage was not so different – the Wife of Bath certainly made her opinions known and not in hushed tones of reverence. The hubbub seemed to me to be that of happy holiday-makers on an itinerary, enjoying a stunning summer's day. The atmosphere was probably not much different from Chaucer's pilgrims as they set off from the Tabard Inn in Southwark for Canterbury.

Once aboard, my Trappist vow was immediately broken by polite-ness as a lady asked me if this was my first trip to Iona. Almost before I could answer, she told me she came, on average, fifteen times a year. Where from? Solihull, near Birmingham, was the unlikely reply. I was not sure what to make of this. More than once a month, she made a very long journey from the old heart of indus-trial England to the Hebrides and Columba's island. Breezy, clearly very cheerful at the prospect of journey's end, she then told me a remarkable thing. She had never stayed on the island, only ever made day trips. 'It's enough,' she said when she saw my eyebrow rise.

Many of the other passengers had come even further. They appeared to be Americans and all to know each other. When the skipper eased the ferry out into the sound for his ten-minute voyage, the level of exchange (not conversation) seemed to grow louder. Far from inducing reverence or contemplation, the prospect of landing on Iona seemed to be the cause of great excitement. As the jetty by Martyrs' Bay loomed closer, I could see a large party of people waving at the passengers on the ferry. Perhaps they were all part of a large touring group from one of the large buses I had squeezed past on the car deck of the Oban ferry.

As we disembarked, the carnival atmosphere heightened, with several warm greetings and even a high five. I was beginning to feel like a version of Private Fraser in *Dad's Army*, doomed to listen to

Americans enjoying rare Scottish sunshine while, it seemed to me, being largely unaware of where they were. In the melee around the jetty, I caught the eye of the lady from Solihull and she smiled. The crowd milled around for a while before beginning to drift towards the abbey, walking through the village, Baile Mor. Led by a tall, tousle-haired man, one group stopped. 'Hey, listen up!' he yelled at the top of his voice and pointing to Dun I, the island's little hill. 'Let's go hike up that sucker!' Now, there is much to like and admire about America and Americans, but I found myself wondering why loud people like that come to this beautiful place. Is it simply another stop on a tour, part of a predetermined West Highland itinerary? Just one more chance to get the phone out and point its camera at something? Another item on the bucket list to tick off?

Behind me a different American voice – this time shrill and camp – gave instructions to another group. 'Now, we will just gather here momentarily to spectate.' Baffled, I turned to see what they were looking at and for the life of me could not work it out. Then I realised that they all had their mobile phones clamped to an ear, listening to goodness knows what. Elsewhere on the crowded slipway one couple met another couple and announced, without much preamble, that they came from New Jersey. The others turned out to be Canadians from Ottawa and there began an animated conversation about ice hockey. Ice hockey!

Suddenly weary after my rollercoaster drive across the Ross of Mull, I sat down on a bench by a shop doing a roaring trade in ice cream. What was I to do? Trying hard to stop my irritation growing into cultural snobbery, I decided that these visitors were only holidaymakers and, on a sunny day, they were going to have a good time in this very pretty location that had plenty to look at. And if that involved talking about ice hockey, then why not? Or listening to a pre-packaged audio tape about the history of the island rather than looking at it, then that was fine. I should stop being so precious and prissy. They were not pilgrims. But their presence, and in such noisy numbers, made my purpose in coming to Iona impossible. I decided to flee.

Instead of turning right to walk through Baile Mor to the abbey, I made my way past the ruins of the medieval nunnery. The sign made me smile. Taigh Chailleachan-Dubha I literally translates as the 'House of the Old Black Women of Iona' or, more unkindly, 'House of the Old Black Hags'. It is a reference not to their age or temperament but to their black habits. The ruins looked warm and well preserved, but they too were well populated. And so I walked on. Beside the road, I noticed several benches with dedicatory plaques.

In Loving Memory of
Martha Elizabeth Shaw
23rd Oct 1934–01st March 2018
Truly blessed to have you in our lives
You'll live forever in our hearts.

On the island of Lindisfarne, where in 635 Iona had founded a daughter house, the monastery of St Aidan, I had seen something similar. Many benches had been placed by roads and paths for weary walkers. They had been set up and paid for by relatives or friends to commemorate someone they loved and someone who loved the island.

After a time, I found myself alone. The sun made the waters of the Sound of Iona shimmer. Several boats bobbed at anchor off the Traigh Mhor, 'the Great Beach'. Iona has a permanent and very tolerant population of about one hundred and seventy and so it was good to come across three new houses. Clad with what looked like larch weatherboarding, with wide windows looking out to sea and a tall, stainless steel flue for a wood-burning stove, one had only recently been completed. Some of the clutter of building waste waited to be cleared away. Brick- or block-built – the white harling made it impossible to tell – another house had even larger windows and someone who looked like they might be the owner was laying down a path. Splendidly situated, with views over the sound to the mountains of Mull, it looked like a good place to live. I smiled at a temporary sign with the house name. Seileastar means 'yellow iris', flowers I had seen on Eileach an Naoimh. The third house was well established, its weatherboarding having turned a lovely light grey, and in the gable was another wide window looking to the sound and Mull.

Beyond a scatter of older houses, the road turned to the west, climbing gently to the low spinal ridge of the island. At a crossroads, I noticed an information board about corncrakes on Iona. While researching a long book on the history of my native place, the Scottish Borders, I had accidentally become interested in this endangered species. In an effort to locate a lost Roman road in Berwickshire, I looked at the cartulary, the landholding records of the medieval priory on the coast at Coldingham. They spoke of a place with a complicated compound name. Crhachoctrestrete is Old English and it means 'the paved road by the oak tree where there are crakes'. The paved road was my Roman road and crakes were corncrakes. With the mechanisation of agriculture, and tractors and reapers cropping grass parks for hay and silage right to their margins, and using chemical fertilisers to enhance growth, corncrake populations crashed during the second half of the twentieth century.

These ground-nesting birds find safety in concealment. Their camouflage is perfect and they are able to hide their nests, eggs and chicks in long grass so effectively that predators can pass close by and miss them. Imported from North America for the fur trade, mink escaped in significant numbers from farms and they became an unlooked-for threat to corncrakes. The distinctive, grating call of these birds used to be heard all over Scotland, including under oak trees by Roman roads in Berwickshire, but now their numbers have shrunk back to the Hebridean islands and parts of the Atlantic shore. Apparently one of the prime nesting sites listed on the information board lay – in the meadow right behind the information board. Perhaps too much information.

Beyond the corncrake meadow, a wide vista of the mighty Atlantic opened before me, the empty road running arrow-straight towards the ocean. There was no one else to be seen. Clearly, the western shore of Iona fell outside most itineraries. Under a cloudless sky, I had removed a light anorak and a body warmer to enjoy a fresh, cool breeze. And just at the moment when I felt I had slipped the surly bonds of too much company, the twenty-first century suddenly roared past me. White Van Man had managed to penetrate Iona. Driving at a ridiculous, reckless speed, skidding to a stop at several houses, some bone-headed clown was making deliveries. Turning, reversing, kicking up clouds of white dust and rending the air with a revving engine, he shattered the peace of this place. When will idiots like him learn to look at their watches? Driving at those speeds in such a small space saves only seconds, perhaps a minute or two at most. I pined for Postman Pat.

Where the tarmac ran out, there was a steel gate and a last house by the road. Beside it grew a lovely yucca tree defended by a post and rail box. It had been kept small by the winds off the ocean but made possible by the Gulf Stream. Beyond the gate ran a track with a grass crest and it led to no houses I could see. Perhaps this was as far as White Van Man could gun his engine, screech his brakes and burn the rubber of his tyres. I hoped so, for on the far side of the gate stretched the glorious wide pasture of the machair.

Unique to north-western coasts, these plains of green grass, flowers and bright white sand are very beautiful. Built up from trillions of shells crushed and powdered by the pounding of the waves on rocky shores, wide swards of fragile fertility have nourished animals, plants and people for many millennia. Forming at the end of the last Ice Age, the machair is characteristically sandy, rich in lime and chalk from all those shells, fertilised by seaweed piled up and left to rot by the high tides and gratefully grazed by sheep and cattle. In some places, it is cropped for sweet, herbal hay. When spring comes and the temperatures rise, the machair is flushed with colour as many species of flowers push up through the grass.

Known as the Bay at the Back of the Ocean, the beach below the Iona machair curves around from a scatter of skerries in the north to cliffs in the south. Its Gaelic name is intriguing – perhaps a memory of the action of the ocean as it grinds up shells and throws them onshore. It is Camus Cuil An T'saimh. In his treasure-house lexicon, Dwelly lists *samh* (*saimh* is the genitive case) as 'a surge, the agitation of the waves on a sea beach'. That may seem like a great deal of meaning packed into a little word of only four letters, but it is often the case that Gaelic's repertoire of terms for the natural world is simultaneously wide and very precise. It was never an urban language and has always dealt with the lives and work of agricultural communities – pastoralists, fishermen, ploughmen and gardeners. All of them depended absolutely on the land, the sea and the weather and describing their seasons and moods accurately was essential. I am not certain how many more words for rain Gaelic has in comparison with English, but I am sure they have more to say about it.

My map told me that there was a golf course on Iona's machair and, as I walked towards the southern end, I could make out an elevated putting green, but there seemed to be no flag in the hole and no sign of any tees or other greens. In fact, there was no one to be seen in the whole panorama of the bay. Below the green I could see where high winds had recently blown white sand inland, and nearby was the dry course of a winter burn whose banks had been much eroded. The machair is delicate, often changed and diminished after severe Atlantic storms. In January 1993, fierce gales and huge waves tore into the coastline of the Uists, Benbecula and Barra and eroded three metres of the machair all the way down that long littoral. It simply disappeared. Climate change and rising sea levels are less dramatic, but nevertheless insistent threats to this fascinating habitat. I love the machair because it is not merely and not only glorious scenery, it is also life supporting – a place where flora, fauna and people survive.

Beyond the raised green of the otherwise invisible golf course, a path wound its way up and into a series of large rocky outcrops, Druim an Aoineidh, 'the Steep Ridge'. As far as I could make out on my map, it led to Port a' Churaigh, 'the Bay of the Curragh', the place where it is said St Columba and his companions first made landfall on Iona. In my haste to flee the crowds at Baile Mor, I had forgotten to check my notes from Ron Ferguson's biography. Part of my plan was to walk the pilgrimage route around the island that George MacLeod had followed. When the workers on the restoration of the abbey buildings assembled each summer, he wanted to make sure that there was a quiet day set aside for meditation and prayer. He devised a six-mile walk that began at the foot of St Martin's Cross outside the main door of the abbey church before setting off southwards to the old marble quarry on the south-eastern tip of the island. From there they walked around to Port a' Churaigh. Turning north, the pilgrims followed the path I could see snaking through Druim an Aoineidh and then they crossed the machair to a place known as the Hermit's Cell. It lies south-west of Dun I. The little hill was the highest point of the pilgrimage. From its low summit, MacLeod led his pilgrims on a careful progress down to the graveyard at Reilig Odhrain.

At each of these stopping places, the leader of the Community offered prayers and some thoughts to encourage peaceful meditation. I am not certain how much the sequence of the stops mattered. Perhaps a theme or themes developed as the party moved on from one to the next. The problem was that in my flight from the hubbub I found myself following MacLeod's route in reverse, walking towards Druim an Aoineidh rather than down from it. I reasoned that only two elements mattered in a spiritual and geographical journey like this – the act of walking and the significance of the places visited. So, it would not matter if I passed the shades of George MacLeod, his young ministers and tradesmen as I tramped up the stony path through the rocks. Our avowed intent was the same.

14

The Graveyard of the Kings

I am not certain where they appeared from, but I found myself followed by a couple, a man and a woman who turned out to be French. Walking quickly, purposefully, they caught up and haltingly asked if the path led to St Columba's Bay. There were no signs. Assuming that this was another name for Port a' Churaigh, I nodded and asked where in France they came from. Parisians, they commented with a broad smile that Iona was not like Lourdes. An odd, jarring remark, it made me think.

A tiny chapel tucked into a corner formed by the abbey church and the conventual buildings, Columba's shrine is modest. When I eventually visited it, it was deserted. Few people seemed to take much notice of it and pass by on their way into the abbey church. Perhaps they were discouraged by the low and narrow doorway. Swallows whooshed out when I went in and I noticed a wide scatter of white droppings on the chairs lining the walls. There seemed to be a nest in the roof. For some reason, I imagined Columba smiling at that.

Lourdes is indeed very different. In 1853, Bernadette Soubirous saw visions. In a grotto near the small Pyrenean town, she saw and spoke with the Virgin Mary no fewer than eighteen times. When she told the parish priest, his initial scepticism soon evaporated. He came quickly to believe Bernadette and, as news of her visions spread, pilgrims quickly began to come. God's Mother had also told the young woman to drink from a nearby spring and, as those who were infirm or disabled in some way drank, miraculous cures were witnessed.

In the twenty-first century, between five and six million pilgrims make a journey to Lourdes. The town now has more hotel space per square kilometre than Paris and an elaborate church was built over the grotto where Mary appeared to Bernadette. I have never been to the shrine, but when I looked at pictures and video online I was immediately struck by a close resemblance. The great church seemed to me like the architecture of fantasy, very like the Walt Disney Company's castle logo that appears in the opening titles of their films and in advertisements for their theme parks.

I make that comparison not out of disparagement. I imagine that the shrine at Lourdes has a powerful air of sanctity and that many are much moved by their visit. And if its power and its waters effect modern-day miracles, then that is, of course, to be welcomed. I suspect that believers see the shrine as a place where the Virgin Mary came down to Earth to talk to a simple young girl, a shaft of heavenly light, bright hope and confirmation of God's love for humanity. But having never been there, I am in no position to offer anything more than a few superficial observations.

The comparison did also prompt a question I wish I had asked the French couple. Having pointed out how different Lourdes and Iona were, I assumed they had been to Lourdes and that made me wonder what had prompted them to come to Iona. What were they hoping to find on this little island on the edge of the ocean? Perhaps I might be able to form some conjectures if not any answers.

Close to the highest point on Druim an Aoineidh is Loch Stanoig, the largest body of freshwater on Iona. I wondered if the Columban monks came up here to immerse themselves in its chill, dark waters to mortify their sinful flesh. Dwelly is silent on any possible meaning of the place-name. As I walked down the stony path, I began to muse on who had labelled this landscape and when. It seems likely that Columba and his men arrived in the kingdom of Lorn sometime after it had been colonised and settled by Gaelic speakers from Ireland. Until the nineteenth century and occasionally after then, the historical origins of Scots Gaelic were remembered. The language was often referred to as Erse or even Irish. But what language did it replace on Iona? Almost certainly natives spoke Pictish but, as far as I could judge, no place-names survived from that era. Much of the very little that is known about the Pictish language derives from place-names.

Iona was certainly settled before Columba came in 563 and archaeologists believe that part of what later became the monastic vallum dates to the first century AD. But what did the original bank and ditch enclose? A henge of some kind? And the name of Dun I is suggestive. In English *dun* means 'a hillfort'. If there was a fortification on the summit, it would probably date from the first millennium BC. On the path to Loch Stanoig, I had passed Cnoc Druidean. It may mean 'the Little Hill of the Druids'. When the Welsh traveller and diarist Thomas Pennant visited Iona in 1772 with his faithful servant and draughtsman, Moses Griffiths, he discovered that 'the Irish name of the island was Inish Drunish; which agrees with the account [he had] somewhere read, that Iona had been the seat of Druids expelled by Columba, who found them there'. This tale has a little more substance than mere tradition. The origin of one of Pennant's sources may lie in a later Irish biography of the saint. According to the writer, upon landing on Iona, Columba was confronted by 'two bishops', probably druids or pagan priests, and he drove them away.

As Griffiths made drawings of the ruined 'Cathedral on Jova' and drew a map of the western coastline of Mull, his employer made detailed notes of all he saw around the ancient church. Although born in Wales, Pennant was not a Welsh speaker, but nevertheless he had empathy and an ear for the Gaelic he heard on his travels in the Hebrides. This made his records markedly more insightful than those of the determined monoglots Samuel Johnson and James Boswell.

Sadly, none of the drawings Moses Griffiths made of the Reilig Odhrain have survived, but Pennant did record in some detail what he saw. It was a scene of conservation by neglect, a landscape littered with relics of a long past but one that was very difficult to untangle from centuries of overgrowth and decay. What is clear from Pennant's account is that a very great deal has been lost since 1772, probably because of a fatal cocktail of ignorance, reforming zeal and thievery. Just as on Eileach an Naoimh, carved stones were simply stolen, torn from their sockets or uprooted perhaps as trophies or outdoor ornaments or broken up for other uses.

More than fifty kings were said to have been buried in the sacred, cleansing soil of the Reilig Odhrain, making it a royal cemetery with no parallel in the rest of Britain and Ireland. Forty-eight kings of Scotland, four kings of Ireland and eight Norwegian viceroys were all interred on Iona over four or five centuries, as well as a great number of the Highland nobility. And there is also a credible tradition that the body of King Ecgfrith of Northumbria was brought to the island after his disastrous defeat at the Battle of Dun Nechtain in 685. His dynasty had close links with Iona through its Northumbrian daughter houses at Old Melrose and Lindisfarne and through Saints Aidan, Boisil and Cuthbert. Here is what Thomas Pennant found amongst the wrack and ruin of the Reilig Odhrain:

On this road [to the burial ground] is a large and elegant cross, called that of MacLeane, one of three hundred and sixty, that were standing in this island at the Reformation, but immediately after were almost entirely demolished by order of a provincial assembly, held in the island. It seems to have been customary in Scotland for individuals to erect crosses, probably in consequence of some vow, or perhaps out of a vain hope of perpetuating their memory.

Arriving at Reilig Ourain, or 'the burying-place of Oran': a vast enclosure; the great place of interment for the number of monarchs who were deposited here; and for the potentates of every isle, and their lineage; for all were ambitious of lying in this holy spot. The place is in a manner filled with gravestones, but so overgrown with weeds, especially with the common butterbur, that very few are at present to be seen.

I am very desirous of viewing the tombs of the kings, described by the Dean of the Isles, and from him by Buchanan: the former says that in his time there were three, built in the form of little chapels: on one was inscribed 'Tumulus REGUM Scotiae'. In this were deposited the remains of forty-eight Scottish monarchs, beginning with Fergus II and ending with the famous Macbeth: for his successor, Malcolm Canmore, decreed, for the future, Dunfermline to be the place of royal sepulture (*sic.*). Of the Scottish monarchs interred in Iona, sixteen are pretended to be of the race of Alpin, and are styled, *Rigbrid Ailpeanaeh.*

Fergus was the founder of this mausoleum (Boethius calls it 'abbatia') and not only directed that it should be the sepulchre of his successors, but also caused an office to be composed for the funeral ceremony.

The next was inscribed 'Tumulus REGUM Hiberniae', containing four Irish monarchs; and the third, 'Tumulus REGUM Norwegiae' containing eight Norwegian princes, or more probably viceroys of the Hebrides, while they were subject to that crown.

That so many crowned heads, from different nations, should prefer this a as their place of interment, is said to have been owing to an ancient prophecy:

> Seachd bliadna romb'n bhra
> Thig muir thar Eirin re aon tra'
> Sthar Ile ghu irm ghlais
> Ach Snamhaidh I cholum clairish

Which is to this effect: 'Seven years before the end of the world, a deluge shall drown the nations: the sea, at one tide, shall cover Ireland, and the green-headed Ilay; but Columba's isle shall swim above the flood.'

But of these celebrated tombs we could discover nothing more than certain slight remains, that were built in a ridged form, and arched within; but the inscriptions were lost. These are called *jomaire nan righ* or 'the ridge of the kings'.

Royal burial on Iona may have completed a ceremonial circle. If kings were ordained and anointed on the island, it may have seemed fitting for the end of their reigns to be marked where they began. The ridges Pennant refers to may have been raised rows of grave slabs, and by the nineteenth century one such was still know as the Ridge of Kings. What is striking now is that there appears to be no trace whatever of any of these royal graves.

In the sixth century, the steersmen of Columba's curraghs set a course for an island known as *Iogh*, an early Irish word for a 'yew tree'. It is also the way that the letter I is represented in the Gaelic alphabet, which is different from the English alphabet. It is also the name of Iona in modern Gaelic. The longer version is I Chaluim Cille, 'Iona of the Church of Columba'. *I* probably therefore means 'Yew Tree Island'. In the pre-Christian era, yews and their groves were sacred, partly because of their great age. They were also associated closely with druids and what little of their beliefs and rituals are understood. What all of these awkward, even tortured half-links mean is that Iona has a much longer association with sanctity stretching back into prehistory, long before the coming of Columba.

Here are more unlikely connections. In his quirky, tremendously learned and endlessly informative *The Celtic Place-Names of Scotland*, W.J. Watson used his instinct and ear for early Gaelic to arrive at the firm(ish) conclusion that Iona used to be known as Ivia, a version of Ivova and also Ioua. Completed around 731, *The Ecclesiastical History of the English People* has something to say about Columba and his island. In his fascinating text, Bede of Jarrow called it Hii. Six centuries later, all of these versions of the name were rounded up and rounded off by a mistake. In the late thirteenth century, a scribe wrote the name down wrongly. In the handwriting script known as insular minuscule, the letters 'u' and 'n' look similar and instead of 'Ioua' he wrote 'Iona', thereby obscuring the name's pre-Christian associations. And it is Iona that has stuck, hiding some history behind a blunder.

George MacLeod and his workers may have passed me going in the opposite direction down the stony path through Druim an Aoineidh, but Thomas Pennant was walking my way. In 1772, he began to

> cross the island over a most fertile elevated tract [the machair] to the south west side, to visit the landing place of St Columba; a small bay, with a pebbly beach, mixed with a variety of pretty stones, such as violet-coloured quartz, nephritic stones [I think he means kidney-shaped], and fragments of porphyry, granite and Zoeblitz marble [grey, possibly fossils]: a vast tract near this place was covered with heaps of stones, of unequal sizes: these, as is said, were the penances of monks who were to raise heaps of dimensions equal to their crimes: and to judge by some, it is no breach of charity to think that there were among them enormous sinners.

From the high ground, Port a' Churaigh looked simply magnificent, perfectly framed by the rocks of Druim an Aoineidh. The stony path led down gently to lush pasture grazed by a flock of sheep. Beyond the beach of bright pebbles, dark skerries reared like old wrecks out of the water, some of them very close to shore. The little bay would have been an impossible anchorage or landing place for conventional boats but a skilled handler of a curragh, with its shallow draught, had no trouble avoiding the tearing rocks. I could see the French couple far ahead of me, one of them on the pebble beach, the other lingering in the sheep pasture.

By the time I reached Port a' Churaigh, they had vanished as quickly as they had appeared, perhaps hurrying their hike because they had a set time to catch the ferry back to Fionnphort. The beach was glorious and I fulfilled the tradition of throwing one pebble into the ocean and keeping another. Wave-rounded, white and veined with grey, it sits on my desk as I write this. There was no sign of Pennant's enormous piles of penitential pebbles, only some smaller cairns built up by pilgrims. I had read that it was possible to see the shore of Northern Ireland from the bay but, even on that crystal-clear day, I could not make it out. On one of the smoother rocks, I sat down to drink some water and eat my cheese sandwiches. I pulled out my map and began to work out where to go next.

Anxious to avoid what I imagined would be peak hubbub at the abbey and its surroundings, I decided to confirm my solitary instincts and re-cross the machair to find what was known as 'the Hermit's Cell'. After half an hour of walking, I found a path at the north end, where there were more obvious traces of golfing, near the farm at Culbuirg. It led me to disappointment.

Rather than a crack in the rock, a low cave or anything resembling the beehive cells I had seen on Eileach an Naoimh, there was a low circle of big stones with a gap as an entrance. Having walked amongst the Cheviot Hills a number of times in the recent past, I had seen several circles that looked very like this. In her beautifully written *Columba's Island*, E. Mairi MacArthur noted that *Cobhan Cuilteach*, the Gaelic and therefore older name for the Hermit's Cell, made no reference to religion – it simply means 'Secluded Hollow'. A passage from her book is very telling and it reinforces my belief that this was no retreat where solitaries prayed through the night and fasted, hoping to move closer to their God. MacArthur tells how two islanders took their curious grandmother to see the Hermit's Cell: 'They walked the old lady out there, across the hummocks and boggy hollows, and her reaction was both spontaneous and down to earth: "But this is just like the circles where we milked the cows in the West End hills when I was young!" So it was. She was growing up on Iona in the 1890s when this practice was common.'

In the Scottish Borders, such circles were known as *buchts*, places where ewes summering out on the hills could be corralled and milked. Far from being hermetic cells, they could be convivial, even places for flirtation and fun. When lasses came up from the farms with their yokes and milking pails, they were met by the bachelor shepherds who tended the flocks and plenty of 'laughin' and daffin'' went on. A place-name on the eastern side of Dun I on the low ground by the shores of the sound offers a much more secure connection with the hermetic life on Iona. Cladh an Diseirt means 'the Graveyard of the Hermitage'. But that might be a reference to Columba's monastery. The monastic vallum lies only a short distance from Cladh an Diseirt.

From Dun I, I had a wide vista over the inner sea of the southern Hebrides. The stubby stump of Staffa lay due north and beyond it were Rum, Eigg, Muck and the jagged edges of the Cuillin on Skye. Out to the west, I could see Coll and Tiree. I watched sightseers' boats returning from Fingal's Cave and the ferry leaving Fionnphort. I reflected that the sea roads between all of these islands would have been much busier on a good, calm day like this in times past. By the time I climbed Dun I, it was late afternoon and I reckoned that the crowds around the abbey precinct might have begun to thin out.

Information boards were everywhere. Some even partly obscured what they were describing. Outside a house called Dunsmeorah, there was a photograph of a middle-aged George MacLeod and his bride on their wedding day. I knew from my reading that Lorna, Lady MacLeod, was her husband's second cousin and she was only twenty-seven when she became engaged to the fifty-three-year-old leader of the Iona Community. Surprisingly and disappointingly, the information board doesn't say who this smiling young woman was. Behind the happy couple – MacLeod is almost smiling – is their family home. It looked to me to be the largest house on the island – something else that surprised me.

There were few people in the Reilig Odhrain, the ancient graveyard by the roadside. Historic Scotland has set up a new ticket office for admission into the abbey precincts but it was possible to avoid the queue, open a low, slightly rickety gate and gain access directly to what was, until recently, reputed to be the last resting place of no fewer than forty-eight medieval Scottish kings. Perhaps because there are much more recent burials in the Reilig Odhrain, it might have seemed crass to charge for admission.

Immediately following his description of the chaotic state of the Reilig Odhrain, Thomas Pennant relates a remarkable tale:

The chapel of St Oran stands in this space, which legend reports to have been the first building attempted by St Columba: by the working of some evil spirit, the walls fell down as fast as they were built up.

After some consultation it was pronounced, that they would never be permanent till a human victim was buried alive. Oran, a companion of the saint, generously offered himself, and was interred accordingly: at the end of three days St Columba had the curiosity to take a farewell look at his old friend, and caused the earth to be removed. To the surprise of all beholders, Oran started up, and began to reveal the secrets of his prison-house; and particularly declared, that all that had been said of hell was a mere joke. This dangerous impiety so shocked Columba, that, with great policy, he instantly ordered the earth to be flung in again: poor Oran was overwhelmed, and an end forever put to his prating. His grave is near the door, distinguished only by a plain red stone.

Despite an undeniably Pythonesque quality, this story is both old and odd, and has been regularly repeated since the twelfth century. As one of Columba's original companions when he landed on Iona, Oran may well have died on the island but his role as a blood sacrifice feels surprisingly pagan. Most famously in the story of Abraham and his son, Isaac, the Old Testament also harked back to a more savage past, but on Mount Moriah it was God who spoke. On Iona it was Columba who suggested that 'someone among you should go down into the soil of the island to consecrate it'. In the earliest version, Oran did indeed volunteer, perhaps as a version of martyrdom, but the nature of his death, of natural causes or otherwise, is not made clear.

Not until the end of the seventeenth century does the tale begin to involve Oran being buried alive. This was apparently done to avoid an impending famine, but when the volunteer was disinterred and began to talk about the afterlife, Columba 'ordered the grave to be closed again on him, and sent him to the other world where he had already made so good an acquaintance'.

A year before Pennant came to Iona, an Irish traveller who clearly had decent Scots Gaelic recorded two quotes which must have come from a version of the story remembered by islanders. The first is said to be from Oran, the second is Columba's response:

> *Cha'n bhuill am bas na iongantas*
> *Na iofrain mar a teistonas*
> There is no wonder in death,
> And hell is not as it is reported.

> *Uir, uir air suil Orain*
> *Mar labhair e tuille comradh.*
> Dust, dust over Oran's eye,
> That he may speak no more.

Strange, even farcical in the Pennant version, but also disconcerting, this tale may have no basis whatever in fact, but it is odd that it survived and that the graveyard is named after Oran.

Part of my reason for going to Reilig Odhrain also involved friendship. I had come to visit the grave of *my* old friend John Smith. Leader of the Labour Party until his early death at the age of fifty-five, John died from a heart attack in May 1994. I met him in 1979 when I was running the Edinburgh Festival Fringe. A man who loved a good party, he was despairing of a dull official reception we were both attending. Minister of Trade in James Callaghan's government at the time, he asked, 'Is the Fringe Club still open? I've got a car and a driver.' A wonderfully convivial evening ended with a remarkable performance. So that they could publicise their shows, Fringe performers did five-minute excerpts as part of a running cabaret. Music worked best in the Fringe Club's packed ballroom and John and I listened to Phil Cunningham, the brilliant accordionist, and his equally talented brother, Johnny, on the fiddle. They were drawing delirious applause, playing on well past midnight. Suddenly, the Minister of Trade felt himself in fine voice. Could he offer the company a song? Did Phil and Johnny know 'Dark Lochnagar'? The audience were at first dumbstruck as this grey-suited, bespectacled figure took the stage, but his voice rang out, the Cunningham brothers smiled and rapturous applause followed. When someone in the front row asked the Minister of Trade where they could watch his show, John, with perfect timing, replied, 'Palace of Westminster – sometimes twice nightly!'

John was a member of and a regular attender at Cluny Kirk, not far from where we lived in Edinburgh. When I walked down to his funeral with our wreath, I was amazed and pleased to see a crowd of perhaps two thousand behind crush barriers. Former Prime Ministers Edward Heath and James Callaghan were followed by John Major and many other politicians. The service that followed was an extraordinary expression of grief at a sudden, terrible loss, an enormous missed opportunity.

Born in Dalmally at the head of Loch Awe in Argyll and raised in Ardrishaig on the shores of Loch Fyne, John never forgot his Highland heritage. What made his funeral all the more poignant was not only the eloquence of the eulogies, it was also the voice of Kenna Campbell. Unaccompanied, she stepped forward to sing the 23rd Psalm, '*Is e Dia Fhein as Buachaill Dhomh*', 'The Lord Is My Shepherd'. In the style of a Free Church of Scotland precentor, her crystal voice rang around the packed kirk, its dramatic cadences swooping and soaring like a flock of birds over the mountains, and it stunned the congregation. They understood nothing of the language and everything about its power and sentiment. Most had never heard the sound of the Gaelic psalmody. Almost primitive, elemental in its power, it is a form of praise that reaches back across millennia to the monks at Bangor in the sixth century – singing that was almost certainly heard on Iona.

In the vestibule after the service, Kenna said to me that she felt she had not sung as well as she wished to. I told her that her remarkable rendition would be in every news bulletin that night, all around the world. And it was. Her voice rang out not only from grief but also in the name of John Smith's West Highland origins. A few days after the funeral, Elizabeth Smith and her daughters, Sarah, Jane and Catherine, went with John's coffin to bury him in the Reilig Odhrain.

His grave seems to be often visited. Lying flat, his gravestone is not large. It is simply inscribed with his name and dates and a quote from Alexander Pope:

An Honest Man's
The Noblest
Work of God

On the day of my visit in 2019, it had been decorated with Iona pebbles laid carefully around the inscriptions, mixed with the remains of dried flowers. I realised that it was twenty-five years since the death of this honest, sometimes witheringly direct and brilliant man who loved a party. He would undoubtedly have been Prime Minister and I believe his country sorely misses him, now more than ever. As I have grown older, I find myself much more easily given to tears and I shed some on that bright afternoon, both at the graveside and again in St Oran's Chapel.

Probably built at the request of the great Somerled, Ri Innse Gall, ruler and creator of the sprawling Atlantic principality of the Isles, the chapel is small and intact, only needing its roof replaced in the late nineteenth century. Its main fabric dates from the middle of the twelfth century, predating the Benedictine abbey by at least fifty years and was probably intended as a dynastic mausoleum. Very simple and with a sanctity needing no adornment, the little chapel was deserted when I entered, lit only by a few votive candles.

The enclosure of the Reilig Odhrain was almost certainly the original burial ground for Columba's monks – and perhaps for Columba himself – and not the Cladh an Diseirt, and for that reason it gathered great spiritual power as the centuries wore on. In the Middle

Ages, Christians believed that holy ground had a tangible, physical effect. If those who were dying or nearing the end of their lives and had the means or money to ensure that they were buried in sacred soil – in Gaelic *an talamh trocair*, literally 'the land of mercy' – then the sins of their mortal flesh might be cleansed as it rotted. The ground had been made holy not only by Columba – before his remains were exhumed and placed in a shrine – but also by the burial of his pious companions and their saintly successors, perhaps including St Adomnán. On the information board, which I had tried to ignore, there is a reproduction of an engraving made in 1849 that shows a very crowded cemetery with many grave markers. Some of the oldest are now on show in the abbey museum.

Inside the chapel, the most sacred ground, the holy of holies, was near the high altar and it may be that under the flagged floor lie the remains of Somerled and his son, Ragnall. Their successors as Lords of the Isles jostle for space with them and, scuffed and smoothed by the penitent feet of many centuries of pilgrims, there seems to be a grave slab by the doorway. Even though the Islesmen are thought to have fought with a type of halberd known as a Lochaber axe, this slab and many others are usually engraved with a *claidheamh-mor*, the long sword called a claymore, and the white wand that signified the authority of the Lord of the Isles.

Since the death of my first granddaughter, Hannah Moffat, in 2015, and the birth of Grace, her little sister, in 2016, I have sometimes lit candles for them, my wee lasses. So that Hannah's memory and Grace's hope burn bright, especially in the peace of ancient churches, I set them close to each other and watch the flames flicker, anxious a sudden draught does not blow them out. In places where generations of mourners have wept for loss, my tears were for the future that was taken from the child we were never allowed to know. It does not matter to me, someone who does not believe in God, that I light candles in a church. I expect no comfort from anywhere and, in any case, where else could I do such a thing? What matters is the peace, the quiet and the dignity. This deserted little chapel seemed to me to have those things and perhaps I could believe a little in the notion of holy ground or at least holy places. There is no sin to wash away, no need for faith in cleansing soil, only grief that will never mend. But, in St Oran's, my tears were for my girls, not for me. I have had my life and I hope that Grace will have hers, but, for Hannah, there will be nothing except remembrance.

15

The Night Before the Morning

I must have spent much longer in the chapel than I intended for when I came blinking out into the early evening sunshine, the abbey ticket office had closed. At first, I cursed myself. How could I visit Iona and leave without looking at the abbey? Even though it is medieval and nothing remains of Columba's monastery except the shadow of the vallum, it does stand on the same site, and where he walked, I could walk, perhaps even see something of the things he saw. Then it came to me that this was not an all-too-frequent episode of absentmindedness but actually a stroke of good fortune. Why not allow the crowds to leave on the last ferries and stay overnight on the island? I could rise with the sun the following morning, at around 5 a.m., and have the island and the abbey to myself. I could hop over the wall and then pay later. The only flaw in my hatching plan was that I did not have a bed for the night. Which was just as well. I did not want to talk to anyone in a hotel or bed and breakfast that might have a room. It was a clear sky and a good forecast for the morning, and it was also the summer dim when the sun stayed only a little below the horizon. I would walk back over to the machair and find somewhere dry and out of the breeze off the ocean.

With only moments to spare before it closed, I puffed through the door of a grocery shop just up the road that led to the slipway and the ferry to Fionnphort. Not wishing to detain the shopkeeper, I quickly bought an eclectic supper – a packet of four small pork pies, a tub of mixed olives, an apple, a wedge of extra-mature cheddar and a large bar of Cadbury's Fruit and Nut. I have never forgotten Frank Muir's advertising jingle about Cadbury's fruit and nutcases, and it plays in my head each time I buy a bar. Having looked for a half bottle and failed to find one – honestly, there was no time – I completed my supplies with a bottle of white wine, with a twist-top metal closure and not a cork. Without a glass or a cup, it would have to be drunk by the neck. Well, who, except for a finger-wagging Columba, would be watching?

When I emerged from the shop, I watched the last ferry cast off, making me a castaway. For the first time that day, I exhaled what felt like a pent-up breath and hoped that the spirit of Iona might begin to reveal itself at last. Once the shopkeeper had locked up, there was no one else in the little street.

I had not had the chance to sit down to check exactly what I had in my backpack, but I knew that I had a good but light and thin Gore-Tex anorak. It had kept me dry many times, but not warm. I knew I had a penknife. The absurd notion that it would come in useful if I wanted to cut firewood flickered through my addled brain and then I remembered I had no matches. And my phone – still with some battery power even after taking scores of photographs that day – had a good torch. I would be fine. I hoped. I had to be – the ferry had gone.

Crossing the machair to the western beaches, I began to look for somewhere sheltered. Little more than a riffle of a breeze whispered off the ocean, but it might freshen overnight. And with no clouds to wrap the day's warmth, it would probably be cold. Climbing up to the raised green of the occasional golf course, I saw what might be a likely spot. Reasoning that it would be better to sleep on the sand than grass that would become damp as dew formed at the end of the night, I thought that a place where a shallow finger of sand reached into the grass of the machair like a tiny sea loch might suit my purpose. The low edges of grass on either side would shelter me from the wind, and the sand seemed to slope a little. My head would be above my feet.

When I reached what I hoped would be my resting place – vaguely wondering if it would be my last, for some reason – I sat on the grass shelf and tipped out the contents of my backpack. In addition to my anorak – which I planned to wear as a version of outdoor pyjamas – I had a thin lambswool pullover, a padded body warmer, several maps and notebooks but no bedtime reading, a compass, a bottle of water, a change of pants and socks, a spare shirt and a towel but no toothbrush. Some of this, I should confess, was not the result of contingency planning but of laziness – not having bothered to repack my backpack for some time.

Much too early to think of sleep or supper, I stuffed all of these contents back into my pack, shoved my groceries on top and twisted off the cap of the white wine. Far from feeling like an idiot, a sixty-nine-year-old boy scout, I found myself slowly relaxing. No doubt the Sauvignon Blanc helped but the silence, the sun westering over the ocean and the fact that I was entirely alone made my shoulders drop and my mind clear. With my legs dangling over the edge of the grassy cliff by my sand bed, I lay flat on my back on the machair and looked up at the deep blue of the heavens. It was almost hypnotic. With no reference point, I felt I had lost focus, was swimming in the skies. Guessing that the tide had turned and was beginning to come in, I listened to the rhythmic surge of the ocean, the strengthening wash of the incoming waves. In Gaelic there is a beautiful verb for the action of sea over the strand, the white sand. *Sluaisreadh an gainmheamh air an traigh* means 'swirling of the sand of the shore'. *Sluaisreadh* is pronounced 'slowashriv'. It is the sound of the ocean.

At 7.30 p.m., the sun still splashed over the beach in all its splendour and, after repacking my backpack and leaving it where I could see it – Who would steal it, for goodness' sake? – I walked down to meet the incoming tide. The sand was pristine and, as far as I could see, only some smooth, bleached driftwood had fetched up on the shore. When I spent a week on Lindisfarne two years before, I walked the northern shoreline of the island – what I came to call 'the Duneland'. Well above the high tidemark, on the margins of the marram grass, I found piles of rubbish collected by conscientious people, probably pilgrims unhappy to see Cuthbert's island so casually defiled. Plastic was of course ever present. But here on Iona, Lindisfarne's mother house, the flower of the west that had brought forth the light of the east, there had been no need for rubbish collection. The current must run from cleaner shores.

The white sands of the long beach are not the sands of Sinai or Syria, the deserts where St Anthony and the other founders of western monasticism first fled from the world. But Columba, Adomnán and no doubt other abbots and brethren who studied scripture deeply will have been comfortable with metaphor. The encircling sea certainly stood for the wastes of the deserts of the East, girding the monastery in solitude, but the uncountable grains of sand also had symbolic power, a part of God's Creation that could never be measured. I wondered if the works of John Cassian were read on Iona and whether his three stages – his approach to God – were understood. It struck me that Dun I and its vast vistas might be a good place to begin the process of *purgatio*, the attempt to triumph over the temptations of the flesh by means of mortification, prayer and fasting. On the summit of the little hill, Heaven was closer and the glories of Creation plain to see. Perhaps brethren also lay on their backs and gazed up at the mesmeric blue of the evening sky fourteen centuries ago.

If monks felt ready to enter upon *unitio*, the complete union of their soul with God, they could retreat to where I had come, to the west side of the island, as far from the monastery as possible. On my map was marked Eilean Maol Mhartuin, little more than a skerry that lay to the south of Bay at the Back of the Ocean, where I was walking. The name is evocative of the deep past for it means 'the Island of the Follower of St Martin' – perhaps a place where an even more profound, wave-lashed solitude might be sought. Nearby are St Martin's Caves, but the inrushing tide prevented me from scrambling over the rocky shore to see them. On Lindisfarne, I had come across a series of small clefts known as 'the Prayer Holes' in a south-facing cliff that was washed by the chill waters of the North Sea. As the salt spray spattered them, making the rocks slick and slippery, monks wedged themselves in these bleak perches as they prayed, feeding the knots of the rosary through their cold fingers. Perhaps St Martin's Caves were used for a similar purpose, the repetitions of the

Jesus Prayer murmured as the waves rolled in, as they faced the eternities of the ocean and the dying sun. Perhaps they hoped and thought of Brendan's 'Land of Promise of the Saints', perhaps it lay only just over the far horizon. After days and nights of trance-inducing fasting and the endless repetition of prayer, it may have shimmered over the waves.

After a time – something I was beginning not to notice – I returned to my resting place and realised that, after a long day of walking and driving a single-track road, I was tired. Having enjoyed my eclectic and welcome supper and a little more wine, I found I could look directly at the sinking gold disc of the sun as its brilliance faded. Searching the sky, I could not see any sign of moonrise. Instead, I sat quiet, watching the hypnotic wash of the waves, listening to them sighing, rising and falling, the ocean breathing. Time seemed to shift a little. Instead of looking at my watch, I felt myself in the midst of the world's clock, moved not by the action of a mechanism but by the four elements. The earth beneath me was cooling, the air around me clean and fresh, the waters of the ocean beating the shore like a drum, the fire of the sun dying beyond the horizon. This was old time, eternal time, the turns of the weather, the seasons and the moods of the land.

Thinking about these things but not thinking, I found myself at last absorbing a sense of Columba's island, the place he made holy, and somewhere that had been sacred before he came. George MacLeod reckoned Iona to be a thin place and I began to intuit what he meant. The veil between worlds, between the spiritual and temporal, between what can be seen and what can be imagined, was gossamer thin for me on that evening by the Bay at the Back of the Ocean. Of course, I knew something of the story of this place and how could that not inform what I thought? But what I *felt* could have been felt before Iona had any history. It is part of its fundamental essence, this thinness, this wispy sense of otherworldliness, and it is what brings pilgrims back again and again. I believed that I myself had shifted, had got on the other side of something – but I had no idea what that something was.

Iona has long been understood as a place with a unique *genius loci*, a place of spirits, a place where spirits brush past like a breath of wind, whispering of a past that existed before time, their form as delicate, insubstantial as morning cobwebs on your face.

On my walks and other journeys, I make notes most of the time and take hundreds, thousands, of photos with my phone, recording everything that strikes me, guarding against a chronic forgetfulness. But the pages for that evening are blank. I made no notes and took no photographs and yet, three months after I returned from Iona, I can recall perfectly what I saw and how I felt.

The silence lulled me, made all that I did slow and deliberate. It had been many years since I had slept the night outside but, without thinking about it, I began to prepare, pulling on my pullover, zipping up my body warmer, slipping my thin anorak over my head. Taking out my spare shirt, I folded it so that it would make a soft pillow to go on top of my backpack. The sand was firmer than I had imagined but when I lay down and stretched out, I found that my drowsiness fled. In the clear sky of the summer dim, I could see some of the brighter stars – I wish I knew their names – and a half moon. I could not tell if it was waxing or waning. It seemed that Heaven lay open above me.

For Columba and his monks, darkness was the time when angels fled and devils crawled out of the shadows. A pantheon of evil existed, and all had names. Some of them, like Behemoth and Mammon, have been remembered, others, like Chemosh and Samael were fallen angels brought down from the glories of Heaven by Lucifer himself. Some took the guise of animals – Azazel stalked the night as a goat, Moloch stamped the ground as a bull. Incubi and succubi hid in the dark places of the world until the light died in the west and black night descended. Darkness hid the realm of Satan, who was vividly real to all believers. The monks' defence was the Word of God, his name repeated over and over again in prayer. Or the psalmody was chanted to create a rampart of praise, and the *laus perennis* could keep evil at bay.

In the half-light, when formless shapes seem to flit on the edge of vision, I found myself not fretting, straining to hear strange sounds, not wondering about a sudden movement amongst the rocks of Druim an Aoineidh, but lying on the sand at peace, for some reason thinking of the deeps of the world. Beyond the beach and the bay, the vastness of the mighty Atlantic shelved down to unimaginable darkness and silence. Not far to the south lay the little island of Oronsay where prehistoric mounds or middens made from shell debris were found. In them archaeologists discovered human bones and also those of seal flippers mixed with the discarded bounty of the ocean. Half-dreaming of wraiths or ancient souls swimming in the deeps with the seals, I fell sound asleep.

In the hind night, as the small hours after midnight used to be known, I woke and shivered. My hands were very chilled. The cloudless sky had brought a cold air and I needed urgently to pee. For some muddled reason, I walked a little way along the shore to find somewhere secluded. Perhaps some ancient instinct warned me not to defile this sacred place. Small, pale shapes moved slowly in the moonlight across the machair, not far from the track, and I saw that they were sheep. Before I had lain down for the night, I realised I should have looked for cattle. Grazing, snuffling sheep are timid and would not have come near me but cows can be a very different matter, especially those with calves at foot.

Using my phone torch to find them, I pulled my spare socks over my hands and put on my spare shirt under my body warmer. Every little would help. Still weary after all those miles and stiff, sore-backed, I fell into a fitful doze, dreaming this time of Bina, my grandmother. The council house where I grew up was a standard size and had too few bedrooms to accommodate an extended family, and when I was a little boy I shared a bed with Bina. Hanging on to the edge of the mattress in a futile attempt to prevent myself from tumbling against her pillowy warmth, I used to look out of the window at the moon. 'You can see the old moon in the shadow of the new,' she used to whisper. That night on Iona's sandy machair, I dreamed of Bina's moon.

16

The Scribes and the Scribbler

Houses have characteristic sounds in the early morning – creaks, inexplicable ticking noises, clicks as water pipes expand or whistles when the winds blow. Waking up slowly in my cleft in the machair, I heard the wash of the ocean, the breeze soughing and, for a few moments, I had no idea where I was. Perhaps I was lying in my last resting place and I had found myself in another world, having passed through a gossamer veil to the other side of something I did not understand. Perhaps I inhabited a dream of Iona. As waves of consciousness began to break over me and I began to remember the magical evening, I realised I was bitterly cold and sore. Unable to push myself up because one arm was completely numb – perhaps I had been lying on it – I rolled over on my side and managed to scramble on to all fours. The pins and needles in my arm were almost painful and so I sagged down on my side to wait for the feeling to return. My flesh had certainly been mortified.

Without intending to, it came to me that I had kept a version of a vigil, the sort of ritual that Columba's monks practised. Like these pious men, but with none of their Christian belief, reciting no prayers, not threading the prayer rope through my cold fingers, chanting no psalms, I had passed the night alone in the darkness, when fell demons were abroad, when Satan stalked the land. And despite my impiety and unbelief, I had felt no fear. There seemed to me to be an inchoate sense of the sacred soil of the Reilig Odhrain flowing far beyond the enclosure of the ancient graveyard, spreading underground like the roots of the Tree of Death, that all of the soil of Iona was sacred and could be a salve to the soul as well as cleanse it of mortal sin.

Even though it is my firm belief that our deaths are final, that no afterlife awaits us and my soul could not be cleansed, full of sin though it must be, because it is not immortal, I could not explain why my night of solitude had affected me so strangely, even deeply. Was doubt nibbling at these lifelong certainties? Although I am sure there is no God, I was coming to understand there are places that are touched by an otherness, that have a unique spiritual atmosphere that seems to have no empirical explanation. I had sensed that on Lindisfarne, grasped at fleeting hints of it on Eileach an Naoimh and on Lismore. But, here, waking alone on the dawn machair on Iona, I felt that otherness powerfully.

After a time, I was at last able to sit on the grass shelf by my sand bed, stretch my legs and roll my aching shoulders. Since reconstructive surgery on my left shoulder in 2017, I have forced myself to follow a morning regimen of exercises and I did manage most of them, irrationally hoping that no one was watching me. Sand is not soft but lumpy and my old muscles were not used to it. Having drained my bottle of water and rinsed my mouth as best I could, I looked around myself at last. In the east, I saw a pale light rising, lighter than the light over the ocean behind me, the beginnings of dawn breaking. It was 4.30 and I reckoned that, if I quickly shoved everything in my backpack and started walking, I could reach the monastery as the sun rose over the mountains of Mull.

As I passed Cnoc nam Bradhan, 'the Hillock of the Brow', the gentle summit of the low ridge between Dun I and Cnoc nam Druidean, it felt as though I was moving from one island to another – from the island of the evening to the island of the morning. Columba chose the eastern side of Iona for the site of his monastery not because the sun's rays would strike there first, but because it was in the east. Early Christians believed that, on the Last Day, Christ would rise in the east and, as they knelt to pray, they faced that way, searching the morning sky for signs of the Second Coming.

By the side of the road that leads from the nunnery to the abbey stands MacLean's Cross. It is not ancient, but it remembers an old belief. Commissioned by the Chief of Clan MacLean of Duart, the sea castle on the eastern tip of Mull passed by the CalMac ferry on its way to dock at Craignure, the cross is tall and impressive. It was amongst the first of many encountered by pilgrims disembarking on the island, places where they could pray on their way to Columba's shrine. If they had come early, they would have seen what I saw. The sun had breasted the mountains and its butter-coloured light washed like a welcome tide over the island. As I stood on its western side, having scrambled over the dyke to see that face of the cross better, the long shadow of the MacLean's Cross stretched over me. I felt I had been blessed, despite my unbelief.

Much weathered but still legible, the centre of the cross head carries an image of Christ crucified. Above is something gentler, a carving of a lily, a flower associated with the Virgin Mary. Nearby stands a building Samuel Johnson was shocked to find that Iona lacked, a parish church. It looked like a functional rectangular box, a good plain kirk, and a little research revealed that it was one of about thirty known as Telford's Kirks. Also called Parliamentary Churches, they were built after the House of Commons voted £50,000 for the construction of forty churches in the poorer and more backward areas of Scotland – which meant the Highlands. Such a lack of awareness of Iona's venerable history is breathtaking but no more so than the fact that the light of Christianity in the west had been so completely extinguished that there no longer existed a place where Columba's God could be worshipped. The great engineer and designer Thomas Telford created a standard template that could be built on a budget not exceeding £1,500, and that would remain reliably weather-tight in the harsher Atlantic winters of the Hebrides. It is an austere little building. Perhaps Columba would have approved.

Turning back towards the nunnery, I saw a roofless shell that I had overlooked. It had been the predecessor of the Telford Kirk. My notes told me that this was Teampull Ronain, 'the Chapel of St Ronan'. The dedication is almost certainly ancient and probably honoured the memory of an extremely austere and courageous hermit who chose to pass his life in prayer and fasting on the tiny island of North Rona. Its name may remember his presence.

Forty-four miles north west of Cape Wrath on the Scottish mainland and the same distance north of the Butt of Lewis, Rona is the
most remote of all the British Isles ever to have been inhabited for
long periods. Its Gaelic name is Ronaigh an Taibh, 'Rona of the
Ocean', probably derived from *tabh*, the Norse word for 'ocean',
which would distinguish it from the other Rona that lies off the
coast of Skye, just north of the island of Raasay.

On the grassy plateau above its dark cliffs, Ronan built an oratory,
a drystane enclosure and cell where he could pray. In photographs,
it looks a little like the beehive cells on Eileach an Naoimh. So much
of the oratory survives that it is the best-preserved example in Britain.
Less spectacular but much more isolated than Skellig Michael, Rona
was the most extreme retreat from the world into the deserts of the
ocean, a harsher place than any that could have been found in Syria
or Sinai. I had considered going there to experience something of
what the saint saw and what he had to endure, but, rather than the
prospect of considerable privation or the difficult logistics of reaching it, it was the dark history of the little island that discouraged me.

With his wife and a full crew, Malcolm MacLeod, the Steward of
St Kilda, was sailing home to the Isle of Harris sometime before
1680. Suddenly blowing up from the south-west, a great storm
chased their ship northwards and they were driven ashore on the
island of Rona. Despite being wrecked on the rocks, MacLeod and
his crew saved themselves and their provisions. Knowing that the
island was inhabited, they were surprised that no one had run to the
shore to help them. When they gained the grassy plateau, they saw
that no smoke blew from the clachans, the blackhouses of the village,
and no one responded to their calls of greeting. Sometime before
MacLeod and his people had scrambled ashore, a biblical scourge
had killed all thirty islanders and effectively ended community life
in this remote place on the edge of the world.

It seems that, after a shipwreck and before MacLeod and his people
dragged themselves ashore, black rats had managed to swim to North
Rona and they devoured the islanders' store of corn. As a result, some
people starved to death and others may have been so enfeebled that they

caught plague from the rats. When all of the corn had been consumed, it is likely that the rats feasted on the corpses of the islanders before they themselves starved to death, unable to hunt for birds and eggs along the shoreline because of the crash and surge of the Atlantic swells in a long period of bad weather. It is a remarkable, chilling tale and, while I understood that it would have been good to know something of the extremes of privation these ascetics suffered, the place sounded sinister, cursed. Not even all the ancient prayers of Ronan could protect its people from evil. North Rona seemed a voyage too far.

Far to the sunlit south, St Ronan's monument on Iona, the roofless little church by the nunnery ruins, turned out to be a fascinating palimpsest that shed a different and fresh light on Iona's history. Between approximately 1200 and the turning point of the Scottish Reformation in 1560, St Ronan's was the island's parish church, the place where the laity worshipped. It seems very small, but it must be borne in mind that medieval Christians did not sit during services. They either stood or knelt in prayer and it seemed to me that the chapel could have accommodated about seventy or eighty people. That probably meant that the lay community on Iona outnumbered the monks, but since the whole island appears to have been granted to Columba, they probably worked in the monastery's fields and tended their flocks and herds.

Beneath where the farm workers stood to worship, archaeologists have found the footprint of a much earlier chapel dating to the eighth century, the time when Ronan fasted and prayed on his tiny island far out in the Atlantic. And beneath those foundations were burials, the graves of women. On the reasonable assumption that these were even earlier, this strongly reinforces the notion that Iona had a significant lay population when Columba's monks dragged their curraghs ashore in 563. It seems also that a graveyard at Teampull Ronain was reserved for women and that may very well be the reason why the nunnery of St Mary the Virgin was founded on that site after 1200 by Ragnall, son of Somerled, and king of the Isles. He installed his sister, Beathag, as the first prioress.

On the road to the abbey I met no one and the sole sign of life came from the St Columba Hotel, where a window was opened by an unseen hand. With some difficulty, I made my way over the wall between the Reilig Odhrain and the abbey precinct. I found myself on a paved road. It is known as Sraid nam Marbh, 'the Street of the Dead', and it led towards the west door of the abbey and the shrine of Columba. A processional way that began at the landing place at Martyrs' Bay, it wended its way past MacLean's Cross – and many other crosses long lost to the image breakers of the Reformation and others – first to Reilig Odhrain and then on to the shrine of Columba. Old roads fascinate me. Ghosts walk beside the living as we follow precisely in the footsteps of the centuries. Those who walked the Street of the Dead have worn down the sacred ground significantly and its level is at least a foot lower than its surroundings.

As the practice of pilgrimage grew, more people walked on from the ancient graveyard to the saint's shrine, and after *c.*1200 to the Benedictine abbey. There was, of course, travel in the opposite direction as funeral processions moved slowly from the church to the graveyard. These rituals are respectfully silent now but it is very likely that the monks sang psalms and perhaps even played instruments as the dead were carried along their last street before being buried in the cleansing soil. Tradition insists that the bodies of many early Scottish kings were brought to Iona for interment, amongst them Macbeth. If Shakespeare's caricature of the blood-soaked usurper is to be believed, then *an talamh trocair* will have had much to do.

Not wishing to leave Columba's shadow, I climbed the little rocky outcrop known as Torr an Aba, 'the Mound [or Mount] of the Abbot'. It is surprisingly steep and it commands the site. The summit is stony, and in the centre lies what looks like a cross socket, the base of a high cross. Whatever its ancient function, this large flat stone was a good place to sit and look at what lay around on either side. I was certain that I was sitting almost precisely where Columba had sat and, if I looked past the Benedictine abbey to the Sound of Iona and the mountains of Mull beyond, I knew that I could see exactly what he saw fourteen centuries ago.

On the Torr an Aba, Columba had his writing hut built. Given the surface area of the rocky mound, it must have been a small structure – and draughty on blustery days. According to Adomnán, it was also cramped:

> One day, shouting was heard from the other side of the Sound of Iona [this was how the ferry man was called for from the island]. The saint was sitting in his raised wooden hut and heard this, saying: 'The man who is shouting across the Sound is too careless to watch what he is doing. Today he will tip over the horn and spill the ink.'
>
> His servant, Diarmait, heard him say this and for a while stood by the door waiting for the clumsy guest to arrive so that he could keep him away from the ink-horn. But soon he moved away for some other purpose, and then the troublesome visitor arrived. As he went forward to kiss the saint, he upset the horn with the edge of his garment and spilt the ink.

Christianity was a religion of the book. 'In the beginning was the Word and the Word was with God and the Word was God' and the copying of scripture, the creation of other manuscripts, such as the lives of saints, and their illumination were understood as powerful, vivid means of praising God. As the vignette from Adomnán illustrates – and it is one of the few passages that is not formulaic hagiography but appears to have been drawn from the life – Columba was a scribe as well as an abbot. It is believed that he copied *An Cathach*, 'the Battler', a psalter which has survived.

He may also have seen himself as a literary stylist; a hymn, *Altus Prosator*, 'Maker on High', has been confidently attributed to him. Taking twenty-three letters of the alphabet (leaving out J, U and W), each begins a verse of a long paean to the power of the Almighty. To my ear – admittedly, my atheist ear – it is a tangled, tortured and lugubrious piece of complicated theology that I find difficult to understand and impossible to enjoy. Goodness knows what Columba's monks made of it as they dutifully chanted or sang. Here are some extracts from what feels like a translation that is equal to the original. It begins with this verse – one of the less cloudy.

Ancient exalted seed-scatterer whom time gave no progenitor:
He knew of no moment of creation in his primordial
    foundation
He is and will be all places in all time and all ages
With Christ his first-born only-born and the holy spirit
    co-borne
Throughout high eternity of glorious divinity:
Three gods we do not promulgate one God we state and
    intimate
Salvific faith victorious: three persons very glorious.

It then goes on with a scatter of impenetrable phrases, such as 'indurated enviousness', the 'lubric serpent' and 'skyey purlieus', and it ends with:

Zabulus burns to ashes all those adversaries
Who deny that the Saviour was Son to the Father
But we shall fly to meet him and immediately greet him
And be with him in the dignity of all such diversity
As our deeds make deserved and we without swerve
Shall live beyond history in the state of glory.

In high contrast, Iona's greatest literary creation may be the most beautiful book ever made. Its words are timeless, and its images close to perfection. And yet the book's association with Columba and his island is a matter for conjecture since it has been named after another monastery far to the south and it cannot be seen in Scotland. The Book of Kells fell into the possession of monks based at what became Kells Abbey and it is now on display at Trinity College in Dublin, marketed as 'Ireland's greatest treasure'.

Scholarship is of course divided as to its origins, but the balance of opinion holds that this gorgeously painted gospel book was begun on Iona and completed soon afterwards at Kells, where it remained. Now bound in four books, one for each of the gospels of Mathew, Mark, Luke and John, the copying of the text of the manuscript was apparently the work of four hands, with a few other, much more minor contributions. Expert analysis has concluded that Scribe A copied the entire text of St John's Gospel. This was probably the first to be undertaken and probably completed on Iona. Like Columba, Abbot Connachtach had a reputation as a talented scribe – he was described in the Irish annals as 'a choice scribe' – and it was to be his hand that would begin the great enterprise.

Connachtach died in 802 and this date may offer some sense of the motivation that lay behind the undertaking of such a costly and time-consuming project. Towards the end of the eighth century, Columba's bones were removed from the Reilig Odhrain and translated to a shrine, the ancestor of the little stone building by the west door of the abbey. This was probably a highly decorated wooden structure, a kind of ark, that took its colourful motifs from the style of the high crosses and illuminated manuscripts. In 797, the 200th anniversary of the death of Columba was celebrated and the Book of Kells may have been commissioned to honour Iona's great saint and endorse and reinforce his cult. A century before, Eadfrith copied the Lindisfarne Gospels and had them painted to add lustre to the name and the cult of Cuthbert.

For the year 793, the *Anglo-Saxon Chronicle* recorded a devastating surprise attack on the monastery at Lindisfarne. The Vikings had sailed out of the sea mists and into history. Two years after they pillaged Lindisfarne, the Vikings rounded Cape Wrath and their dragon ships were seen in the Sound of Iona.

It was the beginning of a time of tragedy for Columba's island. The Sons of Death returned repeatedly, raiding the monastery in the summer of 802 and again in 806, when they slaughtered sixty-eight brethren and lay people.

After the raid of 802, it may be that the Book of St Columba, as it is occasionally known, was stowed in a curragh and taken to Kells. In County Meath, about forty miles north-west of Dublin, the monastery lay far inland, although it was eventually raided by Vikings. If the great manuscript was begun on Iona by Connachtach, it is thought to have been completed by three other scribes with distinctive hands at Kells. Expert analysis judges that three artists were also involved. Known as the Goldsmith – his paintings resemble equivalent images in metalwork – the Portrait Painter – there are many in addition to those of the four gospel writers – and the Illustrator – who seemed to specialise in animals and the intricate, abstract geometric patterns that grace many pages.

Throughout the Book of Kells, there is a great deal of wit. Lions are painted with their paws held up to their mouths when the text relates a direct quote from Christ. Profiles of heads sometimes look in the direction of the next page and there is great playfulness with cats. Scribes and illustrators seemed to like cats. In the ninth century, an Irish monk at the German monastery of Reichenau was copying a Latin commentary on Virgil and a list of Greek paradigms. It must have been a tedious task, for in the margin the bored monk wrote a poem in Gaelic.

> I and Pangur Bán my cat,
> 'Tis a like task we are at:
> Hunting mice is his delight,
> Hunting words I sit all night.
>
> …
>
> 'Tis a merry task to see
> At our tasks how glad are we,
> When at home we sit and find
> Entertainment to our mind.
>
> …
>
> 'Gainst the wall he sets his eye
> Full and fierce and sharp and sly;
> 'Gainst the wall of knowledge I
> All my little wisdom try.
>
> So in peace our task we ply,
> Pangur Bán, my cat, and I;
> In our arts we find our bliss,
> I have mine and he has his.

When the ticket office for the abbey precinct opened, I entered from the wrong side to pay for my visit. The young lady made no comment as I also bought the Historic Scotland Guide, *Iona Abbey and Nunnery* by Peter Yeoman and Nicki Scott. I found it an excellent companion in every way – never intrusive or insistent, always informative. Only in one place did its tone of voice grow a little louder than a gentle, agreeable murmur. Page fifty-nine begins: 'The Book of Kells was the supreme creation of its age, produced on Iona around 800.' There is none of the usual on-the-one-hand or on-the-other-hand equivocation here. This stunning object was definitely produced on Iona by its abbot and his monks and then taken to Kells for safe keeping. Yeoman and Scott believe that there is 'a common symbolic decorative language' shared between the illumination and the high crosses of Iona, fragments of Columba's relics and objects found on the island by archaeologists. It occurred to me that there might be other compelling reasons to rename the Book of St Columba as the Book of Kells.

This was an object that required enormous resources as well as great skill. In addition to the thousands of hours needed to copy and paint, a minimum of one hundred and eighty-five calf skins, the vellum, were used to make the book. It is very likely that this 'supreme creation' had a wealthy patron, perhaps a king or a great magnate. And, if that was so, how did the partly completed book make its way to Kells and out of the orbit of that king? Patronage was very unlikely to transfer so easily because such an expensive object was not only under the control of the monks who were working on it; whoever put their resources behind this great artistic and devotional enterprise will have had a say in its fate. My suspicion is that the Book of St Columba was indeed completed on Iona before it was then carried across the sea for safe keeping.

What also caught my attention when I read the guide was the all-too-common occurrence of displacement. Objects gain a great deal when they are shown where they were made. In the Tuscan cities a great deal of great art has never moved from the churches it was made for and there, rather than in a gallery, it sparkles and lives, its original purpose clear. Just as I have argued for the Lindisfarne Gospels to be moved from the British Library in London to where they were made, so Trinity College should at least share this great treasure with the island where it came to life. Around the abbey precinct or close at hand, skilled scribes and painters found most of the plants and minerals that they needed to make their ink and palette of colours. And the unique atmosphere of Iona itself helped make the great book a beautiful work of art and it deserves to be seen in its original context.

One object that went nowhere fascinated me. Between the Torr an Aba and the shrine of Columba stands St Martin's Cross. For twelve centuries, its great height has been dominant and those who passed along the Sraid nam Marbh in the ninth century as well as those who visit the abbey now walk past its gaze. In the abbey museum, broken high crosses have been brilliantly reconstructed with pale plastic inserted in place of the missing fragments. Overlooking the display is the oldest of them all – St John's Cross. Yeoman and Scott believe that it was the first ringed cross – the sort known as a 'Celtic cross'. Its design may have developed from the chi-rho symbol, and this may have been the origin of the ringed cross.

Most of the carving on St John's Cross is abstract and full of coded references. A lion stands for Christ's royal lineage. He claimed to be a descendant of kings such as David and Solomon, men who called themselves Lions of Judah. Snakes were understood as surprising symbols of wisdom and more obviously of resurrection since they could slough off their skins. Harder to parse, particularly for non-believers, are the three eggs carved on the circular bosses. They represent the Trinity, while the group of five bosses stands for the five wounds suffered by Christ on the cross.

Two other crosses have been reconstructed. St Oran's and St Matthew's carry more figurative carving and this refers to scriptural stories that could be read and recognised by pilgrims and worshippers. When these crosses were first made, they looked very different from the five survivors on Iona. There is good evidence that they were painted in bright colours. At the National Irish Heritage Park near Wexford, many years ago, I saw a free-standing Celtic cross whose carvings glowed with colour. It looked startlingly different from the sombre monochrome in the abbey museum. Clearly, the Atlantic weather will have meant much repainting, but the power of the high crosses and their imagery can only have been enhanced by vivid reds, blues, yellows and greens. In large measure, the illuminated manuscripts sing because they are so brightly painted, and they show how important colour was in glorifying God and all He created.

Although only five crosses survive on Iona, it is certain that there were once many more. And if all were painted and regularly repainted, they will have marked out a striking devotional landscape, somewhere very different and apart from the natural colours of the island and the sea around it. I spent a long time looking at the display of reconstructed crosses in the abbey museum, simultaneously marvelling at the skill of the sculptors who made them and remembering a conundrum. Familiarity almost blinds us to this, but how strange it is that the principal symbol of a religion of love and forgiveness should be a relic of a most hideous form of execution. The adjective 'excruciating' has a grisly derivation and a glance at the appalling reality behind these great works of art makes them all the more remarkable. The familiarity of crosses and scenes of the crucifixion in our culture has almost washed out their historical meaning.

Principally and widely used by the Romans, crucifixion was above all a form of public execution and humiliation. One of the purposes of the unimaginable agonies of its victims was deterrence. When a Roman senator was murdered by one of his slaves, all of the others were crucified, even though there were four hundred, many of them women and children. Like Christ, the condemned were stripped and scourged before being led naked through the streets. There were no loincloths. Sometimes, if they were to be driven by soldiers with whips to a place of regular execution where the crucifixion uprights were already in place, they carried the crossbeam they would die on.

A name plaque, called a *titulus*, was nailed to the top of the cross so that passers-by knew the identity of the victim whose suffering they were witnessing. This can be seen in representations of Jesus's crucifixion, where INRI – *Iesus Nazarenus Rex Iudaeorum*, 'Jesus of Nazareth, King of the Jews' – is frequently depicted.

Nails were more like long iron spikes, measuring between five and seven inches, and they were driven into the wrists of the condemned between the two bones of the forearm, the radius and the ulna. Despite the tradition of the stigmata, it is very unlikely that nails were hammered through the palms. Hanging only by these spikes, the victim's body weight may have caused them to rip through between the bones of the fingers. Ropes may also have been used to secure the arms to the crossbeam, although these are shown only in later paintings and engravings of Christ's crucifixion. Feet were sometimes nailed through the ankles to the side of the cross, sometimes to the sloping footrest occasionally seen in paintings and sculpture. Crucifixion was intended to be a slow death, and the screams and groans of those who hung naked and bleeding were meant to be a horrific and lasting reminder to obey the law.

The mercy of death often came through asphyxiation. The nailing of the wrists on the crossbeam hyper-extended the chest and made breathing very difficult. To take a breath, victims had to endure the appalling pain of lifting themselves up by pulling on the spikes. Blood loss and dehydration also hastened the end of their agonies. The spear that was thrust into Christ's side was not an act of intentional mercy and nor was the habit of smashing the legs with an iron club. The latter was done to kill the victim more quickly, not only with shock but also to force them to suspend all of their body weight from their nailed wrists. The reason guards did these things was not an attempt to put the crucified out of their misery but because they wanted to go off duty. They were not allowed to leave the site of execution until the condemned were dead in case someone tried to save them.

Christ's death was the ultimate, utterly savage martyrdom and nothing that the fasting, flesh-mortifying monks of the disearts and monasteries of the early Christian era could do would ever approach such sacrifice. The agonies suffered by Jesus were in themselves proof of his divinity, as was his willingness to endure them. As I walked around the sunlit precincts of the abbey, amongst the chattering, selfie-taking visitors, I thought about the uncomfortable fact that this very beautiful place was founded on that blood-drenched story. The Passion, the final episode, what made Christ's ministry unique, what made him more than a prophet, what validated everything else that had gone before, was a spasm of appalling savagery, of obscene cruelty. Instead of the most important Christian festival of the year celebrating the birth of the Redeemer or the many glories of his ministry, Easter remembers each detail of his hideous death. I realised at the time that these thoughts swirling around my head were an over-simple interpretation but, in essence, it seems an extraordinary foundation story – one that is not often remembered – for a religion of love and forgiveness.

The abbey museum houses much more modest crosses than those of Oran, John and Matthew and these offer a glimpse of one of the many ways in which Christianity changed society in the sixth and seventh centuries. One of the great mysteries of prehistory in Britain is the relative scarcity of bodies. Over the eight millennia BC, the tombs of single individuals occasionally survive and, particularly in Orkney, there are several substantial ossuaries, where bones from many bodies have been placed. But given the millions who lived and died over that immense span of time, the balance of our history, there is a definite absence in the archaeological record. Where are all the bodies?

The only possible answer is that they were disposed of in places where they simply disappeared, perhaps in lakes and rivers, perhaps the sea or left exposed where wild animals would take them. On Iona, attitudes can be seen to have changed with the coming of Christianity. It may be that it was the first, the earliest place in Britain where believers were buried, and their graves were marked with a cross. In the beginning, these were probably made from wood and have not survived but the oldest grave marker in stone dates back to *c*.600. Some were set upright at the head of the burial – and these were all aligned east–west, waiting for the Second Coming to rise in the east – and others were laid flat. Some have inscriptions. One of those on show in the museum carries a line in Gaelic, '*Orar Anmin Eogain*', 'a Prayer for the Soul of Eogain', and another is in Latin, '*Lapis Echodi*', 'the Stone of Eochaid'. The latter may have marked a royal burial, that of Eochaid, a king of Dalriada who died in 629.

The interior of the abbey church is very atmospheric and very surprising. Perhaps because of the scale of the surrounding landscape and the size and number of the conventual buildings that adjoin its northern flank, the church looked small from the outside. But when I entered the west door, there was a transformation. It felt like a cathedral. It once had been a great and grand church, the spiritual focus of a wide Atlantic principality, the sea kingdom of Clan Donald. The splashes of light from the windows seemed almost celestial, graphic in their crystal clarity. The nature of the light on Iona was much remarked upon by painters. S.J. Peploe, Francis Cadell and William MacTaggart all commented on its luminous quality.

North-east of Iona, across the Sound of Mull, stands Ardtornish Castle, one of a string of coastal fortresses linked by the birlinns of their commanders. These included Dunollie and Dunstaffnage near Oban, and Duart on Mull. Fifteen years ago on another trip into the history of the Highlands, I decided to visit Ardtornish principally because of its appearance in an international treaty, the framework of a plot to overthrow and obliterate a kingdom. It was hatched by the descendants of the noblemen commemorated on Iona.

In 1460, the army of James II laid siege to Roxburgh Castle near Kelso. It was one of the last vestiges of a long English occupation of parts of the Borders after the disastrous and lengthy period of inter-mittent warfare that followed the Wars of Independence. The young king was fascinated by ordnance and a huge gun, The Lion, was dug into a trench on the northern side of the great castle to fire shot over the River Tweed and destroy its walls. But, as sometimes happened when cannon were forced to the very edge of their range, too much gunpowder was packed behind the ball and the bombard exploded. A fragment struck James II in the thigh and it seems that he bled to death.

Only nine years old when he succeeded his father, James III was very vulnerable, and factions jockeyed for control of the regency. Others plotted. And on 19 October 1461 a document was delivered to Ardtornish Castle that could have taken British history in a very different direction. It must have arrived by sea, for when I parked my car at a net-drying station on the southern shore of Loch Aline the road seemed to peter out. There was at least another two miles to the castle and, when it at last came into view, I had to approach it by crossing fields. No direct road, ancient or modern, seemed to exist. The ruined state of Ardtornish and the lack of any plaque, board or information did not disguise an ancient power. It may be forgotten now but its role in our history could have been pivotal. Perched on a headland with long views up and down the Sound of Mull, and a sheltered anchorage below, its position was commanding. To the south-east, I could make out the silhouette of Duart Castle and across the Firth of Lorn a beacon lit at Dunollie would have been visible.

Ardtornish was one of the principal strongholds of John MacDonald of Islay, the Lord of the Isles and the King of Man. His dominion stretched for three hundred and fifty miles down the Atlantic shore of Scotland and reached into the Irish Sea. On his accession, this prince of Clan Donald mustered an army of ten thousand marines and two hundred and fifty war galleys in the bay below the castle. In October 1461, he and his counsellors gathered to consider a half-forgotten plan to destroy the kingdom of Scotland. Recognising the precariousness of the Stewart succession and the powerlessness of the child king, Edward IV of England proposed that he be deposed, that all of Scotland north of the Forth should fall into the possession of John of Islay and that the south of the country should pass to the Earl of Douglas. Both men would swear allegiance to the English king and the kingdom of Scotland would disappear from history.

This moment saw the apogee of the power and reach of the Lord of the Isles, and also the beginning of their downfall. None of these schemes and stratagems came to pass, and by the middle of the sixteenth century it was the lordship that had ceased to exist. Little can now be seen of its administrative centre, the island at Finlaggan on Islay where its councils met, but on Iona, the spiritual capital of the kingdom of the Isles, it is possible to trace the story of this remarkable polity in stone.

In and around the abbey is a series of medieval grave slabs that remember great power. On one splendid example, there is a carving of a claymore, the great sword of the lordship, and next to it what looks like a simple stick. This represented the secular power of the MacDonald sea princes and the slab itself probably commemorates Ragnall, son of Somerled, the founder of the Benedictine abbey. Aonghas Óg, Young Angus MacDonald, chose the right side in the Wars of Independence. At Bannockburn in 1314, the Islesmen under his command swung their Lochaber axes and cut a bloody swathe through the English cavalry. His grave slab is more certainly identifiable by an inscription: 'Here lies the body of Angus, son of Lord Angus MacDonald of Islay'. Robert Bruce believed that the men of the Lordship were crucial to his great victory and he rewarded Aonghas Óg by dispossessing the MacDougalls of Lismore and giving their lands to the MacDonalds.

Through a series of dynastic marriages and failures of succession, the different branches of Clan Donald began to unite and the old dominion of Somerled reassembled. The Reilig Odhrain and its sacred soil gradually filled with the grave slabs of lords and chiefs who swore allegiance to the Lords of the Isles, and whose sins needed shriving. MacKinnons, MacLeans and MacLeods were also buried on Columba's island. In the abbey museum there are five very striking slabs with effigies of great warriors carved in high relief. Each carries a claymore and wears a long-skirted aketon or jack. These were padded coats that could both keep a man warm and repel a blow from a bladed weapon. Below them, soldiers wore jackboots. It is a curious display of raw secular power amidst the peace and quiet of a place of great sanctity

Reflecting on all of these paradoxes as I left the abbey precinct, I decided to walk down to Martyrs' Bay, so called because in 806 sixty-eight monks and lay people were slaughtered in a Viking raid – perhaps they made the fatal mistake of resisting. It is a gentle, pretty place, a strand of white sand fringed by grassy slopes – more paradox. Out in the bay, half a dozen small boats bobbed at anchor, their shapes shadowed against the shimmer of the rippling water of the sound. I sat down to gather my thoughts. The habit of half a lifetime of writing, I always do this in the same way – by making notes and then trying to get them into some sort of narrative order. The camera on my mobile phone is a wonderful addition but it is not until I sift through what I have written that I can begin to recognise what was important.

Sitting on sand that seemed to be as fine-grained as caster sugar, I began to understand that while Iona's beauty and what George MacLeod called its thinness can sometimes confer a sense of settled peace, it is also a place born of turmoil, of struggle and of doubt. Columba's monks led intentionally harsh lives and, at the same time, created great art in the shape of the Book of Kells, their high crosses and much else. But these glories seemed to me to have several wellsprings. The monks copied, painted and carved from a devotion to God that grew out of struggle and arose from great pain, from the agonies of the crucifixion and the cruel deaths of the red martyrs and the privations of white martyrs like themselves. And this beauty also seems to have sprung from the island of Iona itself, from its spirit of place and its gentle loveliness. To many who worshipped in Columba's monastery and to many who come now, it must sometimes have seemed like a glimpse of Heaven.

Despite this, it occurred to me that the island was far from a spiritual filling station, a place where fading or even failing beliefs might be recharged. When Samuel Johnson famously wrote, 'That man is little to be envied, whose patriotism would not gain force upon the plain of Marathon, or whose piety would not grow warmer among the ruins of Iona', he was missing the point as well as self-consciously crafting a quotable quote. Maddeningly, I came across this on a bronze plaque near Baile Mor – as if Iona needed Samuel Johnson's seal of approval. Like Eileach an Naoimh and Lismore, the island seemed to me to be a much more complex experience. Having none when I boarded the ferry at Fionnphort, I had not come to warm up any piety. And nor, I suspect, had Dr Johnson. Instead, I wanted to understand the story of these Irish monks better, to know something of how they lived and how they thought. History, with all its continuities and breaks, its mysteries and confusions, is my religion, my way of trying to make sense of the present.

As I sat on the sands scribbling, scrabbling to make some narrative sense of my journey thus far, I realised that, apart from a diary, what I had were competing impressions, not a progression – as many reverses as advances. When I sat on the Torr an Aba or woke in the machair in the west, I saw the skies and the landscape Columba had seen, and I had walked where he walked, but I could only grasp at straws when I tried to understand the texture of his life and thought.

That difficulty was what attracted me to the story of George MacLeod, 'the self-appointed successor to St Columba'. Adomnán's hagiography of Columba had to follow a formula and could not include episodes of self-doubt, breakdowns and disappointments – that was not his purpose in relating the miracles and good works of an exemplary life. But in his efforts to create something new on Iona, to refashion a mission for the church in the twentieth century, I had the strong impression from everything I had read that MacLeod's road had been strewn with rocks. How I wish I had met him but all I could find was a 1960s documentary about the restoration of the abbey called *Sermon in Stone*. In a clipped, slightly strangulated Scottish version of received pronunciation, he narrated it. His belief in God and himself – and both seemed, at times, provisional – his persistence and his gifts as a leader and a communicator had enabled him to approach his goals. But he did not see them fulfilled in the way he envisaged. In 1965 the abbey's restoration was thought to be sufficiently complete to warrant a service of dedication and that might have been seen as the culmination of the work MacLeod had devoted himself to. For twenty-seven years he had striven tirelessly and without payment, relying only on his private means. However, his goal of seeing Iona as a place to train divinity students was rejected by the Community he had founded and MacLeod resigned as its leader. In 1967, many were shocked when he accepted a peerage and became Baron MacLeod of Fuinary.

This story of what I believe was a saintly life in the twentieth century had obvious insights into the unspoken struggles of Columba, as both men created something new and renewed on Iona. Adomnán was forced to make his subject a hero saint whose success was inevitable since he was blessed by divine grace, but it cannot in reality have been like that. Instead of conjectural reading between the lines, I found it more revealing to think of both men walking in each other's shadows.

Martyrs' Bay witnessed happier times after the sand ran red with blood in 806. The beach where I sat saw boats carrying pilgrims arrive over the centuries and many thousands splashed ashore or were carried by the ferrymen to begin their tour of the sacred island. I watched the CalMac ferry leave the jetty only a few hundred yards to the north. I decided I would leave on the next sailing, but I would use the waiting time to think – to consider how the spirits of this place might have affected me.

And then, time seemed to collapse on itself. As I typed these lines in my office, several weeks after returning home from Iona, I heard the post van trundle down the track to our farm. As always, the postie put the letters, parcels and endless editions of mail order catalogues on the driver's seat of my pickup. Parked near where I work, it was a handy place to collect the post on one of my too-frequent journeys to the farmhouse to make tea. One letter was a rarity. It had a handwritten address on it, and when I opened it I found something breath catching, unexpected, fascinating and timely in every possible sense.

In 2019, an account of a journey I made to Lindisfarne was published. It was not only about St Cuthbert but also something much more personal, a meditation on life and loss, especially the loss of my granddaughter, the wee one whose candle had burned in St Oran's Chapel. The letter was from a reader, Father John F. Doran, a Catholic missionary recently returned to Scotland from South Africa. What he wrote moved me to tears. Father Doran asked:

> Have you heard of Chairos Time? Catholics call it Sacramental Time . . . too hard to attempt an explanation . . . but it is included in, but goes beyond ordinary time . . . Your relationship with Cuthbert, your granddaughter, and her life, then and now, and with God . . . and with death, exist, we believe, in the reality of Sacramental Time.
>
> Reply if you want. Don't worry if you'd rather not.
>
> I'm on my way to chapel now. I will pray for you, and your family and friends, living and dead, through the intercession of St Cuthbert.
>
> God bless
>
> John

Of course I wrote back to him immediately to thank him for his gentle kindnesses and especially his prayers. But I was also very grateful for his insights. He could not know – but perhaps he might suggest that God did – what I felt on the night and morning on the machair, but his introduction of the notion of *chairos*, of sacramental time, more than resonated. Perhaps the atmosphere on Columba's island had at last worked on me.

In classical Greek, there were two ways of thinking about time. *Chronos* was sequential time – the progression of the days and months of the calendar. *Chairos* meant something like 'a moment' – 'a good time for action'. In modern Greek, it means 'weather'. In the New Testament, *chairos* developed the meaning of 'the appointed time in the purpose of God' and that, I think, is how Father Doran was using it. In the Gospel of St John, Christ talked about *chairos* as the moment when He decided to go to Jerusalem to meet His terrible fate and He made a distinction between that and *chronos*, saying that His disciples could go to the holy city at any time.

What I found difficult, almost mystical, was the way in which these different understandings of time had worked on my thinking, such as it was. As I sat at my desk typing what you have just read, wrestling with my inability to make sense of what I had experienced on Iona, an unsolicited, unexpected letter arrived – at that precise moment – that unlocked the logjam. In a secular sense, what I had felt on the machair was perhaps a series of moments of *chairos*, of sacramental time when the *chronos* of the turning world slowed or may have stopped. Father John would no doubt smile at this groping for understanding, believing that God's hand had placed his letter in mine at that precise time – and that that was explanation enough.

Perhaps I am making too much of this, but all my instincts were fully alert to the possibility that there is such a thing as fate. In Scotland there exists a weary phrase that recognises this: 'What's for you won't go by you.' I recoil from that sort of folksy wisdom but can only fall back on something even less substantial. I was simply lucky to have written a book that touched Father Doran and that triggered his letter and, because these notions are of great interest to me, his thinking and belief had a great impact.

I suspect George MacLeod would have made much of my hesitation in accepting that the world could be mystical in the way that it moved, but perhaps my experience and Father Doran's gloss on another like it might lead to a simpler conclusion. Iona is not only a thin place, it can sometimes make time stop.

On the ferry crossing, I watched the island recede, the evening sun slanting on the abbey and Baile Mor.

PART FIVE

INTO EDEN

Applecross

17

The Red Priest

The distribution of a particular place-name charts the extraordinary reach of the early Irish white martyrs. Cognate to *papa* for father and linked to the modern usage of pope, *papars* was how these far-travelled men were known amongst the islands of the North Atlantic. Putting all of their faith in God's mercy and providence, the papars were extraordinarily intrepid, as much explorers as seekers after solitude in the desert wastes of the ocean. Geography traces their progress northwards from Ireland's shores.

In the little archipelago south of Barra lies Pabbay (Pabaidh), likely the site of a rocky diseart that looked west to the vastness of the Atlantic, where the length of fetch could build mountainous waves to crash on its shore. Off Harris is another Pabaidh, and Pabail on the Point Peninsula on the eastern shore of Lewis also remembers where these men dragged their seagoing curraghs above the high tide line. On Orkney, Papa Stronsay and the most northerly island in the archipelago, Papa Westray, were both settled by white martyrs but their next leap of faith was truly remarkable.

Perhaps from Papa Stour, off the mainland of Shetland, their faith launched them into the unknown, into the endless horizons of the ocean, out of sight of land but, as they prayed for His help, always in the sight of God. Somehow, perhaps by reading the run of the currents of the Atlantic or watching the flight of birds, the papars made landfall on the Faroe Islands and the place-names of Paparokur and Vestmanna mark this amazing feat of navigation on the map. Vestmanna was the place of 'the Westmen', those who came from Ireland. By no means all of these voyages succeeded. Some became true martyrs as their curraghs were swamped by the storms of the mighty Atlantic, others died of thirst as their boats drifted, becalmed, lost.

When Norsemen began to colonise Iceland after the 870s, they found that they had not sailed into virgin territory. Early medieval Icelandic sources are rich and detailed, and they speak of Irish monks on the offshore island of Papey and at Vestmannaejyar, the Islands of the Westmen. As the monks fled from the pagan invaders, they were said to have left behind books, bells and crosiers. If accurate, these details describe an established community of some richness. It may be that once found by the white martyrs, Iceland became a holy island, cultivated, visited and perhaps understood as God's country.

Of the many white martyrs who sailed their curraghs from the Irish coast, only Columba was more venerated than Maelrubha – yet no life of him survives. In place-names, there are forty, often wildly different versions of his name and yet it has been almost entirely forgotten. The circumstances and the place of his death are disputed. There are no relics and there is consequently no shrine. And his vital role in the history of the Christian conversion of northern Scotland has been largely ignored. But the landscape remembers Maelrubha, sometimes spectacularly. Over a wide swathe of the Highlands and the Moray coastlands, there are thirty dedications to the memory of his great sanctity.

Maelrubha's name is thought to translate approximately as 'the Red Priest', a name that is commemorated in one of the most distant and well disguised of his dedications. In Crail Castle on the Fife coast, there was a chapel of St Rufus, Latin for 'red'. Those who knew Maelrubha, who listened to him preach and the generations who followed, believed that he was touched by God's hand. That belief persisted across centuries, and off the shores of perhaps his most glorious memorial on Scotland's map, Loch Maree, the loch of Maelrubha, there is a small island, a diseart where the saint's power lingered for a very long time, mingled with memories of the pagan past.

In 1772 the Welsh traveller and diarist Thomas Pennant came to the edge of Loch Maree and boarded 'a six-oared boat at the east end'. Pennant often did good preliminary research, making a point of speaking to local people and recording what they told him, but, in the western Highlands, he needed an interpreter. Many Gaelic speakers were still monoglots in the eighteenth century but, undaunted, Pennant found someone with a little English and before he chartered his boat he had discovered something about the history of his destination.

Landed on that [island] called Inchmaree, the favoured isle of the saint [Maelrubha], the patron of all the coast from Applecross to Loch Broom. The shores are neat and gravelly; the whole surface covered thickly with a beautiful grove of oak, ash, willow, wicken [rowan], birch, fir, hazel and enormous hollies. In the midst of it is a circular dike of stones, with a regular narrow entrance: the inner part has been used for ages as a burial place, and is still in use. I suspect the dike to have been originally Druidical, and that the ancient superstition of Paganism had been taken up by the saint, as the readiest method of making a conquest over the minds of the inhabitants. A stump of a tree is shown as an altar, probably the memorial of one of stone; but the curiosity of the place is the well of the saint; of power unspeakable in cases of lunacy. The patient is brought into the sacred island, is made to kneel before the altar, where his attendances leave an offering in money: he is then brought to the well, and sips some of the holy water: a second offering is made; that done, he is thrice dipped in the lake; and the same operation is repeated every day for some weeks: and it often happens, by natural causes, the patient receives relief, of which the saint receives the credit. I must add that the visitants draw from the state of the well an omen of the disposition of St Maree: if his well is full, they suppose he will be propitious; if not, they proceed in their operations with fears and doubts: but let the event be what it will, he is held in high esteem: the common oath of the country is, by his name: if a traveller passes by any of his resting-places, they never neglect to leave an offering; but the saint is so moderate as not to put him to any expense: a stone, a stick, a bit of rag contents him.

More than a thousand years since Maelrubha died, he was still routinely and regularly – and economically – venerated. Archaeologists believe that during the saint's lifetime an oratory was built on the little island, suggesting it was indeed seen as a diseart, but recent research has confirmed that the well has run dry. Perhaps that is more than a metaphor for changing times and beliefs. The passage from Pennant confirms a second observation. In their attempts to wean communities from paganism to Christianity, saints not only took over pre-existing pagan sites but also often took the place of local gods. Little is known about the pantheon of Celtic deities, except that there were many of them. The names of about four hundred have been recognised. Such quantity strongly suggests that certain places had spirits particular to them, and that around the shores of Loch Maree Maelrubha had become one of them. He probably died in 722, but more than a millennium later local people still swore by him and left little offerings at his 'resting-places'. And not only on the shores of Loch Maree or in Applecross. In his *Celtic Place-Names of Scotland*, W. J. Watson wrote that the Rev. Malcolm MacLean, the minister at Clachan Church in Applecross, had told him that on the Isle of Harris it was common to swear an oath by *Ma Ruibhe*.

More solid evidence of the worship of Maelrubha survives in the records of the Presbytery of Dingwall. In 1678, Hector MacKenzie was cited because he took his sons and grandsons to Eilean Ma Ruibhe, an alternative name for Inchmaree, an island in Loch Maree, in order to enact what was clearly a pagan ritual a thousand years and more after the coming of Christianity to the Western Highlands. No doubt with some difficulty, probably by hobbling its legs, the Mackenzie men manhandled a bull into a boat and rowed across to the island. There, 'in ane heathenish manner . . . for the sake of his wife, Cirstane's, health', Hector and his sons and grandsons sacrificed the poor creature. As the blood gushed from the poleaxed animal's neck and spattered the sacred ground, they dedicated its death to 'the god, Mourie'. Yet another version of Maelrubha, this remarkable conflation of pagan and Christian, mortal man and god, shows not only the ancestral legacy of his ministry but it was probably an exceptional record of a more common practice. More sacrifices were almost certainly made to Mourie than were ever reported. These saints were probably revered for many centuries to the point of outright worship rather than being seen as holy men who might intercede with a higher God. Or perhaps both versions of their roles were simultaneously maintained.

Adomnán was writing his *Life of Columba* at precisely the same time as Maelrubha's ministry was developing not far to the north of Iona. News as well as people travelled the sea roads of the Hebrides and the Abbot of Iona will undoubtedly have had detailed knowledge of the foundation at Applecross on the mainland opposite Skye and the other activities of its community and its leader. It must be the case that he simply chose to make no mention of the work of Maelrubha so that there was no possibility that his achievements might distract from Columba's. Saints and the promoters of their cults competed constantly with each other and, in this case, Iona succeeded in writing almost all others out of history.

In his unsurpassed *Warlords and Holy Men: Scotland AD 80–1000*, Alfred Smyth elegantly summed up the reasons the reputations and achievements of saints such as Maelrubha and Donnan (of whom more later) have faded.

The reason we know so little about Donnan and Maelrubai is that, unlike Columba, they did not earn the official patronage and esteem of that particular Dal Riata dynasty from whom later kings of medieval Scotland claimed descent; and unlike Columba, they never found anyone of Adomnán's stature to write up their lives of toil among the Picts. The outcome of the Viking invasions also had an effect on the development of saints' cults in Scotland for while the ecclesiastical inheritance of men like Donnan and

Maelrubai sustained a shattering blow in the exposed north, Iona
managed to preserve its organisation by the prudent evacuation of
the island by most of its monks in the early ninth century.

Despite Adomnán's wilful blindness, there is no doubt that
Maelrubha succeeded in Pictland where Columba had failed a
century before, as Smyth convincingly argued. Not only was his
influence profound in Applecross, around Loch Broom, Torridon
and Gairloch, it reached far eastwards to Dingwall, Lairg in
Sutherland, Keith in Banffshire and as far south as Perthshire and
Fife. In his *Celtic Place-Names of Scotland*, W.J. Watson made a
determined effort at redressing the historical balance, hailing
Maelrubha as 'next to Colum Cille the most famous saint of the
Scoto-Irish' – not now but in the seventh and eighth centuries.
Watson lists many dedications and place-names that are formed
from versions or elements of the saint's name. Just as with Moluag,
several annual fairs and markets were dedicated to Maelrubha:
Summareve Fair is a lyrical rendition of the name and it is held in
Keith; Feill Ma-Ruibhe in Contin in Strathpeffer was another linked
to him; and Amulree, from Ath Maol Ruibhe, 'the Ford of
Maelrubha', near Dunkeld in Perthshire, saw two fairs established in
his name. There is no St Columba's fair anywhere.

The Irish annalists thought that Maelrubha was important and
took trouble to record the outlines of this holy man's life. It seems
that he too was of noble Irish ancestry, perhaps born either in 640 or
641 near Derry, like Columba. He took holy orders at the monastery of St Comgall at Bangor. In 671, as a mature monk, he decided
to seek white martyrdom in the Hebrides. With a group of like-
minded companions, he launched curraghs to sail north and bring
the Word of God to the heathens. They first spent two years in the
southern Hebrides, when they must have had contact with Iona.
Failbe was abbot but Adomnán probably held some sort of senior
position, for he succeeded him in 679. At that time, Maelrubha may
have founded communities at Arisaig, Kilmelford and perhaps on
Skye. In 673, he came at last to Applecross and made it the centre of

his *paruchia*, a wide parish of chapels and communities founded by the saint and linked by sea. My research told me that, like Moluag's on Lismore, almost nothing remained of the seventh-century monastery, but the place where he settled and its atmosphere might tell me something – might add to the bare bones of the story of this man whom God loved, who glimpsed angels and who seemed also to slip seamlessly into the pagan pantheon.

18

Beyond the Pass of the Cattle

From landlocked Selkirk, not far from the English border, Applecross and the Atlantic shore lie at the other end of Scotland, almost as far away as London. Apart from a helicopter, the only practical way to reach it is by car. I waited and waited for the Met Office to forecast a period of dry and settled weather. I found myself diffident about the prospect of driving three hundred or so miles to wander around a damp landscape or even be drenched by the Atlantic storms that had soaked the early part of September. It was not until the end of that month that a window on the west seemed to open. Fortunate to find a self-catering cottage on the Applecross shore, I set off in darkness on a Monday morning at 5 a.m., anxious to avoid the congestion of the Edinburgh bypass and the commuters of the Central Belt and its cities.

When planning these journeys back into the past, often to remote places, I tend to treat them like expeditions and take far too much stuff. I seem constantly to forget that Scotland and the Highlands are far more connected than they used to be – even if the phone signal is often patchy. All that I really need is a map, a notebook and pen, a camera and a change of clothing, all of which could comfortably be packed into a rucksack. But, instead, I manically duplicate everything, even taking two phones, and my principal comfort luggage is books I feel I will possibly, maybe need. Perhaps to check a reference here, a footnote there, an explanation of a place-name, some background, I pack a small library. I take both of my Gaelic dictionaries – Dwelly and the shorter, handier, quick-reference Malcolm McLennan. But, in fact, I never look at any of them. My copies of Adomnán, Bede, Watson, Smyth or Hamish Haswell-Smith's *The Scottish Islands* all remained unopened on previous expeditions. I suppose I just feel better knowing they are there, lying quiet, undisturbed in boxes in the boot of my car.

By the time I reached the Forth and the glorious, elegant, almost otherworldly new road bridge, the sun was striking the tops of its impossibly tall piers. And, by Perth, I could see only a scatter of high white clouds over the heads of the mountains. It was turning out to be a beautiful morning. I would reach the Atlantic coast in no time at all. Online research had confirmed that a route almost due north from Selkirk to Inverness and then cutting across country to Lochcarron was more than an hour faster than the road through Fort William and by Glen Sheil and Loch Duich.

It was not. Immediately beyond Perth, the A9 was slowed dramatically by a series of convoy road works that seemed to occur at regular intervals until just south of Inverness. By the time I reached the Highland capital, more than an hour later than I had estimated, I was wishing it had been Fort William. And that is a sentence I never imagined I would write.

But the weather was good and the windless afternoon suggested that the Met Office forecast of a fine few days might hold. After a brief walk around the anonymous, shopping mall mess that central Inverness has become, I drove across the Kessock Bridge and the road immediately began to open, traffic thinning dramatically. By the time I turned due west at Garve and into the soft landscapes of Strath Ban, a series of long, empty straights improved my flustered mood and soon I caught glimpses of the shores of Loch Carron and the houses of its pretty little shoreline village, surely one of the longest streets in Scotland. The narrows at Strome Ferry – where famously there is no ferry – give the mistaken impression that it is not a sea loch. Immediately beyond Lochcarron village, the road became single track and climbed into the mountains. A road sign told me I had only eighteen miles to go before reaching Applecross and, before me, the mountains were rising. The rounded hump of Meall Gorm, 'the Blue Lump', reared up in the distance.

Just as the drama of this landscape was beginning to work its magic, an alarm started to ping on the dashboard. Front Left Tyre Losing Pressure. Great. Even though parking there is forbidden, I had no option but to pull into a passing place. No phone signal. So, no AA. Double great. The tyre looked OK – in the sense that it was not flat. I kicked it a few times and then kicked the other three. It seemed no softer or harder than they were. Then I remembered that the car came with a tyre inflator, one that plugged into the cigarette lighter – a strange anachronism. I hooked it all up and pressed start. It showed a PSI (?) of 3.0, vibrated for a bit and then switched off automatically. Was that good? Did that mean the tyre was back at the right pressure? I searched the manual with the words of my younger daughter ringing in my ears – 'RTFM, DAD! READ THE F****** MANUAL!' – for a table that would show the correct tyre pressures but could not find one. A car passed and tooted its horn. Perhaps he thought I had stopped in a passing place to catch up with my reading. There was also no table attached to the door pillars, something I had noticed in a previous car. So, I had no option but to start the engine. No hazard indicators came on. And so I drove on. Computers.

Loch Kishorn came into view, and on the far shore I could see the monumental remains of some industrial archaeology. Because the loch has a clear depth of eighty fathoms, Kishorn was thought to be a good place to build exploration platforms for the North Sea oil fields. A huge fabrication yard was constructed in the 1970s and, at its peak, employed about three thousand people. At first, many were accommodated in two converted car ferries moored in the loch and then a temporary village was built for two thousand workers. Supplied by sea and not by road – hence the reason I was on a single track – the yard flourished for a few years. The Ninian Central Platform, a vast storage facility, designed like a concrete version of a huge medieval concentric castle, was at 600,000 tonnes the largest moving object ever built. It took seven tugs to tow it into position in the North Sea. But the yard boomed and then it bust. Various attempts were made and continue to be made at revival but, like all oil fields, the North Sea's output is finite and will carry on declining.

As I drew closer to the fabrication yard, it surprised me that it had not marked the landscape more dramatically. On what looked like an artificial peninsula, very much wider than a quay, several long white sheds had been built, but I could not make out any sign of the accommodation village. On the western side of the sheds, a ship was moored. There seemed to be activity of some kind.

After a mile or two on a good road and no more alarms, I saw the sign to turn left for Applecross. Looking up at Meall Gorm, it seemed as though I was about to drive over the top of a mountain. The Bealach na Ba, 'the Pass of the Cattle', is, I discovered, the steepest road in Britain, rising very quickly more than two thousand feet from sea level to its highest point. And the signs were not encouraging. As I crossed a bridge over the headwaters of Loch Kishorn, a sign warned 'ROAD NORMALLY IMPASSABLE IN WINTRY CONDITIONS'. OK. As I was shortly to learn, the sign could have safely omitted the last three words and been accurate on that particular afternoon.

At first the road climbed diagonally up the flanks of the foothills below Beinn Bhan, 'the White Mountain', and the views to the south over Loch Kishorn quickly became spectacular and even more dramatic as the Bealach gained altitude. I stopped often to take photographs, both of the views and the road, thinking about how many involuntary stops I had made that day. Would I ever get to Applecross? I had only ever seen roads like this in the Italian Alps.

Then the cattle trail began to fray badly. The edges of several passing places had crumbled to loose gravel and beyond them there was no barrier above steep slopes that could be forty-five degrees for long stretches. When a motor home rounded a corner, going far too fast, its wing mirror clipped mine with a sharp crack as I quickly pulled into a passing place that more resembled a decaying windowsill.

Looking back, I could see how steeply I had climbed, but what seemed to be the really difficult section lay ahead, further up the neck of the narrowing pass. Mercifully there were steel barriers around a series of hairpin bends but, even so, I negotiated them very slowly and carefully as we climbed up to the summit of the Bealach. Too slow for some. Coming in the other direction around a sharp bend was something completely unexpected. A blue, open-top Ferrari was travelling far too fast on this switchback road and, as the sunglasses-wearing driver approached the corner where I had pulled over, he honked his horn and irritably waved his hand in a pushing motion, as though asking me to move aside. Aside to where? Shaking his head, the driver slowed and passed me with exaggerated care. I expect he wanted to gun his rumbling engine and take the bend faster to impress the lady sitting next to him. But a Ferrari! I thought they were all red.

By the time I reached the summit plateau, I had manoeuvred my way past at least twenty other vehicles in a four- or five-mile stretch of what is the most dangerously and dramatically beautiful road I have ever driven. In several places, the drop on either side of the single track is near sheer but there are few barriers. Driving in a high wind must be very challenging. What surprised me was that no one seemed to stop to look at the stunning vistas. It seemed to be the business of driving that mattered.

On the plateau there is a small car park. I got out to stretch my legs, arch my aching back and loosen my brain. I had been driving for more than seven hours and done more than three hundred miles. But it had been worthwhile for the few moments that followed. Across a small lochan and the ridge beyond it was a landscape of epic, breath-catching beauty. Across the Inner Sound and the low island of Raasay, lay the Cuillin Ridge on Skye. From Bla Bheinn ran Sgurr nan Eag, Sgurr Alasdair, Marsco, Sgurr nan Gillean down to Roineval and Arnaval. I have been to Sleat, the southern wing of Skye, many times to visit my friends at Sabhal Mor Ostaig, the Gaelic-medium college, and seen the mighty Cuillin from the south. But I had never seen that astonishing, jagged ridge from the north. And that was only a beginning. More glory waited.

It was late afternoon and the sun was beginning to dip down over the western ocean. When I began to drive over what remained of the summit plateau, I saw a figure walking in the distance, by the side of the road. It was a woman dressed in a bright yellow waterproof and wearing a colourful bobble hat. She walked in a pair of trainers. Thinking that she had parked her car a little way off. I drew alongside and asked if she wanted a lift. 'No, no thanks – I'm enjoying the day.'

Moments later, I stopped again. Below me, at last, lay Applecross. Around a wide, horned bay there was dense woodland and beyond it what I knew to be the small settlement at Clachan, the ancient site of Maelrubha's monastery. It seemed that I was looking down on it not from a steep mountainside but from the heavens. In the still brilliant sunshine, I could make out a white church and its manse to one side. After more hairpin bends, I came down to the shoreline and parked my car. Common sense told me to find the cottage where I was staying and dump my stuff but every instinct prompted me to walk through this glorious land, this Edenic place. From the village by the shore, I made my way slowly around the bay to the little church and my head quickly filled with its singular beauty and intimate detail.

For many decades, after a visit as a schoolboy and many returns, I had thought that the road that winds from Arisaig to Morar and passes the white sands at Camusdarroch ran through the most sublime landscape in the western Highlands. But on that first evening, Applecross seemed to me to surpass it. In the stillness of a gentle early autumn day, when the sea barely rippled and the vistas stretched to the rampart of the Cuillin, I sensed myself in an oasis of peace. *Bealach* means 'a pass' but also has the alternative gloss of 'a gate', one that seemed to me to have opened. On that sunlit evening, it seemed to me that the road from Hell had led me to Paradise.

On my way back to my car, I was astonished to meet the lady I had offered a lift to. She told me that she had walked alone from Loch Kishorn all the way over the Bealach to Applecross.

'Do you live here?'

She shook her head.

'But how will you get home?'

She smiled beatifically, turned and walked towards Clachan and the place where Maelrubha had built his monastery. I never saw her again and all the time I was in Applecross I could not shake the perfectly absurd notion that I had met an angel.

19

The Language of Miracles

Leaving my box of reference books in the car, as usual, I shouldered my rucksack, picked up my bag and pushed open the little wicket gate into the tiny garden of the cottage I had rented. Suddenly ravenous, having had nothing since a sandwich in Inverness, and anxious that the Applecross Inn might have stopped serving supper, I dumped my bags in the kitchen and left without looking around. The bar-restaurant was very busy and, although it was late, the lovely, welcoming lady who seemed to be in charge said they could feed me. The langoustines were perfect, and I filled up with a sticky toffee pudding. When I was young, a walk after supper in the summer months was a tradition and I was glad to revive it, even if only for twenty minutes.

Once I had worked out where everything was in the small, snug, wood-panelled cottage, I sat down at a table by a window to make some notes. But the view over the Inner Sound to Raasay and the Cuillin beyond distracted, captivated me. There was still enough light in the western sky to shimmer off the sea and backlight the ridge and the low hills of the island below it. Finding some candles in a kitchen drawer, I lit several not only to shed a more kindly light but also to allow me to switch off the overhead electric bulb. That dulled the reflections on the windowpanes and made the view across the water more graphic.

One very small book that did make it into the cottage was *Highlands & Islands: Poetry of Place*, a collection of poems edited by Mary Miers. From Walter Scott to Norman MacCaig, it is a delightful, judiciously selected anthology. I found Sorley MacLean's

'Hallaig', about a township that withered and became deserted after the Highland Clearances of the mid nineteenth century. What I love about this poem is how it understands the landscape and its people, the one indivisible from the other, the stands of trees memories in themselves, the deer a metaphor for time. The cruelties of the Clearances may have emptied the townships and their crofts of their people but not of their meaning. And that evening, through the twilight, I could see Raasay and imagine ghosts whispering around the ruins of Hallaig. Here is Sorley MacLean's translation of the opening verses of the original Gaelic:

> 'Time, the deer, is in the wood of Hallaig'
>
> The window is nailed and boarded
> through which I saw the West
> and my love is at the Burn of Hallaig,
> a birch tree, and she has always been
>
> between Inver and Milk Hollow,
> here and there about the Baile-chuirn:
> she is a birch, a hazel,
> a straight, slender young rowan.
>
> In Screapadal of my people
> where Norman and Big Hector were,
> their daughters and their sons are a wood
> going up beside the stream.

As I sat in the glow of the candlelight, looking over the Inner Sound, the rounded shape of Dun Cana faded as the dimness came on the kyles and the sky at last grew darker.

Sadness is inescapable in the Highlands and Islands – a sense of regret and departure is everywhere. The emptied landscape may seem picturesque and even majestic to us now, but, before a brutal aristocracy, some plutocrats and their agents profoundly altered it by removing its people, it was animated, working, sustaining families and communities. As crofters and herdsmen fought the Atlantic weather, the months of rain and storm, they endured a harsh life, but the beauty of their places – the gentleness of the birch trees riffling in the breeze by the burn and the soaring grandeur of the high mountains – these were images printed on their souls. And when they left – many at first herded down their glens to the barren fields of the ocean and seashore – they experienced a hollowing spiritual loss. And when thousands boarded the emigrant ships, some dragged to the quaysides against their will, and the white sails slipped over the Atlantic horizon, bound for Canada and America and a life they could not imagine, a part of their hearts died. In Gaelic, this loss is known as *ionndrainn* and it means something like 'a missing piece', much more than mere homesickness.

'Hallaig' is in some ways a dream poem – a dream of the past that draws its power from loss and an imagined continuity. The township was cleared of its people, Sorley MacLean's people, in the summer of 1854 and a community that included sixty children was evicted on the orders of George Rainy. A slave owner who made his fortune from the sugar plantations of Demerara in Guyana, he was awarded the vast sum of £50,000 in compensation after the passing of the Emancipation Act in 1833. In today's values, Rainy received £5.5 million for the loss of a thousand slaves. He used the money the government gave him to buy the island of Raasay and began to treat its people like the slaves he had lost in Guyana. Ruling by fear, like a despot, he decided to convert as much of the island as possible into profitable sheep runs. Here is the testimony that Donald MacLeod, a seventy-eight-year-old crofter, gave to the Napier Commission, set up in 1883 to reform the law around land ownership and landholding. He was asked what became of the people who were evicted from Raasay:

They went to other kingdoms – some to America, some to Australia, and other places that they could think of. Mr Rainy enacted a rule that no-one should marry on the island. There was one man there who married in spite of him, and because he did so, he put him out of his father's house, and that man went to a bothy – to a sheep cot. Mr Rainy then came and demolished the sheep cot upon him, and extinguished his fire, and neither friend nor anyone else dared give him a night's shelter. He was not allowed entrance into any house.

Rainy's shocking terrorising of his tenants was extreme but not unusual. The Clearances not only reduced a working landscape to barren scenery, they also continued the destruction of a fragile culture and its language. Gaelic had been brought to Argyll from Ireland by the Dalriadan colonists and their kings and its spread further north was spearheaded by white martyrs such as Brendan, Moluag, Columba and Maelrubha as they rowed their curraghs deep into Western Pictland, moved up the Great Glen and brought the Word of God to the North Sea coastlands. When Maelrubha and his companions came to Applecross in 673, they entered a world that almost certainly understood itself in Pictish. As speakers of seventh-century Irish Gaelic, they may have grasped the basics of the native language sufficiently well to communicate but, over time, Gaelic supplanted Pictish to the point of extinction and it came to describe the landscape we see on the Ordnance Survey and that fired the imagination of Sorley MacLean. Its lexicon and usage are firmly planted in the natural world. Never developing into an urban language or much used in commerce, Gaelic is at its most powerful, precise and lyrical when it articulates the rhythms of the seasons, the changing land and ocean, the animals and plants. Trees are more than metaphor in 'Hallaig' and their lore and characteristics form part of the core of *Canan Mor nan Gaidheal*, 'Precious language of the Gael'.

When English-speaking children recite the alphabet, they attach words to each one – A is for apple, B is for ball, C is for cat and so on. In the Gaelic orthography, there are only eighteen letters compared to the twenty-six of English. J, K, Q, V, W, X, Y, Z are absent from the Gaelic alphabet and when children recite it they name the trees of the woods. Here it is:

A is for *Ailm* or Elm
B is for *Beith* or Birch
C is for *Coll* or Hazel
D is for *Dair* or Oak
E is for *Eadha* or Aspen
F is for *Feàrn* or Alder
G is for *Gort* or Ivy
H is for *Uath* or Hawthorn
I is for *Iogh* or Yew
L is for *Luis* or Rowan
M is for *Muin* or Vine
N is for *Nuin* or Ash
O is for *Onn* or Gorse
P is for *Peith bhog* or Downy Birch
R is for *Ruis* or Elder
S is for *Suil* or Willow
T is for *Teine* or Furze
U is for *Ur* also Heather

Gaelic speakers also invented a tree alphabet. Ogham was written with a series of blade-like runes, but its straight-cut lines were arranged like the branches of a tree on either side or through the trunk. Arising in the fourth century in Ireland and spreading to the west of Britain, it was probably used as a means of marking boundaries and asserting ownership of land. Ogham inscriptions were carved on trees but those that survive were, of course, cut in stone. In an old medieval deer park that forms part of our farm, I found the broken top of an Ogham stone and the letters A and H look as though they were inscribed on it. It is now in the National Museum of Scotland in Edinburgh.

So little remains of these Irish saints and their missions that Gaelic has become a vital link, a linguistic thread that can lead us back into the blindness and darkness of the past. Maelrubha and his monks may have prayed and sung psalms in Latin, but they described Creation to each other in Gaelic. But that ancient habit, that link, will soon be severed.

After the calculations on the last census in 2011 had been completed, it turned out that the decline in the number of Gaelic speakers had slowed. In 2001, 59,000 people described themselves as speakers and that had dropped to 58,000 ten years later. But a very recent report has shown that in the last decade the size of the native speech community has plummeted. The heartlands of the Western Isles, Skye and Tiree now have only 11,000 who use Gaelic regularly, perhaps even as a first language. Formerly an important stronghold, Skye has now only one parish where the majority have Gaelic. It is most predominant in Barvas on the Isle of Lewis, where 64 per cent or 2,037 people can speak the language. In essence, Gaelic is dying fast as the numbers who live their lives in it are shrinking dramatically.

Increasing numbers of learners like myself may stave off extinction but our first language will always be English. We live our lives in English, think in English and constantly develop and change the ways in which we use it. If the native speech community disappears, then no one will think in Gaelic and its vitality will drain away, regional variations and dialects will no longer be used and may indeed be forgotten. Rather than being a living language, Gaelic will become an accomplishment.

This means that a historical circle will soon close. Maelrubha and the other saints brought a language and new way of understanding the world to northern and western Scotland more than a thousand years ago. The window will soon be nailed and boarded through which we can see the west.

The most resonant memory of Maelrubha is not a life or even a set of inscriptions or any objects associated with him, like Moluag's staff. It is hidden inside the Gaelic language. It is a tradition of healing, one that endured long enough to persuade Hector MacKenzie to sacrifice a bull on Maelrubha's diseart in Loch Maree. Embedded in the language are similarly long memories of the power of these early saints to effect cures for those who were sick, and the ways in which they absorbed existing pagan beliefs.

In the sixteenth and seventeenth centuries, Scotland was burning witches. Following the Reformation of the 1560s and the creation of what was known as 'the Godly Commonwealth', a spasm of obscene cruelty seized society. In order to purge evil from this new commonwealth, many women and some men were accused, tortured and burned at the stake, some of them while they were still alive. Many of the accused were traditional healers, women who could make herbal remedies for the pains of childbirth, persistent headaches and many other sorts of ailments. It was thought that they practised magic and were in league with the Devil. As a consequence of these appalling persecutions, an entire *materia medica* derived from plants and the natural world disappeared – but not in the Highlands and Islands. For reasons of geography, remoteness and language, the witch finders never penetrated the Gaidhealtachd to any great degree and, as a result, men like Hector Mackenzie continued to rely on ancient methods. And they appeared to work. In another version of the same story, his wife, Cirstane, was described as 'formerlie sick and valetudinairie'.

Eilean Ma Ruibhe became well known as an island of healing. Rituals conducted at the saint's well were a curious confection of Christian and pagan. Prayers were said but libations of milk also poured around the afflicted. When bulls were slaughtered, their meat was given to a group of mendicants called *deirbhleinan Ma Ruibhe*. It translates approximately as 'the lame and the broken of Maelrubha', meaning that they were people who were disabled in some way and under his protection. The sources for this tradition are unclear but the involvement of mendicants suggests that sacrificed meat was given to them before the Reformation, before monastic orders were abolished. Around the holy well, bushes were hung with strips of cloth, a phenomenon still seen in many parts of Britain. Coins were jammed into the bark of an old oak that stood nearby. When she visited the island in the late nineteenth century, Queen Victoria followed the old tradition, not concerned that her likeness was on the sixpence or shilling she used.

Epileptics were rowed across Loch Maree and made to drink well water from the skull of a suicide. Success rates were not reported, but by the early nineteenth century there seems to have been a decline. Sometime before 1850, a pupil in the school at Ullapool suffered some sort of serious breakdown. According to Rutherford Macphail, a member of the Caledonian Medical Society:

> His friends took him away to the famous island with its well of virtues in Loch Maree. He was put into the well, and afterwards tied with a rope from the boat and towed round the island three times, but all to no purpose, for he [Macphail's father] says he can remember vividly the boys waiting on the shore for the return of the boat, expecting to find their schoolfellow all right, but there he was, bound hand and foot, and still a raving maniac.

After treatment like that, they can hardly have been surprised.

Missionaries such as Maelrubha were faced with a dilemma. In order for Christianity to displace paganism, it had to offer more, and while the relative coherence of the New Testament stories may have been attractive, it was not enough. And so the saints were not above accepting pagan beliefs and rebranding them as God-given or at least God-endorsed. And so many rituals, cures and even sacrifices were blessed and even encouraged. The Gaelic language of Maelrubha and the other saints absorbed some pagan terminology and, in one example, one word, a considerable breadth of belief is wrapped up. *Deiseal* literally means 'southwards'. It came to mean 'sunwise', that is, 'moving in the same direction as the sun', and later it acquired the gloss of 'prosperous or correct or ready'. Before Gaelic speakers leave the house, one might ask the other, '*A bheil thu deiseal?*' – 'Are you ready?' In 1703, Martin Martin, a Gaelic speaker, published *A Description of the Western Isles of Scotland* and described what he had seen.

> Some of the poorer sort of people in the Western Isles retain the custom of performing these circles sunwise about the persons of their benefactors three times, when they bless them, and wish good success to all their enterprises. Some are very careful when they set out to sea, that the boat be first rowed sunwise, and if this

be neglected, they are afraid their voyage may prove unfortunate. I had this ceremony paid me when in Islay by a poor woman, after I had given her an alms. I asked her to let alone that compliment, for that I did not care for it; but she insisted to make these three ordinary turns, and then prayed that God and MacCharmaig, the patron saint of the island, might bless and prosper me in all my affairs. When a Gael goes to drink out of a consecrated fountain, he approaches it by going round the place from east to west, and at funerals, the procession observes the same direction in drawing near the grave. Hence also is derived the old custom of describing sunwise a circle, with a burning brand, about houses, cattle, corn and corn-fields, to prevent their being burnt or in any way injured by evil spirits, or by witchcraft. The fiery circle was also made around women, as soon as possible after parturition, and also around newly-born babes.

The incidental reference to MacCharmaig is eloquent about how much of the legacy of the white martyrs has been lost. In 1703, the old lady who embarrassed Martin Martin by walking around him *deiseal* clearly knew of the life of this man more than a thousand years after he died. And Martin seems to have too, for he offered no explanation. MacCharmaig is almost certainly remembered on the map, for he seems to have given his name to the MacCormaig Isles, a scatter of small, rocky islets off the mainland at Knapdale in the Sound of Jura, close to Islay. There are some remains of a chapel that the Ordnance Survey dedicates to St Cormac and perhaps also a hermitage. Tradition recalls that the chapel at Keills on the mainland was also founded by Cormac or Carmaig. The place-name seems to be a corruption of *cille* for 'a cell' or 'a church'. This man was Irish and a white martyr who may have died in 625. But only the map now remembers him. And yet, like Maelrubha, his name was on the lips of ordinary people when they invoked spiritual help or needed a blessing.

The miracle cure was a stock-in-trade for saints, and Adomnán ascribed a few to Columba, but much more revealing is a very specific example. To deal with wounds and other ailments, the afflicted were sometimes given *achlasan Chaluim Cille*, literally, 'St Columba's armpitful'. This was a poultice made from St John's wort and other herbs mixed with butter and grease. It was placed in the armpit or the groin because that is where the skin is thinnest. It was the sixth century equivalent of an injection. The association with Columba comes from his cure of a disturbed young man. After the poultice was placed in his armpit, according to Adomnán, he gradually recovered himself. One of the constituents of St John's wort is rutin and it can affect the flow of adrenalin and the nervous system.

All of these echoes of respect and reverence for the early Irish saints suggest that, as Gaelic has declined, much of their legacy has been forgotten, leaving little more than a scatter of place-names, some dedications and dates. But just as the landscape had remembered Carmaig, Brendan and Moluag, perhaps Applecross would tell a hidden story of Maelrubha.

20

The Sanctuary

I woke to a pink dawn. As the sun climbed unseen behind, Meall Gorm and Beinn Bhan, the mountains to the east, it caught the serrated ridge of the Cuillin not with yellow but a delicate, pale pink light. Both Skye and the sky above it glowed. Pulling on a jumper and taking out a mug of tea, I sat down in the half-dark in the tiny garden in front of the cottage. On the drystane dyke, puffing out his red breast, a robin sang his autumn song and all that accompanied him was the lapping of the incoming morning tide. The bay is so sheltered that there were no waves – only gentle ripples. To sit and gaze, thoughtless, over Creation was a pure experience of unqualified, transcendent beauty.

The name of Applecross has nothing to do with apples even though, on that morning, it looked like the Garden of Eden. It comes from Apur Crossan. The latter is the little river that flows into the bay near the site of Maelrubha's monastery and the first element, according to Watson, means a confluence. In Gaelic and restored on many signs and booklets, I read that Applecross is known as A' Chomraich, 'the Sanctuary', perhaps a place of refuge. Watson adds the gloss of 'a girth', meaning the circumference of the monastic precinct where the unseen frontier between the spiritual and temporal girdled the land. He reckoned it extended for a radius of six miles and was marked with stone crosses. This is a huge area and if tradition reflects reality, the monks owned virtually all of the good land in Applecross. The girth extended north and south of the monastery along virtually the whole shoreline of the peninsula that faces Raasay and Skye. Almost all of the small townships would have been inside the bounds of the Sanctuary.

In a fascinating footnote, Watson added that the stump, or perhaps the socket, of one of the marker crosses could still be seen. Even though he had visited its location, he did not say where it was, except that the cross itself had been smashed by a mason in the early nineteenth century when the school in Applecross was being built. It was still standing in 1885 when Thomas Scott Muir recorded in his *Notes on Remains of Ecclesiastical Architecture* that there was a 'pillar, a rude monolith 8 foot 3 inches in height, showing traces of a cross on its west face'.

I decided to drive down to Camusterrach, where the modern school stands, to see if I could find the stump of the smashed cross, the southern perimeter of Maelrubha's Sanctuary. I would leave the car and walk back up the coast to its heart, the site of the seventh-century monastery at Clachan. When I parked at the post office that serves Applecross, at Camusteel, I asked about the location of a cross socket or a stump, but the otherwise helpful lady shook her head.

I spent a pleasant hour in the sunshine looking around the tidy little township at Camusterrach. The layout of the roads looked old, not made for cars but carts, people and ponies. On an uphill bend, the tarmac was so close to the gable end of a cottage that I was surprised to see no scuffs or damage to its white harling. My reasoning for following the roads and lanes was that a cross had to be placed where it could be seen by travellers. There was no one about to ask and so I climbed up to a higher road that ran parallel to the coast road so that I could get a better view of the second reason I had decided to begin my journey in the shadow of Maelrubha at Camusterrach.

Out in the bay lies the low island of Eilean an Naoimh. There is a story in what the Gaels know as *beul-aithris* – meaning something like 'mouth-history', the oral tradition – that the Saint's Isle was where Maelrubha and his companions first made landfall in Applecross. Small and sufficiently remote to have been a diseart, the place-name may commemorate a prudent beginning. Even though the Irish annalists are emphatic – *673 Mail Rubai fundavit Apor Croosan*, '673 Maelrubha founded Applecross' – it may have been a process rather than an event. He and his brethren had come to Pictland and most likely a part of the kingdom not visited by Moluag or Brendan – a place that had yet to hear the Word of God. Bridei map Beli had succeeded to the Pictish throne only a year before Maelrubha had sailed into his territory. The king was certainly a Christian, for Adomnán composed an elegy when he died in 693. And he had been a child of the Christian family that ruled Strathclyde from Alt Clut, Dumbarton Rock. The arrival of missionaries in the western regions of Pictland at the same time as Bridei took power in the north is unlikely to have been a coincidence. But royal patronage was probably a matter of diplomacy and therefore will have taken time. Someone owned the fertile fields of Applecross before 673, and if they were to be given to God and Maelrubha, then negotiation and compensation will have been needed.

Politics may have strengthened or even extended the monastery's control of its patrimony. In 664, at the Synod of Whitby, King Oswiu of Northumbria presided over a dispute. Northern and Irish churchmen had developed one formula for calculating the date of Easter and the bishoprics of the south, western Europe and the Mediterranean had adopted another. This disparity mattered for two reasons. Easter was the most important, pivotal festival in the Christian year and all the others in the calendar were dated from it. And so the disagreement meant that all of the dates of the festivals in Northumbria and in other kingdoms were not uniform. Lindisfarne might celebrate Christmas at one time, and York would celebrate it a few days later or earlier.

That was certainly inconvenient but most compelling was the matter of numbers. When Christians prayed at Easter, the time of Christ's Passion, they attempted to rally devotional troops against the forces of evil. In order to defeat and confound Satan, as many Christians as possible needed to pray together – at the same time. Two different dates for Easter divided the army of Christian soldiers and made them weaker in the face of the hosts of Hell.

Oswiu ruled in favour of the southern or Roman method of dating and, even though monasteries like Old Melrose and

In Search of Angels

Lindisfarne were originally founded by Aidan, a monk from Iona, they had to conform. Iona did not and it took some time for the Celtic Church to adjust. One of the other areas of disagreement resolved at Whitby was the monastic tonsure. Oswiu ruled that all churchmen, bishops, priests and monks should adopt the habit of shaving the crown of the head and leaving a fringe around the sides. This was done in imitation of Christ's crown of thorns. Celtic monks like Brendan, Moluag and Columba shaved across the crown of their heads, from ear to ear, giving themselves very high foreheads and leaving their hair long at the back. Some scholars believe that this was similar to the Druidical tonsure. It may be that at Bangor Maelrubha had his head shaved in this way, and when he began his ministry in Applecross he may have had a comforting resemblance to pagan priests. Change came slowly in the north and this probably made good sense in the fragile early years of conversion.

In 685 King Ecgfrith of Northumbria rode north with his Northumbrian cavalry to challenge Bridei. It seems likely that Pictland had been subservient to the Northumbrians, probably paying tribute. That may have ceased, and when Bridei led his warriors to Dun Nechtain near Forfar, he aimed to reassert his dominance. Instead, the Pictish infantry withstood and drove back the charging cavalry. Ecgfrith was killed and Northumbrian power shrank back south to between the Forth and Tweed valleys. Few battles are truly pivotal, but if the Pictish army had been overrun by the Anglian cavalry, what became Scotland might now be known as Northern England. As he re-established his control of Pictland north of the Forth, it may have suited Bridei to be supported by a Church that was different from Northumbria.

By granting so much land to the Church and having it consecrated as holy ground, Bridei – or a local lord acting with his approval – had not only stored up personal virtue but had also been politically astute. Since 313 and the promulgation of Constantine's imperial edict that made Christianity the state religion, it had been associated with power. And in the minds of monarchs in Western

Europe, there had been no greater power than Rome. A tide of conversion was washing over northern and western Scotland and rulers sought legitimacy by being closely associated with Christianity. According to Adomnán, Columba was commanded by God and his angels to ordain Aedan macGabrain as king of Dalriada:

> The holy man obeyed the word of the Lord and sailed from Hinba to Iona where Aedan had arrived at this time, and ordained him king in accordance with the Lord's command. As he was performing the ordination, St Columba also prophesied the future of Aedan's sons and grandsons and great grandsons, then he laid his hands on Aedan's head in ordination and blessed him.

Aedan succeeded to the throne in 574 and reigned for at least thirty years, all of Columba's remaining lifetime. If true, this is an account of the earliest example in European history of a religious ritual being used to reinforce the legitimacy of a royal inauguration. If it is an invention and merely an example of a biblical trope – in the Old Testament, the prophet Samuel anointed kings – being woven into Columba's story, it probably reflected the political realities of Adomnán's time, more than a century later. By that time, the Church and temporal power had become closely intertwined.

Maelrubha had no biographer to chronicle his life and there exists not a shred of evidence that Bridei sanctioned the establishment of a monastery at Applecross. But he must have. Linked by the sea roads of the Hebrides and the Atlantic shore, it became the centre of a network of foundations on Skye and along the sea lochs of the north-western mainland and as far afield as Wester Ross and Moray. Maelrubha's mission was the first to settle and prosper at Applecross, but it was not the first attempt at the Christian conversion of the north-west Pictland. Sixty years before, many red martyrs had been made amongst the islands not far to the south.

Most famously memorialised by the much-filmed castle at Eilean Donan on the north shore of Loch Duich and by at least six Kildonans, St Donnan is principally remembered from accounts of

his death on the island of Eigg in 617. Here is an extract from the
Book of Leinster:

> Eigg is the name of a spring in Aldasain [obscure]. And there
> Donnán and his community suffered martyrdom. This is how it
> came about. A rich woman used to dwell there before the coming
> of Donnán and her flocks grazed there. On account of the ill-
> feeling she had towards Donnán and his community, she
> persuaded a number of bandits to kill him. When these bandits
> arrived in Eigg, they found them chanting their psalms in the
> oratory and they could not kill them there. Donnán however said
> to his community: 'Let us go into the refectory so that these men
> may be able to kill us there where we do our living according to
> the demands of the body; since as long as we remain where we
> have done our all to please God, we cannot die, but where we
> have served the body, we may pay the price of the body.' In this
> way, therefore, they were killed in their refectory on the eve of
> Easter. Fifty-four others died together alongside Donnán

The dialogue may of course be entirely fictitious, but even if the
sense of it is accurate, there is a whiff of red martyrdom being
welcomed. After all, if, as Donnan seemed to claim, the monks would
have been safe in the sanctuary of their church, why did they consent
to leave it and meet their deaths? The answer may lie amongst the
debris of faded beliefs. Early Christians were certain that it was only at
the End of Days, at the Last Judgement, that the dead would rise from
their graves and know their fate. Their resurrection would be the
beginning, with those brought back to life either rising or falling,
bound for eternal life in Heaven or eternal torment in Hell. But
martyrs were different. Those who died in God's name, spilling their
blood for His sake, did not have to wait until the last days to learn
their fate. Immediately upon death, they would fly on the wings of
Heaven, borne aloft in the arms of angels to take their place by God's
side. As the slaughter on Eigg ended mortal lives, monks dying with
hands clasped in prayer, it signalled the beginning of life ever after.

A slightly different version of this shocking incident appeared in the *Martyrology of Donegal*, compiled in the seventeenth century from much older sources.

Donnan, of Ega, Abbott. Ega [Eigg] is the name of an island in which he was, after his coming from Erin [Ireland]. And there came robbers of the sea on a certain time to the island when he was celebrating mass. He requested of them not to kill him until he should have the mass said, and they gave him this respite; and he was afterwards beheaded and fifty-two of his monks along with him. And all their names are in a certain old book of the old books of Erin, AD 616.

And a little more can be added to this blood-spattered tale from a tradition that a pagan queen from the mainland had Donnan and one hundred and fifty of his followers burned. The saint's body may have been taken to Kildonan on the island of Arran for burial.

These accounts have a number of telling elements in common. On the island of Eigg, Donnan had founded a community, and in 617 its monks were all martyred. Probably at the instigation of pagans – and only women are mentioned – a group of bandits or 'sea robbers' killed everyone and their leader. But there was some hesitation. Perhaps because it would have been an ill omen even for a pagan to commit the sacrilege of murder in an oratory or when mass was being said, they waited with their weapons while the terrified monks completed their devotions. There was also a dispute about land and its appropriation. But the most obvious conclusion to draw from this attack was that the early attempt at the conversion of north-western Pictland met with such violent resistance that no other mission appears to have sailed north for almost sixty years. If Maelrubha made a tentative landfall on Eilean an Naoimh before moving to the mainland, he may have been wise to be cautious.

By the time I left Camusterrach, it was mid morning. I wanted to have a look around Applecross School to see if there was any trace of a cross socket or stump. On my way, I came across a roadside sign for the Applecross Free Presbyterian Church of Scotland. The minister's name was not on it but two weekly services were advertised – one at 7 p.m. on Tuesdays and the other on the 'Lord's Day'. A simple, white-harled building with a grey slate roof, the little church lay at the bottom of a short lane. There were two cars parked beside it and I wondered if there might be someone I could talk to. But the door to the church was locked, although the key was hanging from a hook beside it. That made me smile, but the door being locked meant no one could be inside and I did not want to go poking around without permission.

But I did want to hear the Gaelic psalms again, one of the cultural glories of the Gaidhealtachd. Sung unaccompanied, they have a bleak, soaring, elemental beauty that seems the only possible overture for the dramatic, natural theatre that is the landscape of the Atlantic shore – the places where the saints made cathedrals from islands, mountains, rivers and the ceaseless surge of the ocean. To begin each psalm, a precentor stands before the congregation – *air ceann na seinn*, 'at the head of the singing'. It is always a man, and when he sings a line, the worshippers pick it up and sing it back to him hung with grace notes. There are only a handful of tunes and often the precentor does not know which he will use until he stands up. There has always seemed to me to be a great deal of improvisation. Or perhaps it is simply the spirit moving. And only the biblical psalms are sung. Each time the interplay begins between the precentor and the congregation, the music is interpreted so differently that it is made anew.

The Free Presbyterian churches are the pre-eminent keepers of this tradition and the raw, emotional power of the psalms seems to be of a piece with the history and beliefs of this Highland form of Protestantism. In 1843, the Church of Scotland split over the issue of patronage. Should the congregations and the elders control the Church and appoint its ministers, or should the local lairds continue to have that power? The ministers of what became the Free Church of Scotland walked out of the General Assembly in Edinburgh and began the huge task of building the infrastructure of a new national

Church from nothing. In 1893, there was a further schism that was sparked by moves towards reunification. There had been indications that the Disruption of 1843 might be healed, but the necessary compromises were unacceptable to two Highland ministers, both associated with Applecross. The Rev. Donald MacFarlane was minister on Raasay and the Rev. Donald MacDonald was at Shieldaig on the north coast of the peninsula. They were followed out of the Free Church of Scotland by dozens of elders and congregations across the north. From that time onwards, the Free Presbyterian Church of Scotland defined itself unshakably as the spiritual descendant of the historic Church of Scotland.

A central tenet of the new Church was its adherence to the Westminster Confession of Faith of 1646 and its belief in the absolute infallibility of Scripture. This uncompromising adherence seems to hark back to the early history of Christianity, the religion of the Word and the Book. And sometimes the harshness of doctrine is extremely detailed. For example, it is considered a sin to use public transport to go to the church on the Sabbath, presumably because it meant that the driver of the bus was working on the Lord's day of rest. In 2014, the Synod of the Free Presbyterian Church castigated itself when it quoted from a report to the Religion and Morals Committee: 'We must acknowledge the low state of religion among ourselves.' And then it went on to castigate others: 'We found that many professing Christians in the Churches are actively encouraged to continue their former worldly interest in professional and amateur sport, worldly music, entertainments such as the cinema, dances, the use of public houses, concerts and ceilidhs, and that many speak and dress like the world with little distinction to be found between them and their former companions.'

The Gaelic psalmody is certainly unworldly music and it may be ancient – in the eighteenth century, it was known as 'the old way of singing' – and its form was seen as a means of facilitating worship for those who could not read. This may mean that precenting predated the Reformation of the 1560s. One of the principal aims of Knox, Melville and the other reformers was the creation of a school in every parish – something that was achieved by the end of the seventeenth century. Education and the ability to read were not made available to all Scots for their own sake. There was a clear religious purpose. Martin Luther had promoted the notion of a priesthood of all believers. Removing the exclusive role of the clergy in communicating or interceding with God, he wanted to make everyone responsible for their own salvation. This involved reading the Word of God, Holy Scripture, directly and without help. Literacy would pave the road to Heaven.

If congregations could read, then there was no need for a precentor. What trips up this line of conjecture is language. If worshippers were either monoglots or had only a little English, then a precentor who had versions of the psalms in Gaelic would indeed be needed. All of the one hundred and fifty biblical psalms were first published in Gaelic in 1694 as Sailm Dhaibhidh, 'the Psalms of David'. A revised edition was brought out in 1826 and it is the version usually sung in churches now.

Lacking evidence, I am forced to fall back on little more than instinct. Having heard the psalms sung in church and felt their raw power reverberate through me as the metrical verse soars into the huge Hebridean skies, I am certain their origins are old. Almost primitive, needing no instrument or formal music of any kind, sung by groups of ordinary people and not choristers or professional choirs, they are closer to perfect praise than anything else I have listened to. The psalms inspire awe, are transcendent and, on the Sabbath, God can hear them. Perhaps He has been listening for many centuries. It may be that the psalms are a distant echo of the ancient music of Comgall's monastery at Bangor.

Brendan, Moluag, Columba and Maelrubha knew only the biblical psalms. They probably did not involve musical instruments in their worship, and I wondered if they did indeed sing in the same way as the congregations of the Free Presbyterians of the west. I hope they did. There is one psalm that speaks to me more powerfully than others. I first heard '*Cha'n Fhaigh Mi Bas Ach Maiream Beo*' – 'I Shall Not Die But Live' – in a small church at Letterfearn on the shore of Loch Duich a long time ago. As a teenager on a school trip anxious to find shelter from the rain on a Sunday morning, I was made welcome by the congregation. Thinking about this more than fifty years on, it occurs me that they had probably had several visitors from the youth hostel along the road at Ratagan. In those days, the warden chucked everyone out after breakfast, no matter the weather.

Smiling, knowing that I had no Gaelic, an old man opened the hymn book at the appropriate page for me moments before the precentor stood forward. Not even able to mutter the words, for, not only did I not understand them, I had no idea of pronunciation, I listened open-mouthed, the hairs of the back of my neck prickling. The singing rolled around the walls of the little church in waves. I may not have understood it but I felt it.

Even if the Psalms of David do not reach back fourteen centuries into the past, there is no doubt that a continuity of profound sanctity does. Even though the Westminster Confession obliges Free Presbyterians to believe that the Pope is the Antichrist and that Roman Catholics are idolaters, their music transcends all doctrinal daftness, it seems to me. When the psalms soar, angels take flight.

There was rain over Skye. Across the Inner Sound, a grey curtain was drawn, but behind it, over the ocean, blue sky stretched into the distance. Loch a' Mhuillin forced the coast road at Applecross to run between fresh water and salt, but the little isthmus I walked on did not seem natural to me. The name means Mill Loch or Milltown Loch and its creation seems to have been the solution to a problem. Nowhere in a convenient place along the Applecross coast did there seem to be a fast-flowing run of water that could reliably turn a mill wheel to grind corn into flour. And so, as often happened, a stream was dammed, a millpond created and the outflow canalised into a downhill race where a wheel could be positioned.

Milltown Loch filled up to become more than a pond because it lies in a natural catchment where several streams run down the hills behind it. Older dams have been replaced by concrete, but the outflow was still visible. I could see where the mill race had once run, and against the garden wall of one of the houses by the shore two huge stone mill wheels had been propped. It is impossible to say when this mill and its loch were established, but Maelrubha and his monks will have needed to grind their corn somewhere. Bread was not only the staff of life, it was also a necessary ingredient in the Eucharist – as was red wine. Applecross may have seemed Edenic but I suspected I would look in vain for rows of vines.

Beyond Milltown, the road led me past a series of boatsheds shelved into the rising shoreline. Nearby, a concrete slipway reached out into the waters of the bay. It used to be a lifeline for Applecross until very recently. Before the coast road around the north of the peninsula as far as Shieldaig was completed in 1975, and when the Bealach na Ba was still a gravel track and often impassable, the townships' only means of supply was by ship. The CalMac mailboat that plied between Stornoway, Kyle of Lochalsh and Mallaig brought passengers and goods into the bay. But there was no quay with deep water where it could dock. Instead, it lay off the slipway at Milltown and a seagoing rowing boat went out to ferry people and goods back to the shore. In bad weather, this could be a dangerous business – especially at the moment when people had to move from the mailboat to the rowing boat in a heavy swell.

In the 1950s, a boat operated between Toscaig in the south and Kyle of Lochalsh and it ceased operations when the coast road opened. Perhaps the most spectacular arrival was the coal boat. Carrying vital winter fuel for twenty townships, it sailed into the heart of the bay at high tide, ran itself aground and waited for low tide. For a frantic few hours, horses brought out carts to be loaded with as much coal as possible before the sea filled the bay once more and the boat refloated.

All that traffic has gone now. The sea roads to Applecross are still open and passable even in winter but no one uses them except for the pleasure of sailing and cruising. Until 1975, another remarkable continuity was maintained. Maelrubha and the other white martyrs thought of the sea not as a barrier but a highway. Applecross was not as isolated or difficult to reach but a crossroads, a hub for the churches of the sea, a *paruchia* of foundations linked by the ever-flexible, shallow-draughted curraghs. Unlike the chancy exchanges between the CalMac mailboat and the rowing boats off Milltown, the skin boats could sail close inshore and be unloaded by those willing to kilt up their tunics or habits and wade. That must be how the red wine for the Eucharist made its way to Maelrubha's monastery. It was brought from the vineyards of western Gaul, the Bordeaux and Loire regions, up the Biscay coast, across the English Channel, up into the Irish Sea and on to the inshore waters of the Hebrides, transferring to curraghs at some lost entrepôt.

Through the welcome shade of an avenue of hardwood trees, I came to the Shore. Often miscalled Applecross village, it is the largest township and, like Lochcarron, it has a long row of cottages set on a narrow shelf that all look out to sea. Beyond the road that ribboned past them, many had built summerhouses on the very edge of the bay, where the stony foreshore rises high enough. Across a dyke, several had been set up, some with barbecues and tables and benches. The long summer evenings in Applecross will have seen many sitting outside in the clear air looking across the Inner Sound to Raasay and the Cuillin Ridge. Not so long ago, the space taken up by the summerhouses would have been where a boat was pulled up above the tideline. Opposite the Applecross Inn were some tables and chairs and, with some coffee, I sat in the sunshine making notes but thinking that the better course would be to take my time, experience this place slowly and record later what I thought about this gentle, majestic landscape. After the rain had moved through, a rainbow arced over Skye.

About a hundred yards along the shore road, where the Bealach na Ba joins it, there was something that surprised me, a community petrol station. There can be few industries so cutthroat as petrochemicals. A notice on the pump made a point of principle.

This vital filling station belongs to the community and is run by volunteers on a not for profit basis. We keep the price of fuel as low as we can, while allowing us to cover our costs. Please buy your fuel here. The more we sell, the more certain the future of the filling station will be. Thank you for your support.

Behind the petrol and diesel pumps, which I used later, was a display of old photographs. These ranged from the previous petrol station that had closed down to two ancient, open-top sports cars negotiating the Bealach when the surface was still gravel. Another plaque thanked the Applecross Historical Society for supplying the photographs and carefully listed the names of who owned copyright in what.

When I'd had supper at the Applecross Inn the night before and my coffee that morning, I had the impression that many of the customers seemed to live locally. Most were older and, over the following two days, I realised that there was probably a substantial community of retired people living in the townships. Perhaps through a family link or simply having spent happy holidays in Applecross, these people had decided to spend their evening years in this beautiful place. Evidence of their vitality was clearly there in the community filling station and other initiatives I began to notice.

Even though the nearest hospital is eighty miles away in Inverness, it seemed to me that people had come to spend their last years by the bay and the Inner Sound. Applecross had become a different sort of sanctuary – a place from where the edge of eternity can be glimpsed in the skies of the west. Perhaps, like Brendan, these retirees sought to live amongst the Isles of the Blessed – somewhere they can reflect on a past that is much longer than their future.

I was snapped out of this reverie by the throaty roar of another sports car as a Maserati pulled in to fill up with fuel. The driver told me he was doing the North Coast 500, a tourist route that begins in Inverness, strikes north through Dingwall to John o' Groats, along the north coast and then down the west to Ullapool, Applecross and then back to Inverness, or it can be done in the clockwise direction by leaving Inverness and going along Loch Ness. It is five hundred miles of stunning views and, I suspect, inadequate roads. Apparently it had been driven by Jeremy Clarkson, who declared it 'wonderful'.

The irascible man in the Ferrari on the Bealach had probably been following the route, perhaps as fast as he could. There are apparently already record times. The Maserati driver told me that the owners of classic cars often organise trips around the NC 500 and he had seen a group of Lotus cars parked in Ullapool earlier that day.

Beyond the filling station, the shoreline sweeps around the bay towards Applecross House and Clachan, the site of Maelrubha's monastery. A path took me off the road and through a long planta-tion of monumental, white-barked beech trees. Very striking and clearly with a good grip on the sloping ground, resilient in the face of winter storms that blow straight off the bay below, these trees seemed to be loved, even revered. Further along the path, an infor-mation board shed some light, telling the story of the Four Trees of Applecross. New plantings commemorate four long-lived sweet chestnuts that originally stood at each corner of a square approxi-mately a hundred yards across. They were said to remember a clearly fictitious but intriguing yarn about the claiming of land at Applecross, one that is mirrored on Lismore. Moluag and Columba were appar-ently in a race to claim the island and the former won because he cut off his little finger and threw it ashore so that his 'blood and flesh' landed there first. In the contest for Applecross, the competitors are not named but the winner cut off his arm, or perhaps his hand or his belt and threw that ashore. These tales must come from some forgot-ten trope.

What caught my attention was this quote from the information board:

Significantly the Four Trees were universally respected in Applecross. Such was their reputation (or the superstition surrounding them) that no one would remove the first tree to fall, or indeed the others and they were all allowed to fall and rot away naturally.

Walking the shore path, I wondered about the reverence for trees, its role in the pagan past and its long continuity from the holy places of early Christianity to the observations on the information board. Iova, Iona, Yew Tree Island, the tree language of Ogham, the trees of the Gaelic alphabet, the oak studded with coins on Eilean Ma Ruibhe and much else. Yews in particular live to a great age. At Fortingall in Perthshire, an ancient tree in the churchyard may be four thousand years old. Often found around churches and in graveyards, yews seem like religious metaphors, their topmost branches reaching for the heavens and down amongst their roots bodies are buried and rot to dust. They seem to stand between spheres. The respect for the Four Trees of Applecross is not superstition but an unwillingness to interfere with the long life of these majestic plants and their slow death as they themselves sink into the soil and turn to dust.

On the northern edge of our little farm in the Scottish Borders, a wood was clear-felled in the summer of 2017 because of the danger from trees being blown down. It was a brutal process, as gigantic machines rumbled amongst the trees, felling them in seconds with a saw that dangled on the end of a hydraulic arm. The harvester looked like a dinosaur thrashing, crashing through the primeval forest. At the fringe of the wood, twenty-eight Scots pines stood tall and, with the birches, geans and rowans we planted opposite them, they made a beautiful avenue on either side of the tracks that leads to our farmhouse.

When the sun dappled on the rich, red bark of these mighty trees, I thought their trunks glowed with years and memories of what had passed below them. And when the swinging arm of the dinosaur-harvester at last reached them, I am not ashamed to say that I wept to see them fall. In moments, a sheltering horizon had thudded to the ground, branches cracking and breaking, and the wood had suddenly gone. Instead of shade, a green canopy and the soughing of the breeze through the boughs of the trees, we saw the churned mud of destruction, the landscape of no-man's-land in Flanders. These old pines were my friends and sometimes I sat in the bole of the tallest to read and enjoy the evening sun. I never failed to touch them, running my hand over the rough scales of their bark. When the big tree had fallen, I cut a wedge from its stump and it sits by me on my desk as I write this.

Trees have a real and present spiritual power that seems to me to have endured for millennia, perhaps ever since our hunter-gatherer ancestors first rustled the leaves of the wildwood. In remembrance of those that have fallen, I have planted many trees over the years on our farm. Up in the old deer park, I had two hundred saplings, ashes, oaks and Scots pines, put in the thin soil and protected with fencing. I will never see them in their mature majesty. No one will remember who caused them to be planted but I know that it was more than an act of land management. It was done out of love, respect and renewal.

Crossing the tarmac, on my way to the site of Maelrubha's monastery in Applecross, looking and listening for the roar of sports cars, I happened on something mysterious. The salt-washed turf of the foreshore that reached right down to the high tide line around the curve of the bay was pockmarked by a series of hearths. All circular, ringed by large stones, set at regular intervals and blackened with rain-soaked cinders, these fires may simple have been lit by campers to cook an evening meal. There were two tents pitched further along the shore. But something told me they were more than that. I sensed they were beacons of some sort, a welcoming semicircle that looked out to those who sailed the waters of the Inner Sound.

When I turned back up the road that led to the sea bridge that crossed the River Crossan, I caught a glimpse of something I had seen the day before. Just on the edge of my vision, no more than a flicker of movement, I thought I saw the bright yellow waterproof of the woman who had walked the *Bealach* all the way from Kishorn to Applecross. She seemed to disappear into a copse of willows and gorse by the bridge. The magic of *genius loci* works in inexplicable ways.

Beyond a stock fence stretched a flat, wide field where lush grass grew and a few hardwood trees flourished, offering shade. On what looked like the policies of Applecross House, a flock of large geese was grazing, perhaps a refuelling stopover on a long migration. The sense of fertility around the horned bay was reinforced by the surprising sight of a farmer cutting a field of tall grass for silage. Despite

being very late in the year and so far north, it seemed like a worthwhile job since the reaper was leaving thick dreels of rich green grass
behind it. These big fields seemed to me to be the productive heart
of the Sanctuary, of Maelrubha's monastery. They were valuable, well
drained and flat, able to support the flocks and herds through the
winter after they had come down off the summer pasture in the high
country.

An unprepossessing steel and concrete bridge crossed the River
Crossan but the view inland and up to the sheltering mountain ridge
was heart-catching as the trees bent over the banks and the river
glinted in the sunshine. I leaned over the parapet to look at the clear
water. It looked wholesome, cool and good enough to drink. The
grove below the bridge was shaded but instead of somewhere to sit,
I found another information board and more evidence of an active,
vibrant local community. Before I drove over the Bealach, everything I had read about Applecross was historical and so I had missed
the existence of a central reason for such vibrancy – the Applecross
Trust. It was set up in 1975 when the peninsula began to open up in
the wake of the completion of the coast road from Shieldaig. Run in
the interests of the whole community, the landscape and its animals,
the trust owns the 26,000 hectares (64,000 acres) Applecross estate
that used to belong to the Wills family. It manages a wide range of
activities from farming to tourism to conservation and they contributed £5,000 to the setting up of the community petrol station in
2010. These heirs of Maelrubha aim to create a twenty-first-century
Sanctuary that not only preserves and sometimes restores the best of
the past but avoids the depredations of the future. Applecross feels
alive, capable of growth and change, not frozen in time's aspic, and
that atmosphere may well be a consequence of the work of the trust
and the judicious use of their resources. However, I doubt there is
much they can do about rude Ferrari drivers.

The information board told me that the Applecross Trust is specifically trying to improve the quality and nature of the stocks of
salmon that swim into the bay and spawn in the clear waters of the
River Crossan. The eggs of the last wild salmon to be caught in the

river in 1995 (presumably preserved in some way – and how did they know it was the last salmon?) have been gradually introduced in an effort to restore native bloodlines. The thousands of resulting smolts are tagged and followed so that research into their movement helps improve the project's chances of success. It is a glorious application of modern wisdom to ensure the future of what Maelrubha and his monks called *Am Bradan Mor*, 'the Great Salmon', 'the Wise Fish'. This accolade springs from a charming, atmospheric tale – even if it is a nineteenth-century romantic invention and not genuinely old, I don't care.

Hazelnuts were thought to be nuggets of wisdom. When some fell into a pool where salmon were swimming, the silver fish ate them. Not only did they acquire at that moment the red spots on their scales from the nuts, they also became wise. And it is an attribution, a tradition, that has persisted across millennia.

Many years ago, in another life as Director of Programmes at Scottish Television, responsible for creating a new schedule of Gaelic programmes, I argued that to build returning, regular audiences, a soap opera had to be central to that schedule. Writers came up with a storyline that revolved around the life and work of a Gaelic-medium further education college in the islands. Its proposed name was *Am Bradan Mor*, The Great Salmon, a puzzling name for an English-speaking viewer but all Gaelic speakers immediately understood the link between the fish and knowledge, wisdom and education.

It may be that the association of wisdom with the salmon arises from its remarkable life cycle. When young fish leave their home river, they swim far out into the Atlantic Ocean, sometimes as far as Greenland and the Denmark Straits. After approximately four years, doubling its weight annually, the wise fish swims homewards to find the river of its birth where it will spawn. How it does this is a matter of essential mystery. Scientists conjecture that the salmon swim so close to the surface of the ocean that they can see the stars of the night sky and that, in some unexplained way, their instincts for home are pulled along by the configurations of the heavens. When at last they come near to their destination, it is thought they recognise the contours of the coastline and finally the smell of their home river. But no one knows how they achieve this extraordinary journey over thousands of miles.

The origins of the tales of the Wise Fish are Irish and are told in the poetry of what is known as the Fenian Cycle. These were almost certainly composed in the north in the Dark Ages and may be drawn from much older stories. Some scholars have described them as a window on Iron Age Ireland. Maelrubha and his companions will have known these tales and been well versed in the lore of *Am Bradan Mor*. And they also recognised the importance of the salmon to monastic communities. In dozens of medieval documents associated with monasteries in Scotland, great care was taken to protect their rights to fishing beats on the great salmon rivers. The abbeys at Melrose, Dryburgh and Kelso all claimed *stells* or fishing pools on the Tweed, their locations and extent meticulously detailed. The reasons for this were religious rather than culinary. By the twelfth century, dietary regulations in monastic orders forbade the excessive consumption of meat, and fish was an allowable substitute. These rules were complicated and qualified but had their origins in the habits of fasting in the early monasteries. In the seventh and eighth centuries, the bay and the River Crossan will have been teeming with salmon, especially when the great fish were finding their way back from the wastes of the North Atlantic to spawn. The Applecross Trust are not only restoring a lost natural resource as they re-stock the river, they are also bringing back a part of its history to the bay.

More restorative work will help return the landscape to its origins. As I walked on from the sea bridge to Clachan and the site of the monastery, I was passed by the thunder of a long log lorry. These leviathans are a necessary intrusion, even on single-track roads not designed for all those wheels, because they need to reach remote places where commercial forestry is being planted and harvested. Since it is so hardy and fast growing, the Alaskan Sitka spruce has been planted all over Scotland, sometimes in vast blankets of forestry. So dense that they create a dark, sterile environment, the trees are scruffy and ugly. But the timber industry desperately needs more Sitka and it must continue to be grown so that an important Scottish industry remains viable. But the Applecross Trust is beginning to clear-fell commercial timber and replace it with native broadleaf trees such as oak, ash, birch and alder. Not only will this restore the way the landscape looked for many centuries, it will also encourage the return of the fauna of ancient woodland. The total carrying capacity for tree planting in Scotland is difficult to compute, but I suspect that many hundreds of thousands of acres of both Sitka forests and native woodland could be created. On all levels, ecological and economic, this mixture should become a priority.

Near the gates of the graveyard around Clachan Church and the watermark of Maelrubha's monastery, a small truck and trailer were parked. The scent of freshly cut grass greeted me as I made my way up the track.

The driver rolled down his window. 'Visiting the graveyard?'

I was but, in the unhurried manner of the Highlands and Islands, there was time to pass the time of day.

The man in the passenger seat told me they had driven down from Gairloch that morning and taken the coast road from Shieldaig. With a trailer and a big grass cutter on it, that route was 'less exciting' than the Bealach.

Guessing that his accent was from Lewis, very like that of my Gaelic teacher, I asked, '*A bheil Gàidhlig agaibh?*' He nodded, but even though I followed his mute response with '*Cò às a tha thu?*' –'Where are you from?' – he doggedly stayed with English. In the company of his monoglot colleagues, I wondered if he felt awkward in Gaelic and thought it rude to talk to me in a language they did not understand. It is an all-too-common reaction.

The men told me they were staying overnight in Applecross, having driven the long, twisting coast road south to cut the grass in all of the peninsula's graveyards. They agreed it would probably be the last cut of the year. And, like all polite and interested people, they asked me what my business was at Clachan. To my pleasant surprise, the Lewisman was well aware of the story of Maelrubha and pointed out where the saint's grave was reputed to be.

To the left of the gate into the graveyard stood a strange ghost from the long monastic past. A tall cross slab had been erected even though its carving had barely begun. More like a prehistoric standing stone, blotched with patches of white lichen, it had the faint, roughed-out marks of a cross on the crusted surface and only the head of the stone had been worked on to any great extent. It must have been raised to stand sentry by the entrance to the country of the dead sometime after the monastery had disappeared, perhaps as a memorial to the original foundation.

The unfinished cross is known as the Abbot's Stone and has a tenuous link with Ruaraidh Mor MacAogan. It is said to have marked the grave of this abbot, who died around 801. That seemed to me unlikely, an incomplete cross slab for a successor of Maelrubha, a man whose writ ran over a wide *paruchia* of churches in north-western Scotland.

Particularly in the northern half of the graveyard, there were several new headstones and room for more beyond them. The cleansing soil of the sacred precinct seemed endlessly, even magically receptive. Beneath the freshly cut grass lay the bones of thirteen centuries, eighty generations since the monks came, the mute sediment of history and belief. Beyond the grave-markers of Tina Jessie Maclean (*Lena an Ochain*), James Thomson Baxter (Keep dancing, wild thing) and the beautifully worked granite stone of William George Greig lay the supposed site of the tomb of St Maelrubha. There was no headstone, no sign, no information board, nothing but the two rounded stones the size of footballs that the reluctant Gaelic speaker from Lewis had told me to look out for. If I had not met him, I would not have known where to look.

The contrast with Columba's memorials on Iona could not have been starker. The erasure of Maelrubha and his monastery from the landscape was almost total, while the richness of Columba's legacy has inspired not only streams of pilgrims and literature but also a movement in the shape of the Iona Community. Here, there was next to nothing to remember a great mission of conversion, probably greater even than Columba's. Immediately to the north of the forlorn stone footballs was the roofless ruin of a small fifteenth-century chapel. Perhaps it was originally dedicated to Maelrubha, but if there was a connection, it is now lost. Kenneth MacRae, a local historian with strong opinions, was appalled at the neglect of the site of the monastery, writing, 'What the illiterate natives commemorated . . . one educated generation despised and forgot.' He has a point. MacRae was sexton of the graveyard and his head-stone told me that he died in 1982, no doubt content to be planted in a place whose lost history he championed.

So that I could concentrate on the seventh century and the foun-dation of the monastery, I decided not to visit the early nineteenth-century Clachan Church that stood in the middle of the graveyard and, instead, go to the Heritage Centre behind the manse. It was crammed with exhibits, information panels, old photographs and a very comfortable armchair in front of a slide show of good views of Applecross. Above the screen, a surprising coracle had been jammed into the roof space and labelled as a curragh. On the floor, leaning against the wall, were the remains of great richness – fragments of intricately carved stone from one or perhaps two of the many crosses that had once marked the bounds of the Sanctuary. Equally impres-sive were three panels listing almost forty sites across Scotland that had associations with Maelrubha, the result of a sustained programme of real scholarship.

At the far end of this busy room, near the window looking over the graveyard, I was astonished to discover that a wide circle was quickly closing. Beside a very good model of what the early medieval monastery looked like was a drawing of the location of the original monastic vallum made by Professor Charles Thomas in 1963. Here was the early work of the man whose passion, learning and brilliance had introduced me to St Patrick and inspired me to undertake these journeys up the western coasts of Scotland. I had ended with Maelrubha and it seemed that Charles Thomas had begun with him.

Amongst the Edenic glories of Applecross, I had found myself occasionally straying from the path of forensic investigation into the misty realms of *genius loci*, conjecture, even apparition, but here was something that was surely more than a coincidence. Quite what it was, I am not sure. I had no idea that Charles Thomas had done a ground survey of this site, and his simple plan of the monastery seemed to bring Maelrubha and his monks out of the half-light and into history.

Anxious to have a guidebook for the exhibition so that I had a tangible record of Thomas's work and to buy all and any books about Applecross, I returned to the ticket desk and the little shop at the entrance. There were few to be had and no guidebook, and those I did buy mostly contained information I already knew, which was scant enough. The most incisive and thoughtful summary of the work and significance of St Maelrubha is to be found in Alfred P. Smyth's *Warlords and Holy Men*. He made much sense of the few scraps of sources that exist for the saint's life. But at the Heritage Centre I did come across a welcome and living link with the coming of the Irish monks in 673.

When I paid for the two booklets that looked most likely to be helpful, I asked the lady at the desk in Gaelic if she had Gaelic. After the disappointments on Lismore, I expected the usual blank look, but instead was cheered and surprised when she said, in English, that she did and was also a native of Applecross who had been raised in Gaelic. Like the Lewisman, she was nevertheless reluctant to speak to me in her native tongue – 'I will have to think before I can say anything.' But slowly and with much deliberation, almost whispering, she switched and began to tell me that at school she had not only been scolded for speaking Gaelic but the teacher also criticised the way in which she made herself understood in English. As a little girl, she had been translating in her head and producing sentences with a Gaelic word order. Instead of saying 'I am thirsty' she came out with 'There is a thirst on me.'

Concentrating, becoming increasingly comfortable and more clearly audible, this lady began to talk of her early life in Applecross, remembering the CalMac ferry lying off the slip at Milltown and the coal boats in the bay. Determined to be precise, her Gaelic was also

very different and much more mellifluous than mine. I lack vocabulary, and if I cannot think of the Gaelic word for something, I shove
in the English equivalent without hesitation or much shame. As we
talked quietly, the Heritage Centre suddenly began to fill with
people, probably from a bus party on a tour, and I became aware of
someone behind me. 'Excuse me! Excuse ME!' barked a lady, clearly
irked not only that she was waiting but also that she could not
understand what transaction was taking place between me and the
lady behind the desk. That irritable intervention immediately shut
down what had been a brief but quiet and very pleasant encounter,
and as I retreated the impatient lady glared at me.

More than many practical things, such attitudes are damaging
Gaelic. With the early death of Pictish, it is the first language of the
Highlands and Islands, one that describes the north more completely
than any other and the last thing its use should inspire is exaspera-
tion. The lady visitor cannot have been in a hurry. She had just
arrived. What annoyed her was that she could not understand. That,
in turn, fosters suspicion. She knew that we both spoke English but
why had we chosen to speak to each other in Gaelic? What were we
hiding? It will never have occurred to her that the mouth-filling
syllables of this most beautiful of languages are worth uttering
because they describe Applecross more precisely and appropriately
than English ever could. Such deep-seated suspicion may be a consequence of history, an insular society ill at ease with multilingualism.
But that did not persuade me to excuse this woman and with the
sentence '*Bha e uamhasach math d'fhaicinn*', I told the lady behind
the desk that it had been very good to see her. I walked out into the
sunshine and sat down on a bench to look over the Inner Sound to
the Cuillin ridge.

21

The End of the Rainbow

This was my last day in Applecross and the shadows of the evening would soon begin to lengthen and the light on the waters of the bay start to soften. Before the long walk along the shore for supper and a welcoming bed, I wanted to flush out my irritation and I decided to visit Clachan Church after all. To my surprise, it was open and empty. And in the vestibule was another surprise. One of the information boards carried a splendid photograph of the historian Kenneth MacRae. With a tam-o'-shanter bonnet, at a ridiculously rakish angle, barely covering his rebellious black hair, a pipe clenched horizontally between his teeth, holding the shaft of a scythe over his shoulder, a shovel resting against his thigh and wearing shorts and what looked like gym shoes, he was grinning broadly. A handsome man, knowing full well how daft he looked, it was an unexpected image. No sombre, black-robed minister or group of glowering elders here – instead, I found myself welcomed to this church by good humour. Even though it was a black and white photograph, the shadows showed a sunny day at Clachan many years ago.

The church itself, the body of the kirk, was a stunning revelation, entirely unexpected. As the late afternoon sun streamed in through plain glass windows, it lit an interior of cleaned and repointed rubble-built walls, a pale white wooden floor and a wood-panelled roof. Instead of rows of fixed pews, chairs had been angled in two sets of rows on either side of an elegant white pulpit, a lectern below it and what might have been an altar table.

It was, without doubt, the most perfectly beautiful church interior I have ever seen. There was no decoration of any kind, no stained glass, no bright colour, not even an altar cloth. The effect of all of this washed-out simplicity was to make a stillness. After a time, I sat down on one of the chairs and slowly this empty space began to fill with atmosphere, with a sense of spirituality, with silence and gradually, it seemed to me, with the shadow bodies of the long past. Here was none of the richness of Iona or the bleakness of Eileach an Naoimh but, instead, an unexpected warmth. As dust motes danced in the sun splashing through the windows, I felt as though time was collapsing on itself once more.

In the vestibule I had read that Clachan Church was built in 1817 on the footprint of an earlier church and Charles Thomas's tracing of the monastic vallum placed it near the centre of the sacred ground. Was this simple little church built over the first, the place where Maelrubha and his brethren prayed and chanted, where they played their rosaries through their clasped fingers? In the silence, I felt as though I had joined hands with centuries of generations, *linn gu linn*, 'from one to the next'. When Father Doran wrote, 'I feel that you know you are on a journey, Alistair. Your eyes are open, your heart is open. And you are not walking alone, as I suspect you already believe', he was half right. I do not and never have felt the presence of God, any god, but, in the late afternoon of that last day in Applecross, I sensed the presence of the dead in every part of that church. Maelrubha, Brendan, Moluag, Donnan and even Columba – all of these men who lifted up their eyes and searched for angels in the huge Highland skies. Their spirits danced with the dust in the sunlit air. For a few fleeting moments, they were with me.

Many years ago, when I was a student, I visited a church in Florence. Away from the crowds around the Uffizi gallery and the Piazza della Signoria, Santa Maria del Carmine is on the south bank of the River Arno. There is a small side chapel decorated with frescoes by Masaccio, Tommaso di Ser Giovanni di Simone – 'Big Tom'. Some of the other work is by Masolino, Tommaso di Cristoforo Fini – 'Little Tom'. Painted in the early fifteenth century, the frescoes show a series of biblical scenes. Very powerful is Masaccio's *The*

Expulsion of the Garden of Eden – Adam and Eve's grief-stricken expressions are unforgettable.

In those far-off days, there were no barriers or even much supervision and, alone in the chapel, it was possible to stand close to these magical works of art. To my inexperienced eye, the appearance of these images was mysterious, possessed of an uncatchable strangeness or perhaps otherworldliness, certainly outside the everyday, far beyond the bustling streets of the city. For a fleeting moment, I felt that, as I looked at his work, Masaccio was looking through his paintings directly back at me.

For all my time in Applecross, scrambling around the rocks of Eileach an Naoimh, walking in Lismore and Iona, I had sensed a similar reflection, more than a sense of *genius loci*. Through these landscapes, flitting between the mighty trees, half-hidden by the swales and undulations of the machair, I felt the presence of Maelrubha and the other saints more than once. As I looked out over what they had seen, from the places they had made, I felt them looking back at me, their faces ghostly, like a momentary pale reflection in a windowpane.

In the silence of the church, I began to hear music. Faintly at first, the rich, remarkable voice of Donnie Munro filled my head. He was singing the first piece of music that really stirred me and, many years ago, hinted that the dying Gaelic language might have a future if it could remember its past. '*An Ubhal as Airde*', 'The Highest Apple', sings of religion and memory as its cadences pick up the lines given to congregations in Highland churches for centuries.

> At present
> All you were is with me
> My eyes closed, my memory confident
> Standing here watching
> Each hill and shoreline
> With the seed you left still growing
> The garden is well stocked
> With mighty trees

With fruit growing for the whole world
Ripe, sweet
And bitter apples
And the one apple that is beyond reach
Who amongst us
Can exist a single day
Beyond our own time and our own limits
Countless and futile
Are times I've climbed
To reach and taste the forbidden fruit
The winds will blow and the sun will shine
From generation to generation
Through the trees of the garden
But the day and the hour will surely come
To take the highest apple
From the knowledge tree

In the place-name of Applecross there are no apples, but in the late sunshine of the evening it did seem to me to be like an orchard, a place where God had once walked amongst the trees and a place where knowledge of Him might once have been glimpsed or grasped. Earlier that day, I had wandered into the tangle of the walled garden near Applecross House and been struck by its riotous fertility. Berry bushes, twisted old apple, plum and pear trees, raised beds overflowing with greenery, trellised arcades and a curragh-shaped boat stacked oddly in a corner all spoke of bounty and plenty.

I had imagined that John Cassian's state of *unitio,* a perfect union with God, would happen only in remote places, alone and far into the desert or on a wind- and rain-swept island in the Hebrides. But '*An Ubhal as Airde*' offered other images. Guarded and sheltered by the half-ring of high mountains, Meall Gorm and Beinn Bhan, behind it, the garden that is Applecross may have been a better, more human setting. Amongst the green and golden glories of Creation, the salmon in the river, the fruit of the trees and the beasts of the field, *unitio* might have been found in a different way, with joy rather than through suffering and privation. And, if it was found in bountiful Applecross, then it was understood in Gaelic, the language of Eden.

Maelrubha and the early saints made us. Even though churches are emptying and prohibitions are being dismantled, there is an enduring consensus across Europe, in the Americas and elsewhere about decency, good behaviour, about what constitutes right and wrong. Overwhelmingly that consensus was formed by the centuries of Christianity. As doctrine and belief evolved, and as far too much blood was spilled, the Church largely formed our morality. There were and are, of course, other influences, not least from other religions, but the teachings of the Church have been enormously determinant in the operation of a generally accepted code of conduct, both in private and public life.

In trying to form a picture of the life and work of the early saints on my voyages to Eileach an Naoimh, Lismore, Iona and Applecross to complete a complex jigsaw with only a few pieces to hand, I found myself interrogating the processes of compiling that moral code in the early centuries of Christianity, often testing it against my own sensibilities. Historically, the sources for this story and the physical remains are vanishingly scant but the cultural legacy of the saints, especially in north-western Scotland, lies all around us. It seemed to me, on that soft and gentle evening, that we are all Maelrubha's children and in the words written by Calum MacDonald for '*An Ubhal as Airde*',

> All you were is with me
> My eyes closed, my memory confident
> Standing here watching
> Each hill and shoreline
> With the seed you left still growing

As I packed my bag and rucksack next to the box of unopened books in the boot of my car, rain clouds were gathering over the Cuillin ridge and a westerly wind was bringing more in off the ocean.

When I began the long climb up the *Bealach*, it started to rain heavily, and I felt sorry for the two cyclists I passed. But as I reached the plateau, the cloud suddenly thinned and the arc of a complete rainbow appeared over the road. The gates of Eden seemed to open as I slowed to turn the sharp bends of the cattle trail and leave the garden behind me.

Rainbows are entirely optical phenomena and do not exist in any tangible sense. The eye of every person who sees one will create its own individual rainbow with a unique position in the sky that is always exactly opposite to the sun and behind the observer. No two rainbows are the same, even if they are seen at the same time. As I reached the plateau of the Bealach, the seven colours of the spectrum glowed red, orange, yellow, green, blue, indigo and violet. And then, in a moment, I was beyond the arc, and the rainbow had disappeared. When I began the descent to Loch Kishorn, the rain stopped and the sun lit the farther shore.

Epilogue

The Blood of Blathmac

'*Barbare, duc gladios, capulum cape, iamque trucida!*' shouted Blathmac. 'Barbarians, draw your swords, grip the hilts, and now kill!' Standing on the altar step, having prayed and perhaps celebrated mass, the Abbot of Iona had just seen many of his brethren slaughtered by a Viking raiding party who had broken into the monastery at dawn. Like Blathmac, they had chosen not to flee, to stay in their church and await their blood-spattered fate. Others had chosen life and 'by a foot-path through regions known to them' had presumably taken refuge in the west of the island beyond the open machair, perhaps amongst the rocks, crevices and sea caves of Druim an Aoineidh. As the Viking warriors laid hands on Blathmac, their blades slick with blood, he cried out, 'To your aid, gracious God, I commend myself humbly.' And then the pious sacrifice was torn limb from limb.

The Latin is precise, more lexically tight than most monastic texts. It is quoted from a poem composed by Walafrid Strabo, the abbot of Reichenau, a monastery on an island in Lake Constance in southern Germany. Blathmac died in 825 and it is likely that the account of his martyrdom was written soon after it took place. It seems that the monk was not simply killed or cut down or slaughtered when the Vikings crashed into the church. Elsewhere in the poem, Strabo wrote that the brothers had buried the valuable reliquary of Columba and perhaps other precious objects: 'The violent, cursed host came rushing through the open building, threatening cruel perils to the blessed men; and after slaying the rest with mad savagery, they approached Blathmac to compel him to give up the precious metals wherein lie the holy bones of St Columba.'

To extract information about the location of these treasures, the Vikings questioned Blathmac. Strabo related that he told them he knew nothing of where the reliquary had been buried, and that even if he did, he would not say. It is very likely that, at this point, Blathmac was tortured before he was 'torn limb from limb'. Strabo offered nothing more than that phrase, but in other accounts of atrocities, victims had their testicles squeezed excruciatingly hard and then cut off with a dagger. And they were told that unless they gave up information, when their inevitable death came, it would be slow and even more agonising. It may be that the Vikings carved the blood eagle on Blathmac's back.

A hideous ritual and a deliberate affront to the god who these men called 'the White Christ', it was committed as a sacrifice to Odin. He stood for war and brutality as opposed to peace and love for fellow men. The blood eagle ritual began when a victim was tied to a stake or a pillar face first. With an axe or a very sharp sword, a Viking warrior then hacked the ribcage from the spine before pulling out the lungs and draping them over the shoulders, like the wings of an eagle. This was done to King Edmund of East Anglia in 869 and to others in Orkney in the 870s. Unless they died of shock, those who suffered this appalling death may have stayed alive until the moment their lungs were ripped out.

In Strabo's poem, there seems to have been an inevitability around what took place on Iona in 825. It was intended that blood be spattered on the floor of Columba's church, monks were expected to scream when their testicles were cut off and their bodies hacked with swords and axes. It is clear that Blathmac and those who refused to flee were actively seeking red martyrdom. They consciously chose to give up their lives to God amidst all that savagery and their abbot 'stood before the sacred altar as a calf without blemish, a pleasing offering to God, to be sacrificed by the threatening sword'. Blathmac decided to come to Iona because the island had been repeatedly raided. He and his brethren knew that the Vikings were coming on that fateful dawn – they had buried the abbey's treasure. They were not only prepared to accept their fate but to welcome it. The agonies were unimaginable but then so were Christ's on the cross. Like Donnan and the monks who died on Eigg in 617, they knew that immediately after death, no matter how prolonged the terrible pains of torture, their souls would soar up to Heaven. Not for them would there be any waiting and no judgement to be made after resurrection on the Last Day. At the moment of red martyrdom, God waited to welcome them to eternal life.

Throughout Strabo's poem, there is a clear sense of the terrible slaughter on Iona being a set-up, deliberately sought, even encouraged. Only rarely available in the centuries since the adoption of Christianity as the imperial religion in the early fourth century, red martyrdom had returned and, despite the destruction, despoliation and the theft of scared treasures, it was welcomed by those ready to suffer death for Christ.

The other, somewhat contradictory, thread that runs through the poem written on Reichenau Island is shock. The story of Blathmac's martyrdom in the *sanctum sanctorum* of Columba's Iona reverberated across Western Christendom and inspired pious poetry from Walafrid Strabo.

In 793, as though from nowhere, Viking ships had sailed out of the eastern horizon and attacked Cuthbert's monastery on Lindisfarne. The sleek, fast and highly manoeuvrable warships known as *dreki*, 'dragon ships', had rasped up on the shingle beach below the monastery and warriors had raced towards the undefended church before the monks could bar the doors. What chroniclers called 'a shower of Hell' had burst over Christian Britain and Ireland and the *Anglo-Saxon Chronicle*'s entry for the events of 8 June 793 is apocalyptic.

This year there came dreadful forewarnings over the land of the Northumbrians, terrifying the people most woefully: these were immense sheets of lightning rushing through the air, and whirlwinds, and fiery dragons flying across the firmament. These tremendous tokens were soon followed by a great famine: and not long after . . .

the harrowing inroads of heathen men made lamentable havoc in the church of God in Holy Island by rapine and slaughter.

Lindisfarne may have been unlucky. When the first fleets sailed 'westoversea' from the rugged fjords of Norway, their sails filled and they aimed for a long target. The British archipelago runs nine hundred miles from Shetland to the English Channel and, even with contrary winds and a strong-running sea, it is hard to miss. It may be that the raiders who attacked Lindisfarne splintered from a larger fleet, perhaps in stormy weather, because more attacks were reported in the Western Isles in 794, when Donnan's monastery on Eigg was desecrated, and a year later the Vikings first made landfall on Iona. As Alfred Smyth wrote in *Warlords and Holy Men*, the monasteries were 'shop windows crammed with the loot of centuries and occupied by unarmed monks who worshipped the White Christ', a very different god from the warlike, ruthless Odin. The Vikings were heathens, 'barbarians' in Blathmac's reported speech, and they cared not a jot for the sanctity of the monasteries, their relics and their churches. What they sought was portable loot – gold, silver and gems. When they raided Lindisfarne, they probably tore off the jewel-encrusted metal binding from the great gospel book, but miraculously, the worthless painted pages of calfskin were cast aside.

At first there was a shocked bemusement. As news of these savage desecrations flickered across Western Europe, churchmen were at a loss to understand why Almighty God had allowed such foul deeds to be done. The monasteries may have been undefended but surely there was no need. The sacred precincts were ringed by centuries of prayer and psalm singing that hung in the blessed air around their churches, cells and scriptoria. Having given their lives to worship of God, mortified their flesh to honour his sacrifice on the cross and striven to achieve *unitio* with Him, their holiness was surely armour enough.

When Alcuin of York, a very great scholar who had found his calling and his home at the court of the new Emperor Charlemagne, heard of the attack on Lindisfarne, he furrowed his brow and lifted his pen. In letters to Higbald, the Bishop of Lindisfarne, he wrung his hands: 'The church of St Cuthbert is spattered with the blood of priests of God, stripped of all its ornament, exposed to the plundering of pagans.' He also came up with a reason for the atrocities. Almighty God had had no choice but to leave the island undefended because the monks had brought down this calamity on their own heads. 'Either this is the beginning of greater tribulation, or else the sins of the inhabitants have called it upon them. Truly it has not happened by chance, but it is a sign that it was well merited by someone. But now, you who are left, stand manfully, fight bravely, defend the camp of God.'

Sin must have infected many more monasteries. Sometime after Eigg, Skye and Iona were raided in 794 and 795, the dragon ships sailed into Applecross Bay and pagan warriors overran Maelrubha's precinct. It may have been a very rich prize and the destruction great. The sources are scant and somewhat contradictory. Ruaraidh Mor MacAogan, the abbot associated with the unfinished cross slab still standing at Clachan graveyard, probably fled to Bangor, where he appears to have become abbot. He died there in 801 and tradition relates that Big Rory's body was brought back to Applecross for burial. More open and exposed than other foundations, the monastery contracted in the decades after the Viking onslaught. Instead of rule by an abbot, Applecross's land and its wide *paruchia* of daughter houses and churches dedicated to Maelrubha seem to have been administered by a line of hereditary lay abbots, perhaps best understood as estate managers rather than spiritual leaders. It may be that destruction was so great that no monks survived it and none came to take their places. All that remained was their great patrimony. Obeolan was the first of the lay abbots, and place-names such as Cul an Dun, 'the Field behind the Fort', suggest that he and his successors built refuge fortifications near the monastery. Eventually these men morphed into lordly landowners.

Iona was raided again in 802 and, four years later, more carnage took place on the island when sixty-eight brethren and lay people were butchered by Vikings. Bloodletting on this scale was exceptional since slavery fast became a more lucrative business than mere robbery. There can have been only so much gold, silver and precious stones to be stolen and it could be easily and quickly hidden. Eventually, a busy slave market was established at Dublin, a port easily accessible for sellers from the north and buyers from the south. Fair-haired northern Christian slaves were apparently much in demand in the Emirate of Cordoba that governed much of modern Spain.

The mass martyrdom of 806 compelled Abbot Cellach to make the heart-breaking decision to abandon Columba's foundation and move the community and such treasures as were left, like the famous gospel, to Kells in Ireland. By the later ninth century, Lindisfarne was also deserted, as was the mother monastery of St Martin at Marmoutier, too easily accessed by the shallow-draughted dragon ships that could be rowed far up the Loire.

As well as forcing exposed monastic communities to shrink back from exposed coastlines, the Vikings reshaped Scotland's geopolitical landscape. By the middle decades of the ninth century, the Dalriadan kings had begun to exert pressure on parts of Pictland and, probably in 848, Columba's relics were divided between Kells and the old Iona foundation at Dunkeld. The church there became a focus for pilgrimage and, ultimately, a great and very beautiful cathedral was built on the banks of the Tay. Columba's legacy had crossed the mountains and come a long way from the dangerous Atlantic shore.

Iona was never completely abandoned and, as Viking raiders became settlers and converted to Christianity, some of their lords were buried on the island. By the later ninth century, a tradition of burying Scottish kings in the Reilig Odhrain had begun. Chroniclers noted that when Constantine I died in 877 he was interred in the cleansing soil of the old cemetery. A year later, a cortege made its way down the Sraid nam Marbh with the body of King Aed. Over the following two centuries, others followed. Perhaps one of them was Macbeth. Clearly, the memory of Columba's great sanctity was powerful, fuelled not only by consistent royal patronage but also by the much-circulated *Life* by St Adomnán. But this survival was sadly singular. The Viking raids almost completely destroyed the traces of others who sailed the western seas to found disearts, monasteries and churches. Little or no record of Brendan, Moluag, Donnan and Maelrubha remain – and almost all that does survive is to be found in the Irish annals – and there are others whose legacy has faded near to invisibility. At Applecross, tradition recalls that the scriptorium was burned by Viking raiders and, since each major foundation will have had such a store of written knowledge, it is very likely that much has been lost in the flames of ignorance.

All that remains are names, the memories of the landscape and echoes of great sanctity, sacrifice and bravery on the Atlantic shore and amongst its islands and skerries. The lives of those men who searched the skies for angels have long faded – their grey shapes are little more than fleeting shadows in the darkness of the past. But their devotion and determination not only laid the foundations of churches, they also formed many of the building blocks of our society. Scotland was made by the convulsions of geology, the eruptions of fire and the grinding movement of ice but its people and their communities were given much of their character by ideas and their power to shape behaviour. One of the most determinant factors was the coming of Christianity and its beginnings were overwhelmingly in the west. And then, forced over the mountains by the depredations of the Vikings, the beliefs, the cults and the relics of the saints had an enduring influence.

When Hector MacKenzie sacrificed a bull and called down the power of Maelrubha to help cure his wife, Cirstane, and as the Presbytery of Dingwall wagged its finger at him, both recalled the legacy of these remarkable holy men. A belief in the power of an ancient martyr was as much a legacy of the sixth and seventh centuries as the asceticism of the reformed Church in Scotland. Their monasteries have been long lost and reclaimed by the grass and the heather, their stories destroyed or forgotten, their names barely remembered, but the influence of the old saints of the west has not yet fled.

Further Reading

There is surprisingly little accessible written on this period of Scotland's early history, so the selection of books below can but serve as a basic introduction. Many of the early saints' lives are unavailable in any modern edition, or even at all. However, exceptions to this are two towering contemporary works, the second of which appears in two good editions with interesting ancillary works:

Adomnán of Iona: *Life of St Columba*, tr. and ed. P. Sharpe, London 1995

Bede: *The Ecclesiastical History of the English People*, tr. L. Sherley-Price, ed. D.H. Farmer, rev. R.E. Latham, London 1990

Bede: *The Ecclesiastical History of the English People*, tr. and ed. B.J. McClure and R. Collins, Oxford 1994

Another useful work, which includes a number of sixth- and seventh-century texts giving a good idea of the world of the Holy Men is:

The Age of Bede, tr. J.F. Webb and D.H. Farmer, London 1983

Poetry from Scotland in this period can be found in:

Clancy, Thomas (ed.): *The Triumph Tree: Scotland's Earliest Poetry AD 550–1350*, Edinburgh 2008

Markus, Gilbert and Thomas Clancy: *Iona: The Earliest Poetry of a Celtic Monastery*, Edinburgh 1995

Good introductions to the period can be found in:

Clarkson, Tim: *The Makers of Scotland: Picts Romans, Gaels and Vikings*, Edinburgh 2013

Clarkson, Tim: *Columba: Pilgrim, Priest and Patron Saint*, Edinburgh 2019

Marsden, John: *The Sea-Roads of the Saints: Celtic Holy Men in the Hebrides*, Edinburgh 1995

General books on Iona are:
Crawford, Robert (ed.): *The Book of Iona*, Edinburgh 2016
MacArthur, E. Mairi: *Columba's Island: Iona from Past to Present*, Edinburgh 1993
Marshall, Rosalind: *Columba's Iona: A New History*, Edinburgh 2014
Yeoman, Peter and Nicki Scott: *Iona Abbey and Nunnery* (HES official souvenir guide), Edinburgh 2020
Ritchie, Anna: *Iona* (official Historic Scotland guide), London and Edinburgh 1997

Separate treatments of the peoples of Early Historic Scotland can be found in:
Carver, Martin: *Surviving in Symbols: A Visit to the Pictish Nation*, Edinburgh 2005
Campbell, Ewan: *Saints and Sea Kings: The First Kingdom of the Scots*, Edinburgh 1999
Foster, Sally: *Picts, Gaels and Scots: Early Historic Scotland*, Edinburgh 2014
Lowe, Chris: *Angels, Fools and Tyrants: Britons and Anglo Saxons in Southern Scotland*, Edinburgh, 1999

A variety of other books I have enjoyed or found useful are listed below:
Athanasius of Alexandria: *Life of St Anthony of Egypt*, London 1892
Bartlett, Thomas: *Ireland: A History*, Cambridge 2010
Cahill, Thomas: *How the Irish Saved Civilization: The Untold Story of Ireland's Heroic Role from the Fall of Rome to the Rise of Medieval Europe*, London 1993
Colgate, Isabel: *A Pelican in the Wilderness: Hermits, Solitaries and*

Recluses, London, 2002

Dillon, Miles and Nora Chadwick: *The Celtic Realms*, London 1967

Dwelly, Edward: *Illustrated Gaelic to English Dictionary*, Glasgow 1994

Ferguson, Ron: *George MacLeod: Founder of the Iona Community*, Edinburgh 1990

Haswell-Smith, Hamish: *The Scottish Islands*, Edinburgh 1996

Hay, Robert: *Lismore: The Great Garden*, Edinburgh 2009

Lethbridge, T.C.: *Herdsmen and Hermits: Celtic Seafarers in the Northern Seas*, Cambridge, 1950

Mackenzie, Iain A: *Applecross, A' Chomraich, The Sanctuary: a Glimpse of History*, Applecross 1990

MacLennan, Iain: *Applecross and Its Hinterland: A Historical Miscellany*, Applecross, 2008

McCaffrey, Carmel: *In Search of Ancient Ireland: The Origins of the Irish from Neolithic Times to the Coming of the English*, Chicago 2002

Meehan, Bernard: *The Book of Kells: An Illustrated Introduction to the Manuscript in Trinity College Dublin*, London 1995

O'Brien, Jacqueline: *Ancient Ireland from Prehistory to the Middle Ages*, London 1996

Severin, Tim: *The Brendan Voyage*, London 1978

Smyth, Alfred P.: *Warlords and Holy Men: Scotland AD 80–1000*, Edinburgh 1984

Watson. W.J.: *The Celtic Place-Names of Scotland*, Edinburgh 2011

This list can only be a taster of the material that is available, and an intrepid explorer will find much material in essay collections and other volumes.

Index